Tobias Faix, Johannes
G. J. van Wyngaard (Eds.)

Reconciliation

Interdisziplinäre und theologische Studien
Interdisciplinary and Theological Studies

herausgegeben im Auftrag der

Gesellschaft für
Bildung und Forschung in Europa (GBFE)

von

Prof. Dr. Tobias Faix, Prof. Dr. Volker Kessler und Dr. Debora Sommer

Band 3

LIT

RECONCILIATION

Christian Perspectives –
Interdisciplinary Approaches

edited by

Tobias Faix, Johannes Reimer
and G .J. van Wyngaard

LIT

Cover image:
Coventry, UK – July 26th 2018: The Reconciliation statue
in the grounds of the ruins of Coventry Cathedral in the UK.
chrisdorney / Shutterstock.com

Bibliographic information published by the Deutsche Nationalbibliothek
The Deutsche Nationalbibliothek lists this publication in the Deutsche
Nationalbibliografie; detailed bibliographic data are available in the Internet at
http://dnb.dnb.de.

ISBN 978-3-643-91303-6 (pb)
ISBN 978-3-643-96303-1 (PDF)

A catalogue record for this book is available from the British Library.

© LIT VERLAG GmbH & Co. KG Wien,
Zweigniederlassung Zürich 2020
Flössergasse 10
CH-8001 Zürich
Tel. +41 (0) 76-632 84 35
E-Mail: zuerich@lit-verlag.ch   http://www.lit-verlag.ch
Distribution:
In the UK: Global Book Marketing, e-mail: mo@centralbooks.com
In North America: Independent Publishers Group, e-mail: orders@ipgbook.com
In Germany: LIT Verlag Fresnostr. 2, D-48159 Münster
Tel. +49 (0) 2 51-620 32 22, Fax +49 (0) 2 51-922 60 99, e-mail: vertrieb@lit-verlag.de

Table of Contents

4

Forward

Peace and reconciliation is a highly discussed topic at the moment. No other issue lately has received as much attention among missiologists, both Evangelical and Ecumenic, as the issue of Peacebuilding and Reconciliation. Praised as the new paradigm of Christian mission on the one side, it is ascribed to the field of Christian ethics by the other. A heated debate is in process.

In this volume, we want to examine this important question from different interdisciplinary and international perspectives in order to develop an overall understanding that will contribute to reconciliation in various cultural and religious fields of conflict in the world. Particular attention will be paid to the theological perspective on reconciliation, in which justice and restoration of relationships play a central role.

Surprisingly few authors provide proper theological foundation for their views. At the same time the practical suggestions seem to stay preliminary.

Reasons enough for an international symposium of theologians from Europe, Africa and North America to explore the issues on a deeper level. This volume represents their views from different angles and perspectives in theological thinking. Papers read in biblical theology present both Old and New Testament views on the issue. Added are systematic theological, practical theological and missiological as well as interdisciplinary perspectives.

All in all, a thought-provoking conference which may move the discussion a step on. Interested readers will find a wealth of theological thinking and some challenging practices.

Many thanks to Elke Meier and Manuel Reimer for all work on the manuscript.

Editors, in May 2020

Theo Witvliet as Hermeneutic Guide for White Theologians Engaging Black Theology of Liberation

George J (Cobus) van Wyngaard

Abstract

This chapter discusses the theological hermeneutical model which Dutch theologian Theo Witvliet developed for white theologians to listen to black theology of liberation. Witvliet's important contribution for such a dialogue is recognized. His Christological argument for keeping together the universality and particularity of theological claims and for the empty middle as a guiding metaphor for dialogue between theologians from different contexts and backgrounds is described. Critical questions are raised concerning how this argument allows a settlement with whiteness, and in particular on how a different interpretation of the art of South African artist Azaria Mbatha might call for a guiding metaphor different from the empty middle. This argument is set within the conference theme of reconciliation, with the work of Witvliet used as guide for one aspect of what might be named Reconciliation, while the critique presented on Witvliet's Christological model points to an approach to reconciliation which requires a deeper transformation of relations of power.

1 Introduction[1]

This chapter will discuss Dutch theologian Theo Witvliet's response to black theology of liberation as guide for white South African and European theologians in continuing such an engagement into the present. While reconciliation as a concept has received sustained critique for the ways in which it has been employed in the service of maintaining historic inequalities and undermining Christian work for justice, the Christian emphasis on bringing people together

---

[1] This chapter also forms part of my PhD, *In Search of Repair*, from the Vrije Universiteit, Amsterdam, and the University of South Africa (2019). The chapter was first submitted for this book during the period of PhD research. This work is based on the research supported in part by the National Research Foundation of South Africa; the author acknowledges that opinions, findings and conclusions or recommendations expressed in this publication, generated by NRF supported research, are that of the author, and the NRF accepts no liability whatsoever in this regard.

nonetheless carries potential to form deeper commitment to the struggles of others. As far as race is concerned, I would argue that 'reconciliation' would partially imply the way in which those made white through the modern and colonial process of racialization listen and respond to Christian voices from the 'underside of modernity'.

More specifically, this chapter seeks to open a conversation within the concrete relations which (at least in part) informed the conference on reconciliation from which these chapters emerged – those of European, predominantly German-speaking, theologians connected to the *Gesellschaft für Bildung und Forschung in Europa* and South African theologians at the University of South Africa.[2] I myself am approaching this conversation as a white South African, in many ways connected to the very white supremacy underlying the history of European colonialism, thinking alongside others on what it would mean for white theologians, whether South African or European, to responsibly listen and respond to black theology. Lastly, in this particular chapter I am approaching this question through the work of a continental European (Dutch) theologian as guide.

I therefore advance to this chapter noting that while the meaning of whiteness is indeed shaped by particular social and national contexts (Garner, 2007:1), whiteness per definition acts as an attempted universal identity[3]. This universal racialization is cause for similar questions being raised to those considered white within the context of a world shaped by Western colonialism – even while race takes form in particular ways in specific contexts.

After making some brief introductory comments on the problems with reconciliation and the need for white theologians in particular to have a more attentive ear to such a critique, the main section of this chapter will introduce key arguments from the work of Theo Witvliet. Finally, by pointing towards certain limitations in Witvliet's approach, I will highlight potential questions for ongoing engagement within the relations that form the background of this reflection.

---

[2] While this dialogue is broader than theology, and specifically involves colleagues from development studies, there are predominantly theologians involved. My own focus here is on the particular encounter between theologians.

[3] The process of tying bodies together aesthetically regardless of a shared geographic location and representing vastly different histories informs such a universal racial identity construction.

1.1 Reconciliation, ideology, and openness to the other

On the one hand, Christian reflection on reconciliation is caught up in conceptual, theological, and confessional confusion. Christians mean vastly different things when they speak of reconciliation (Conradie 2013; Solomons 2018) – and this before various public debates on reconciliation are drawn into our conceptual consideration. However, while greater clarity would assist our reflections on reconciliation, the tensions around the use of this concept are not in the first-place tensions about clarity, but rather about the ideological work that we make this concept do. Within South African theology *The Kairos Document* stands as the most symbolically important critique of reconciliation as response to histories of oppression (Kairos Theologians 1986:pp. 17-18).

It is this second problem, the question of which ideological and political ends reconciliation has been made to serve, more than the problem of clarity, which causes Willie Jennings to declare that this notion should be used with utmost caution, if used at all (Jennings 2011:pp. 9-10). I do not propose a solution for this problem, but a few comments are important to bring us to the main section of this chapter. Despite the contamination of reconciliation, there remains a Christian impulse, which at times was captured with this word, that requires our attention. Jennings, for example, uses the language of "intimacy" to capture this impulse. Christians should "know" each other (Jennings 2011:3) – an intuition at the heart of Christian community, but with a devastating history in modernity, in particular of colonial mission.

The very critique of reconciliation as potential response to histories of injustice already reminds us that the meaning of reconciliation is deeply intertwined with social location: where we are speaking from has a profound effect on what we see as the place of reconciliation in our response to histories of oppression. As far as race is concerned, in a particular way for those racialized as white, the double bind is that a commitment to one form of reconciliation – of openness to another, openness to listen to and learn from those whose lives were disrupted by the history of race and colonialism – requires us, somewhat ironically, to also hear the critique against what often goes under reconciliation as paradigm for our life together. Finding ways in which such critical responses to a too hasty reconciliation can be truly heard and engaged is therefore, in this reading, exactly a commitment to a deeper reconciliation.

2 Theo Witvliet as Guide

Theo Witvliet was associated with the University of Amsterdam throughout his academic career – 1977-2000. Preceding this, he worked as journalist with IKON (*Interkerkelijke Omroep Nederland*), known amongst other things for its focus on racism. Through this engagement, he was involved with many ecumenical gatherings, among other things making a television series on the ecumenical movement. One of these gatherings, which he explicitly names as an inspiration to write *The Way of the Black Messiah*, was a 1973 symposium in dialogue with black theology and Latin American liberation theology, which was also attended by around 50 European theologians. Witvliet notes the particular struggle of white European theologians[4] to grapple with the hermeneutical challenge, which black and Latin American liberation theologians were posing (Witvliet, 1987:ix).[5] It is this problem that receives sustained attention in his work.

Witvliet was often mentioned in South African theology – mostly by black theologians from the late 1980's and early 1990's. These references are always positive, but mostly just drawing from either of his two initial books as reference work in the history of black and liberation theologies.[6] He was also on the

---

[4] We observe a certain vagueness in how Witvliet refers to whiteness. He quotes James Cone from the end of the already mentioned 1973 WCC meeting as saying "What is black theology? Or, what is Latin American theology of liberation? This is what Europeans want to know. Or, if I'm in America, this is what white people want to know." (Witvliet, 1974, p. 197) Whether this is a direct quote or a paraphrase is not clear, and given that Cone would have spoken in English, what the exact formulation is that Cone would have used is even less clear, so my focus is not on Cone but rather on Witvliet's use of these words. Witvliet does not discuss this distinction between European and white, and in other places he does clearly refer to himself and to Europeans as white – for example in noting that Sartre discovers his own colour as white (Witvliet, 1980, p. 501). A page earlier another potential synonym is found. Witvliet writes "If a western theologian wants to go into dialogue with a black theologian" (Witvliet, 1974, p. 196), but whether 'Western' here refers to white, how it relates to European or white earlier, and the different ways black is opposed to each of these, is not clear.

[5] Elsewhere he indicates that the word that best described this event is "*incommunicatie*", an impossibility of communication (Witvliet 1974:197).

[6] See for example Goba, (1988), Mosoma, (1992), Maimela, (1994), Botha, et al., (1994) and Koopman, (2008).

editorial board of the (short-lived) *Journal of Black Theology in South Africa*. James Cone described Witvliet with the words "No other white European interpreter of liberation theology equals his sharp spirit and deep involvement. His book, *The Way of the Black Messiah*, is the most informative and challenging interpretation of black theology written by a white theologian" and Jim Perkinson credits him with the words "[a]mong white theologians in general (and certainly among white males in particular), Dutch journalist-theologian Theo Witvliet has offered the most sustained and in-depth response to the claims of Black Theology's explicitly black christology" (Perkinson 2004:38). For white theologians, Witvliet remains an important guide in thinking through, how the challenge of black theology can be heard, or more generally, how we hear theologians from vastly different contexts than our own.

While Witvliet's interest has been on liberation and contextual theologies in general, it is black theology in particular that he focused on most in his early work. His first book, *A Place in the Sun* (Witvliet 1985)[7], contained chapters on various movements in contextual theologies. However, it is black theology which receives the longest treatment in this text, and the questions of race typical of black theology emerge again in different forms in the chapters on African and Caribbean theology (e.g. (Witvliet 1985:89, 115-116)). *A Place in the Sun* is then followed by *The Way of the Black Messiah* (Witvliet, 1987)[8], a book length treatment of black theology in the United States of America.

Key to Witvliet's entire project is the hermeneutical challenge posed by the "other". While this is not limited to ecumenical encounter – to encounter between those who profess to be Christian, whether as local, national, or international level – it is the questions that emerge when Christians encounter each other ecumenically that receives particular attention in his work. This Witvliet describes as a hermeneutical problem or the problem of knowing the other (Witvliet 1992:50).

The next section will first outline the way in which Witvliet drew on Chalcedonian Christology to develop a hermeneutic lens for listening to black theology of liberation, drawing mostly from the already mentioned earlier work on black theology. The second part of the section will start at his 1999 publication *Gebroke Traditie*, critically examine his use of Azaria Mbatha's *Stations of the*

---

[7] Dutch edition published in 1984 as *Een plaatz onder de zon*.

[8] Dutch edition published in 1984 as *De weg van de Zwarte Messias*.

Cross for Africa as Christological guide for a hermeneutic of mutual understanding, and briefly relate this to his most recent study of Martin Buber
(Witvliet 2017). By pointing out a key problem in his use of Mbatha, I will also
raise questions about Witvliet's proposal, and through this return to the question of reconciliation.

2.1 Chalcedon as hermeneutic for reading Black Theology of Liberation

A key line running throughout Witvliet's work concerns the relationship between universality and particularity, developed in relation to Chalcedonian
Christology, and drawn into the work of thinking through, how black theology
would have implications for European theology.

Specifically, his focus is on the criteria "without confusion, without change,
without division, without separation" – in Witvliet's work translated as "unconfused, unchanged, undivided, unseparated" and often shortened to "unconfused and undivided". What Witvliet seeks to do is to draw from such an incar-
national theology a lens for reading contextual and liberation theologies in general, and black theology in particular. These two notions Witvliet relates to the
universality and particularity of theological claims and to how theology emerging from particular contexts can speak to the Church universal. From this, a
theology in which a white European theologian can hear the challenge of black
theology can then be developed.

The one side of his approach lies with an emphasis on "undivided and
unseparated", which should reject any separation of "Word and world" in doing
theology. This is an insistence, no longer strange today, on a theology fully
committed to *this* world. On the other hand, "unconfused and unchanged" calls
up the Barthian critique of religion and warns against denying the gulf between
modern bourgeois society and "the appearance of God's love for humanity in
the midst of a specific people (the people of Israel), in a specific person (the
Jew Jesus of Nazarath)" (Witvliet 1987:65). Both is however a commitment to
history – the present context and the particular history of God's revelation.

The theological frame within which Witvliet thinks through the engagement
with black theology of liberation insists on the particularity of the one doing
theology, both as a limitation to what we can see, but also as a commitment
which we should hold to – we must speak in the particular about this world
when doing theology. Simultaneously, it insists on the universality of God's

incarnation into this world, doing so specifically by insisting on the particularity of this revelation in history – in Israel and Jesus.

This reading of the incarnation allows for a particular openness to the diversity of theological voices while drawing all into a universal logic – although, importantly, this universality is found in a story which is not our own, the particular story of God's relationship with Israel and Jesus: "Both elements of truth need to be maintained: the story of God's humanity comes to us as one of the many stories in which our consciousness is entangled ('undivided') and this story is a unique story because of the uniqueness of the name ('unconfused')." (Witvliet 1987:72)

The preface to *A Place in the Sun* introduces the basic elements of how Witvliet draws these notions together. All theologies of liberation start with a very particular situation in mind. But they have a universal dimension, and this universal dimension is found in their specific commitment to the "rejected of the earth". Through this commitment, they do justice to the gospel. Witvliet then continues to write that "[w]e are concerned with this universal dimension, but… it is only accessible to those who take the trouble to grasp the particularity seriously and put up with it" (Witvliet 1985:viii).[9]

Within the Chalcedonian space Witvliet uses as lens, where both, our particular experience and God's wholly other story, remain in constant tension, Witvliet proposes constant listening to and dialoging with the particular stories of those with very different experiences and perspectives from ourselves as a way for hearing God's wholly other story. To be clear, such a dialogue is not a nice addition to the normal work of theology, to Witvliet's mind. Rather, the only possibility theology as a discourse has of speaking about God without reproducing ideology is through constant dialogue with 'the other'. The place where such an encounter may occur is – both, sociologically and theologically – ecumenism.

What Witvliet proposes throughout his work is the possibility for ecumenicity, on local, national or international level, to be a place where voices from very different contexts and social locations can encounter each other, and where we

---

[9] When returning to the relation between particularity and universality, he names this we "Western European" (Witvliet 1985:41).

14

can learn to understand one another, in spite of vast differences. Quite specifically, ecumenism could be, as it was for Witvliet personally, the place in which the critical voice of black theology can be heard.

3 A Hermeneutic of Mutual Understanding and the Limits to the Empty Middle

The hermeneutical quest for understanding those who are 'other' than ourselves runs through Witvliet's work. From the beginning it is the hermeneutical challenge resulting from a meeting between European and liberation theologians which draws Witvliet's attention – in brief, European theologians fail to *understand* what is being said by different liberation theologians.

In the midst of reflecting on the problem of the enlightenment and our understanding of the 'other', Witvliet makes this brief comment which illustrate his own focus: "the attempt to achieve a hermeneutics of (mutual) recognition based on the biblical covenantal idea deserves to be seriously investigated" (Witvliet 1999:74).[10] It is not the search for what is Biblical, or questions on whether such a covenantal idea might do the kind of work Witvliet has in mind, which I want to highlight here, even though that does deserve reflection. Rather, it is the strong emphasis on "mutuality", highlighted by its insertion in parentheses, that we need to note.

Perhaps the most developed reflection on this hermeneutic of mutual understanding is found in Witvliet's most recent book on Martin Buber's humanism, but most importantly for this argument, in Witvliet's attempt to go beyond Buber by drawing from him that which was not said but which rightly should have been expected: the relation between "us and them". While Buber is known for his work on the relation "I and thou", Witvliet notes the strange silence in Buber's work on "the world of the 'us'" (Witvliet 2017:65).

He seeks to trace the potential for reflecting on this "us" through Buber's work, focusing in particular on Buber's attempts to think through Jewish and Arab community in Palestine – searching for ways for Jews and Palestinians to be in a community of equals. What Witvliet highlights in the end is that "a *person* is someone who is in relation to other persons and is capable of real encounter" (Witvliet 2017:79). What Witvliet envisions is a continuation of his past work and the argument above: community which is not bound to fixed identity, but

---

[10] This, and all subsequent translations from Dutch originals, is my own translation.

which is open to others, yet not afraid of loss of identity for the self (Witvliet 2017:80).

A brief personal reflection then illuminates Witvliet's entire project on ecumenical encounter as the place in which the challenge of black theology should be heard and the place where people who are very different can meet each other:

> For Buber community does not mean that people share the same norms and values. It is exactly important not to silence personal, cultural, ethnic or religious contradictions, but to commit to accept each other as a person. The latter is an art, but it is worth the effort. That's also my own experience. I did not often experience real community. But the few times that I really felt something of communion were exactly those moments where people from different backgrounds and cultures were together. (Witvliet 2017:81)

A key critique from Kameron Carter on the possibility of drawing on Buber to disrupt whiteness becomes important at this point. Carter, while discussing the work of James Cone, refers to Cone's use of Buber to present the work of black faith as transforming "a relationship in which black people are cast as Its into relationships that recognize them as Thous" (Carter 2008:189). However, the key problem that Carter point out is that it normalizes the "I". "[I]n I-Thou structures, the I relates to the other but allows it a separate-but-equal status in relation to itself as I. In this way, the I positions the other as Thou. But something more that this is needed, for on its own, this really is only a settlement with whiteness, not its overcoming" (Carter 2008:190). In effect, the white 'I', even when relating to others as 'thou', remains in relation 'as white' – whiteness is not (necessarily) disrupted.

Witvliet's ecumenical dialogue and hermeneutic of mutual understanding runs into the very same problem. While it allows for a deeply respectful dialogue with others, and allows others the space to truly bring their own voice to be heard, it also makes such a settlement with whiteness possible. I illustrate this further by turning to Witvliet's discussion of the art of South African artist Azaria Mbatha.

If for Witvliet ecumenism is the *place* of encounter, then the *empty middle* is the guiding metaphor in his later work for what might happen in that encounter. In *Gebroke Traditie*, a book published a year before his retirement, the empty middle is explored in dialogue with the work of philosopher Theodor Adorno, artist Azaria Mbatha, and theologian Karl Barth. For Witvliet it is however the middle of this exploration which is key to his understanding of the empty middle. Towards the end of *Gebroke Traditie* he writes:

> The philosophy of Adorno and the theology of Barth cannot be brought to a synthesis. The tension remains between the philosopher, who takes his starting point in the universal and tries to do justice to the particular, and the theologian, who takes his point of departure in the specificity of a particular event and seeks to show the universal implications later. However, the work of Mbatha, placed in the triptych between philosopher and theologian, makes both thinkers representative of a modern European culture in which the way of the Black Messiah remains invisible. (Witvliet 1999:283)

So how does the artist Mbatha's Black Messiah inform Witvliet's ongoing Christological reflection in relation to his hermeneutical problem? Witvliet's focus is on Mbatha's 1995 *Stations of the Cross for Africa*. My concern is not in the first place with Mbatha's art, but rather, with how Witvliet's theology engages and draws from Mbatha's stations of the cross – yet this requires brief comments on Mbatha's work. More specifically, I want to focus on a problem in Witvliet's use of *Stations of the Cross for Africa*, but not primarily for the sake of highlighting the problem, but rather because it highlights a particular response to the question of race and reconciliation.

The stations of the cross traditionally consist of fourteen stations. It is therefore immediately obvious why Witvliet focusses his attention on the fact that Mbatha included a fifteenth station to the traditional fourteen stations of the cross. In this fifteenth station, titled *Jesus rises from the dead*, the focus is on an empty middle, which Witvliet draws from to further develop his own ecumenical theology and hoped-for dialogue.

Figure 1 Azaria Mbatha, Stations of the Cross for Africa.
Station XV - Resurrection (from MacDonald 2016:156)

The fifteenth station consists of three elements: an empty circle, a crowd gathered around the empty circle, and in the foreground a black and white person embracing and kissing.[11] Witvliet notes the visible absence of the risen Christ in this representation of the resurrection – always present but not presented.

---

[11] The figures in the embrace draws from earlier works – *Crucifixion/Reconciliation* from 1967-1968 and *Between Hope and Despair* from the 1980's – in which the estrangements of these figures were depicted (MacDonald 2016:108). For *Crucifixion/Reconciliation* Mbatha has confirmed that the black figure represents himself (MacDonald 2016:92).

While the empty middle will be mentioned repeatedly from 1999 onwards when interpreting Mbatha's work, Witvliet notes that the circle is not empty. Rather, the circle represents Christ, the one who disappears after breaking the bread and thanking God (Luke 24), and the circle therefore a Eucharistic gathering (Witvliet 1999:234-235). But, Witvliet argues later, Christ is also in the people gathering in the circle, and in the black and white individuals embracing in the foreground. Important for Witvliet is that the empty centre implies that the centre of power remains unoccupied (Witvliet 1999:239). For Witvliet such an empty circle is an image for a place where all can gather as equals since no one occupies the center of such a gathering.

But at this point a particular problem with Witvliet's interpretation of Mbatha's *Stations of the Cross for Africa* must be noted. Witvliet only mentions one addition to the fourteen stations, while Mbatha had two. The fact that this was not known by Witvliet creates immediate problems with his interpretation of Mbatha, but that is not my primary concern.[12] Rather, noting station XVI can highlight Witvliet's own theological project, which could interpret station XV as culmination of the stations. Simultaneously, it points us to a possible limit to Witvliet's work, since he might have needed to make a very different theological argument had he been aware of station XVI and if he wanted to use this as guiding metaphor for what might happen in ecumenical encounter. Station XVI in part duplicates station fifteen, with the gathered community both in a circle and in the foreground. Most importantly, while the circle is still present, it is no longer empty – it is now occupied by a United Nations icon and a black and white hand shaking.

It will not be saying too much to argue that if Witvliet sees in station XV the prerequisite of embrace for the gathering of people around the empty circle, then in Mbatha's station XVI we have to add the reorganization of the global world order – of the structure of global society, the decolonisation of the world – as fundamental aspect of such a gathering. In his 1993 article on the future of South African foreign policy, Nelson Mandela explicitly called for a restructuring of the United Nations as part of the making of a more democratic world. He writes that "[t]he United Nations should not be dominated by a single power or group of powers, or else its legitimacy will continuously be called into ques-

---

[12] It seems like a lesser known version of the *Stations of the Cross for Africa* was indeed published with only fifteen stations, and this version was used by Witvliet.

tion" (Mandela 1993:89). To see in Mbatha's art an explicit call for such a re-structuring of the global relations of power as a fundamental part of making a more humane society should therefore not come as a surprise. Sabelo Ndlovu-Gatsheni, in his interpretation of Nelson Mandela as a decolonial humanist, places this call by Mandela within a longer trajectory of working for a more humane and democratic world, a key aspect of the struggle against Western colonialism and its ongoing effects (Ndlovu-Gatsheni 2016:139).

What is raised by noting either station XV or XVI as the concluding moment of Mbatha's *Stations of the Cross*, when read through Witvliet's question of how people who are different, but more specifically, how people on different sides of the process of Western colonialism, relate, is whether the focus on gathering around the empty circle, even when that circles is occupied Christo-logically, doesn't inevitably reproduce the power that precedes such a gathering – in returning to Witvliet's earlier work: whiteness.

For Mbatha, the empty middle is associated with resurrection – *Jesus rises from the dead*, but in line with the salvific narrative, resurrection is not the final word. What follows resurrection is ascension, church, and return. It is clear that station XVI is also intended as a Christological moment: *Reconciliation*. As a moment in the stations of the cross we could also have named this Pentecost, or ecclesia; the gathering of a concrete community after *Resurrection*. As *Acts* have reminded its readers over millennia, this gathering involved quite explic-itly working out the implications of the resurrection for our relations of power within this resurrection community with implications for broader society. Mbatha's vision of reconciliation seems to explicitly require a restructuring of power – including its global dimensions.

What Witvliet's empty circle can do is provide a theological and ecumenical vision[13] for a gathering of equals for the sake of listening and doing the difficult work of knowing the 'other'. This might open up possibilities of doing the dif-ficult work of confronting the eurocentrism within the self, but it does not in and of itself allow envisioning the theological and political process of forming a world which is not founded on this eurocentrism. The *Stations of the cross for*

---

[13] This ecumenical vision does not remain limited to a gathering of Christians (Witvliet, 2003:147), although such a broader engagement across faith traditions does not receive sustained reflection in Witvliet's work.

Africa, however, seem to call for this further work as well. In fact, the empty circle as *Resurrection*[14] can be described as eschatology – even while having as prerequisite the real forgiveness and embrace of black and white, while the concrete work of Reconciliation happens not around the empty circle, but around a different political arrangement – which still has the empty circle as backdrop, as hope.

4 Conclusion

For white theologians in general, and for those working from within the continental European context in particular, Theo Witvliet is an important guide for exploring theology in all its global diversity, and black theology of liberation in particular. The hermeneutical challenge which Witvliet noted in the 1973 gathering has not disappeared, even though almost a half-century has passed. Such a gathering around the empty circle, where voices from vastly different contexts can speak as equals, should indeed remain part of a Christian hope. However, Mbatha's sixteenth station, missing from Witvliet's reflection, should also caution against a too easy faith in a hermeneutic process disconnected from a political and economic restructuring of a world still marked by the history of colonialism.

Such hermeneutic work does indeed remain important, and Witvliet's empty middle a profound Christological reflection around which to imagine such an engagement. But the question any reflection on reconciliation today should engage is contained in Mbatha's sixteenth station on *Reconciliation*: how do those gathered around the resurrected Christ imagine the concrete organization of our lives together. In a globalized world, this question would have to be global as well.

Bibliography

Botha, N., Kritzinger, J.N.J., & Maluleke, T.S., 1994. Crucial issues for Christian Mission - A Missiological Analysis of Contemporary South Africa. *International Review of Mission,* 83(328), 21-36.

Carter, J.K., 2008. *Race: A Theological Account.* Oxford: Oxford University Press.

---

[14] Mbatha's title for station XV.

Conradie, E.M., 2013. Reconciliation as one Guiding Vision for South Africa? Conceptual Analysis and Theological Reflection. In: E. M. Conradie, ed. Reconciliation. A guiding vision for South Africa. Stellenbosch: SUN Media, 13-84.

Garner, S., 2007. *Whiteness: An introduction.* s.l.:s.n.

Goba, B., 1988. Toward a Quest for Christian Identity: A Third World Perspective. *Journal of Black Theology in South Africa,* 2(2), 31-36.

Jennings, W.J., 2011. *The Christian Imagination: Theology and the Origins of Race.* London: Yale University Press.

Kairos Theologians, 1986. *The Kairos Document Challenge to the Church: A Theological Comment on the Political Crisis in South Africa.* s.l.:World Council of Churches.

Koopman, N., 2008. On violence, the Belhar Confession and human dignity. *Nederduitse Gereformeede Teologiese Tydskrif,* 49(3 & 4), 159-166.

MacDonald, J., 2016. *Tracing the Passion of a Black Christ: Critical reflections on the iconographic revision and symbolic redeployment of the Stations of the Cross and Passion cycle by South African artists Sydney Kumalo, Sokhaya Charles Nkosi and Azaria Mbatha.* Cape Town: Masters Thesis, University of Cape Town.

Maimela, S.S., 1994. *What is the human being?.* Pretoria, University of Pretoria.

Mandela, N., 1993. South Africa`s Future Foreign Policy. *Foreign Affairs,* 72(5), 86-97.

Mosoma, D.L., 1992. Black Power and Justice. *Journal of Black Theology in South Africa,* 6(1), 32-45.

Ndlovu-Gatsheni, S.J., 2016. *The decolonial Mandela. Peace, Justice and the Politics of Life.* New York: Berghahn.

Perkinson, J.W., 2004. *White Theology: Outing Supremacy in Modernity.* New York: Pelgrave Macmillan.

Solomons, D., 2018. *Reconciliation as a controversial symbol: An analysis of a theological discourse between 1968-2010.* Unpublished thesis from the Vrije Universiteit Amsterdam and the University of Western Cape.

Van Wyngaard, G.J., 2019. *In search of repair: Critical white responses to whiteness as a theological problem – a South African contribution.* Unpublished thesis from the Vrije Universiteit Amsterdam and the University of South Africa.

Witvliet, T., 1974. Zwarte theologie en blanke theologen. *Wending,* 29(1), 190-201.

Witvliet, T., 1980. Sartre en de strijd tegen racisme. Wending, 35(9), 501-511.

Witvliet, T., 1985. *A Place in the Sun.* Maryknoll NY: Orbis Books.

Witvliet, T., 1987. *The Way of the Black Messiah.* London: SCM Press.

Witvliet, T., 1992. Europa en de anderen: Bespiegelingen over een kentheoretisch probleem. *Wereld en zending,* 21(1), 51-63.

Witvliet, T., 1999. *Gebroke Traditie: Christelijke religie in het spanningsveld van pluraliteit en identiteit.* Antwerpen: Ten Have.

Witvliet, T., 2003. *Het geheim van het lege midden: Over de identiteit van het westers christendom.* Zoetermeer: Meinema.

Witvliet, T., 2017. *Kwaliteit van Level.* Vught: Skandalon.

The Gospel of Reconciliation in the Gospel of Mark

Morten H. Jensen

Abstract

The term "gospel" is arguably the most prominent Christian keyword, at least in the Protestant tradition. But how should it be understood? This has been fiercely debated for more than a century, especially with reference to the Gospel of Mark, which is the only one of the four gospels to frame its narrative from the first verse as a "gospel-narrative". In this article, it is argued that "gospel" should neither be understood as sin-management nor a subversive message aimed at countering the Roman gospels of its day, but instead as a relational category, as reconciliation.

1 Introduction

The Gospel of Mark does not at first glance seem the obvious place to kick-start a conference on "reconciliation", since none of the Greek words for reconciliation (the καταλλάσσω word group) appear in Mark, who instead chose to open his narrative with the distinct notion, "the gospel" (τὸ εὐαγγέλιον). While this is not to be denied, the burden of my argument is that Mark could have used reconciliation words, since exactly the notion of "reconciliation" helps us to understand Mark's theological "gospel" agenda. Once recognised, this will help us to see that there is no Gospel without reconciliation.

To approach this argument, we must first notice the long acknowledged striking difference between God/human interaction in ancient Greek writings compared to the New Testament writings. For instance in what is sometimes referred to as 'the Greek Bible', Homer's writings, the Greeks and Trojans do not seek reconciliation with the Olympic gods. They sacrifice to them, placate them, appease them and even pray to them for protection. But they never reconcile with them. Because reconciliation involves friendship, and, in the Homeric world, you just do not have the terrifying, magnificent Zeus as your buddy. This observation is supported on a linguistic level. As noted almost a century ago by Friedrich Büchsel (1933) and recently by Moisés Silva (2014), the various reconciliation words are practically never used in a Greek religious context to describe god-human interaction. According to Büchsel, they "play no essential part in even the expiatory rites ... of Greek and Hellenistic pagan religion ... The relation between divinity and humanity does not have this personal nearness" (1964:254). Instead, reconciliation words are used more or less entirely in the Greek tradition to describe reconciliation between people.

It turns out that it was Paul, who was the first person to use the concept of "reconciliation" on a deep level, when describing God's interaction with humans in the Christ-event (cf. e.g. Rome 5:11; 2 Cor 5:18-20), with just a few forerunners in earlier Jewish literature. As phrased by Silva, an important "element is the theological novelty of the NT in comparison with non-Christian religious thought, which knows the deity only as the object of the reconciling or appeasing work of human beings" (2014:245). When Paul chose to theologise this non-religious word group formerly used to describe human-human-interaction, he intrinsically came to stress the Christ-event as relational at its core level.

It is precisely here, the theme of "reconciliation" connects to the Gospel of Mark. Though reconciliation words are never used, my argument in the following will be that Mark's favourite key-term, "the gospel," should be understood exactly in the Pauline sense of "reconciliation," as an interpretation of the Christ-event as a story of how God has brought himself near to the world, offering reconciliation and fellowship in and through the life, death and resurrection of Jesus.[1]

One might ask: What are the alternative understandings of Mark's "gospel"? As we shall see in just a moment, there is presently and has been for more than a hundred years a huge discussion of how to understand "the gospel", with two strong competitors in each their corner: One side portrays "the gospel" as another word for "justification by faith" or "atonement" in the sense of a transaction between God and humans. If formulated carelessly, this picture easily resembles the aforementioned Greek tradition of appeasement of the gods. The other takes a completely different route, understanding the gospel as a rival claim for political emperorship over the world tailored to knock the

---

[1] There is a long-standing discussion in New Testament research on the relationship between Paul and Mark (cf. e.g. Marcus 2000 and Bird and Willits 2011). This study would thus add to the argument of Pauline influence on Mark.

emperor off his throne in Rome. According to this view, "the gospel" is a human-human endeavour; it is political action.[2]

I am not going to counter that there are elements of truth in both views. My basic contention is this: We get off on the wrong foot, if we do not observe how "the gospel" is a "gospel of reconciliation" presented by a God, who seeks proximity and fellowship to and with humans on which basis interpersonal proximity, fellowship and reconciliation are lifted to the centre stage of Christian praxis.

2 From Athens to Rome: What Does the Gospel Mean?

2.1 The turn of a century and the quest for the gospel

In order to establish this case, we shall begin by outlining how a huge discussion of the understanding of the gospel-notion has evolved within New Testament research during roughly the last 120 years. Though the understanding of this New Testament keyword naturally was investigated before (cf. Horbury 2005:9), something decisively happened around the turn of the 20th century that provoked a hitherto unseen amount of interest in the root and meaning of "the gospel".

According to Hubert Frankemölle, the sudden change was caused by two publications (cf. 1984, 1671). One was Gustav Dalman's first of his *Die Worte Jesu* series from 1898, in which he argued, on the basis of Hebrew and Aramaic word investigations, that exact gospel nomenclauture used by especially Paul and Mark was coined after the death of Jesus in the early Hellenistic congregations (cf. 1930:84). The case is that the specific New Testament *Stichwort*, τὸ εὐαγγέλιον, is nowhere to be found in a religious sense in the Hebrew Bible, neither in the Masoretic text nor in the Septuagint. It is used a few times in a secular manner as referring to good news from the battlefield (but kept unarticulated). Only when we move to the book of Isaiah and a few of the Psalms does the picture begin to change. Here we find a specific use of the verb that brings us closer to the NT *Stichwort* – but, alas, only in the form of a verb, not the articulated noun of the NT. Since it is also used only by some NT-authors, the question is: Why did *some* of the first Christian writers begin to use this notion?

---

[2] For an overview over the discussion of the "gospel" notion, see, besides the literature mentioned below, Frankemölle (1988) and Stanton (2004).

The other publication was published the following year in the journal of the German, archaeological institute in Athens. It reported the discovery of an inscription found in Priene, Turkey, and records a salute to emperor Augustus issued by the government of the Roman province of Asia Minor. In this rather lengthy tractate, there is a line, which in a remarkable way hails the emperor as "god", stating that his birthday was the beginning of "good news" (εὐαγγελίων) for the world.[3] While the publishers confined themselves to making a, for scholarship typically downplayed remark at the end of the article stating that this discovery should not be of any insignificance (Mommsen and Wilamowitz-Mollendorf 1899:293), the most preeminent theologian, Adolf von Harnack, immediately felt the profound implications and wrote a far more spirited evaluation. Propelling the news out to the German, Lutheran, theological community with exclamation marks, he noted that a one-to-one resemblance of Mark's bold opening line had been found, only saluting the emperor in Rome, not the crucified Christ (cf. Harnack 1904:302, originally published in 1899). In other words: with the discovery of the Priene inscription in 1899, the gospel-word was demonstrated to be in use in the religious context of the imperial cult.[4]

2.2 Two competing gospels

In the wake of the discovery of the Priene inscription, a heated debate unfolded among especially German, Lutheran scholars (cf. Stanton 2004:2) battling over the root of the gospel word. Two competing explanations soon emerged. One elaborated on Harnack's interpretation of "the gospel" as coined to counter the emperor's claim for fame. In the imperial cult as attested in the Priene-inscription and other long-known sources now dusted off, the gospel word was used in the pluralis, unarticulated – that is, "gospels of the emperor". When Paul and others of the first Greek-speaking Christians moved the message of Jesus from the Aramaic environment to the Greek, they at some point felt forced to counter the religious "pax Romana," being in effect a "pax Deorum," by

---

[3] Schorlarly representation of the Greek text is provided by Sherk (1969:328-37, adopted from Dittenberger 1905:48-60). For translation of the entire text, see Danker (1982:215-22).

[4] Since other examples of gospel nomenclature in the context of the imperial cult have been found (cf. Llewelyn and Horsley 1978:10-5; Stanton 2004:33). To this comes an occasional attestation in the writings of Josephus and Philo (cf. Stanton 2004:28-9).

making one small but subtle change: the verbal "to preach good news" of the Hebrew Bible became the nominal "*the* good news". As if they were reasoning: "People may hail the emperor as good news, but we proclaim Christ as *the* Good News for the world."[5]

The other explanation was indeed a reassertion of the Isaianic explanation of the root of the Gospel. And to cut a long story short, for the bulk of the 20th century, this explanation became dominant due to the masterful entry in *Theologisches Wörterbuch zum Neuen Testament* by Gerhard Friedrich. The main arguments are that, firstly, the "Roman explanation" is too far-fetched after all and that, secondly, the leap from verb to noun is not that much of a step that it can bear such a radical reunderstanding. As an aside, it might be said that the shift from the liberal to the kerygmatic tradition of Barth, Bultmann and others undoubtedly contributed to the victory of the Isaianic interpretation in the 20th century German tradition; political theology became outdated.

Exactly this has changed in recent decades through the introduction of postcolonial and anti-empire readings into New Testament studies.[6] One of the areas in which this tidal shift is felt, is precisely in the understanding of "the gospel", where once again the Roman political explanation has gained renewed attention.

In turn, the competing historical reconstructions of the gospel nomenclature have huge implications for the way in which we envision gospel praxis and reconciliation. On the one end of the spectrum, the Gospel slides towards an other-worldly, religious sentiment. On the other, it slides towards a defined political program.[7]

---

[5] For examples of this interpretation, see Strecker (1975); Dechow (2014).

[6] For an introduction to such readings in regard to the Gospel of Mark, see Evans (2006), Horsley (2008), Winn (2008), Leander (2013) and Winn (2018). For a recent introduction to the same issue in relation to Paul, see Heilig (2017).

[7] While examples of the first are foremost to be found in devotional literature, examples of the latter are, surprisingly, to be found in scholarly literature, as when Richard Horsley defines present implications of the gospel as a fight against the (at the time of writing) regime of Bush and Chaney (cf. 2003:5; 2008).

3 The Gospel of Reconciliation and Proximity

3.1 Case to test

The case I will present and test in the following comes with a corrective to both, the imperial/political reading of Mark as well as to the kerygmatic/Isaianic understanding, arguing the following: While Mark does indeed tell his gospel-story as a continuation of "the gospel of Isaiah," the driving principle is not sin-management in itself, but the question of how God draws near to his people. This process is casted as a re-enacting of Israel's old exodus-narrative (often referred to as Isaiah's New Exodus-theology).[8] During this process, the question of the Roman Empire is dealt with, just as sin and cultic atonement are deeply embedded, but neither are able to bear the burden as the hermeneutical key to Mark's gospel. On different levels, they are both "means to an end," but not "the end" in themselves. Instead, Mark's gospel is a story of divine nearness – a story of reconciliation. In other words: Mark's gospel is a relational category.

I intend to unfold this claim by observing a three-fold division of Mark into a prologue (1:1-15), a Galilee section (1:16-10:52) and a Jerusalem section (11:1-16:8).[9]

3.2 The Gospel of Isaianic proximity (Mark 1:1-15)

Approaching Mark's Gospel, the first thing to notice is the preeminent position of the gospel-notion that encapsulates the prologue in one of Mark's typical sandwich constructions (cf. Williams 2006:515). The entire narrative is labelled as "the gospel" (τὸ εὐαγγέλιον) in Mark 1:1, just as the initial summary of

---

[8] For a treatment of Isaiah's New Exodus-theology, see especially Lim (2010), Watts (1997) and Smith (2016). For references to Isaiah, see especially 44:13-16; 48:20-21; 52:4-13. Smith has been able to detect the use of a "new exodus"-phrase back to a commentary on Isaiah from 1847. Otherwise from that, it is a trend of more recent studies from the 1950s and onwards (cf. 2016:208). Critique of the consensus was presented recently by Lund (2007). Also the new study of the theology of Isaiah by Andrew Abernethy makes clear that other motifs are at play in Isaiah 40-55 (e.g. Yahweh as a righteous king, as supreme to other gods, as creator, cf. Abernethy 2016).

[9] Despite intense efforts, there is no consensus regarding Mark's main structure; neither the length of the prologue, the number of main sections and their precise location, nor if Mark has an intended structure at all (for an overview, see Larsen, 2004). For our purposes, this discussion is out of focus since the argument pursued does not rest on any exact structure of Mark, besides the obvious observation that Jesus moves from Galilee to Jerusalem.

Jesus' ministry and message is described as a proclamation of "the gospel of God" in order to believe "the gospel" (Mark 1:14-15). In a unique way compared to the other gospels, Mark is telling a "gospel-story".[10]

The second thing to notice is how eager Mark is in presenting the book of Isaiah as the interpretative key to his gospel by following his initial gospel-reference with the statement "as is written in the prophet Isaiah" (Mark 1:2). While all New Testament gospel-writers cite Isaiah 40:3, Mark alone places this quotation at the very beginning, even before John the Baptist is introduced, who is presented as the Isaianic voice in the desert. As a matter of fact, the grammar of the entire pericope is stressed by Mark's eagerness to begin with Isaiah, making it difficult to judge if the cluster-citation in Mark 1:2-3 is at all an expounding of John's ministry (Mark 1:4-8) or rather an expounding of the gospel of Jesus (Mark 1:1).[11]

For our purposes, the important question is: Why Isaiah? Judging from the available Jewish sources from the Hasmonean and Herodian periods, the book of Isaiah had become immensely popular and 40:3 a kind of shorthand for the blooming hope of what has been termed "a new exodus"-expectation, a new leading out from bondage through the desert: "A voice cries out: "In the wilderness prepare the way of the LORD, make straight in the desert a highway for our God" (Isaiah 40:3, New Revised Version).

As is evident from Josephus' descriptions of messianic figures (cf. e.g. *War* 2.261-63), the Qumran community (cf. Community Rule 8-9) and the Psalms of Salomon (cf. 11:1-9; 17:1-10), there was at the time of Jesus a longing for the day in which Israel's God would arrive at the door step of Jerusalem and take up his throne once again as king of his people (cf. Isaiah 52:7). No longer would God and Israel be separated "heavens apart," but the presence of God would dwell yet again in the midst of his people. This is what the "New Exodus" expectations were all about.[12]

---

[10] This emphasis on "the gospel" becomes even more peculiar when comparing to the other New Testament Gospels. Matthew is the only other Gospel to use the gospel-notion, but only four times and not in the same distinct manner. Luke confines himself to using the verbal form only, whereas John eschews both altogether.

[11] For a discussion of the complicated syntax of Mark 1:1-4, see Wikgren (1942), Guelich (1982), Boring (1990), Klauck Hans-Josef (1997:27ff), Elliott (2000) and Croy (2001).

[12] For an introduction to the use of Isaiah 40:3 in Jewish texts, see Watts (1997:82-4).

Mark not only begins his narrative with a direct reference to Isaiah, besides the already implicit Isaiah reference hidden in the gospel nomenclature (cf. Isaiah 40:9; 52:7; 61:1-2). He also saturates his prologue with Isaianic notions of Isaianic proximity language. This is obviously the case in regard to the Kingdom proclamation speaking of the kingdom that has "come near" (1:15). But on a deeper level, the very centre of the prologue is the theophanic vision of the heavens that rend open over Jesus bringing upon him proximity of "first degree." As a matter of fact, the splitting of the heavens is part of Isaiah's vision of a new exodus but formed as a prayer (63:19). Here it is fulfilled. In this way, Mark presents his narrative as a sequel to Isaiah's vision of the arrival of God's nearness to Jerusalem.

This observation propels us into the next two sections of Mark with one overarching question: In which way does Jesus bring the nearness of God into the world? Or to phrase it differently but topically identical: In which way is God reconciling himself to the world through the ministry of Jesus?

3.3 The Gospel of Isaianic subversion and new beginnings (Mark 1:16-10:52)

We shall answer this question by surveying Mark's Galilee and Jerusalem sections respectively. Beginning by tackling Mark's long Galilee section, the reading I am proposing here will confront the tendency in Protestant reading to view the gospels as passion narratives with extended introduction.[13] Recent postcolonial readings of Mark have rightfully highlighted how Jesus in Galilee embodies a mission of "subversion" and power-negotiation, making Galilee an intrinsic part of "the gospel" Mark is telling. Phrased in the themes of proximity and reconciliation, Jesus embarks on a mission of the renegotiation of powerbases of old, clearing the way for an encounter between his kingly rule and people from the margins.

Mark uses two words in particular to denote the powers at work in Jesus' mission. One is the concept of power or authority (ἐξουσία), which is immediately attached to his ministry (cf. Mark 1:22.27). Another is the adjective "newness" used to oppose the powers at work in Jesus to the powerbases of old (cf. Mark 1:27; 2:21-22).

---

[13] As famously stated by Martin Kähler (cf. 1892:33).

In this, I see a valid point in postcolonial and anti-imperial readings of Mark. However, in their effort to understand Mark as a coded resistance message against the Roman empire, they fundamentally misconstrue the way in which Mark brings Jesus to engage powers of old in a process, where Jesus as a warrior king engages in battle with a wide array of these old powers, who all are subdued or overthrown by the new beginning of the gospel of Jesus. Rome is simply not Mark's focus, but only one of the powers addressed by the newness and authority of Jesus.

To briefly list some examples of this power renegotiation:

a. The family, which according to the Biblical as well as the cultural standards of the day was one of the unnegotiable powerbases, is relativised by Jesus in the calling of the disciples (Mark 1:16-20) and in the reinterpretation of who his true family is (Mark 3:30-35, see further Jensen, 2011).

b. Another renegotiated powerbase is the Scribal and Pharisaic authority over the interpretation of the law (cf. e.g. Mark 1:22, 27; 2:10). In particular, this confrontation is felt over the issue of purity (cf. e.g. Mark 7:1-23), under which umbrella we also find Jesus' fellowship with the outcasts, degraded and unclean (e.g. Mark 1:41; 2:14-17; 5,6.27.41) producing questions for the legitimacy of his actions (Mark 2:16; 7:5, cf. e.g. Kazen 2013).

c. In continuation of the issue of purity, we find Jesus' intentional contact with the pagans in Decapolis (Mark 5:1-20; 7:31-37) and the area around Tyre and Sidon (Mark 7:24-30).

d. A special acute area of power confrontation concerns Jesus' defeat of demons, evil spirits and the ruler of demons himself, whose kingdom is robbed (cf. Mark 3:27). Connected to this theme, we find the way in which Jesus applies his authority and the newness of his kingdom to sickness, death (often mentioned in connection with exorcism, cf. Mark 1:34; 6:13) and even the destructive forces of nature (cf. Mark 4:35-41). In the same way as Jesus' kingdom fundamentally confronts Satan's kingdom (Mark 3:22-27), it fundamentally confronts the consequences of evil as an integral part of his ministry (cf. the summaries in Mark 3:10-12; 6:56).

e. In the string of subversions and renegotiations, we find Jesus' encounters with the Roman Empire. As already outlined, an intense discussion is presently unfolding in the research of Mark, and some are claiming that the evil of Rome is the actual target of Jesus' mission.[14] Without going into a discussion of the suggestions for more subtle references to Rome,[15] there are a number of instances in which Jesus is brought into direct contact with the Roman empire such as the question of imperial tax (Mark 12:13-17) and of course the crucifixion itself. Two things are important to notice in this regard. Firstly, crucifixion was the most severe Roman punishment used solely on slaves and rebels.[16] In the eyes of the Romans, Jesus died a rebel's death.[17] Secondly, the centurion's proclamation in Mark 15:39 is likely to be heard against the emperor's claim of being *divi filius,* son of a Divine. However, for two reasons the anti-imperial readings of Mark fail to persuade. On the one hand, it is obvious from the string of confrontations above that the Roman power is only one of those subverted and confronted by the authority of Jesus. On the other hand, these readings struggle to come to grips with Mark's key interpretative statements (especially Mark 10:45; 14:24 and 15:38), which all connect the death of Jesus to the temple cult in Jerusalem.[18]

[14] For instance, Stephen D. Moore labels Jesus' exorcism of "a legion" of demons in Mark 5:9 "a 'hermeneutical key' with which to unlock the gospel as a whole" (Moore 2006:73). Here Mark shows his true colours. He is not targeting evil spirits but the Roman powers as such.

[15] For instance, the dove coming upon Jesus in the baptism has been interpreted as a covert opposition to the eagle of Rome (cf. Peppard 2011).

[16] For an introduction to Roman crucifixion, see Samuelsson (2011). Hans Leander has labeled crucifixion pointedly "the material density" describing it as "the most repressive aspect of imperial discourse" (2013:246f).

[17] This is obvious from the reference to the political title "king" in the Roman process (Mark 15:2, 9, 12), whereas "Messiah" is used in the Jewish interrogation (Mark 14:61), just as Jesus aligned with another rebel from "the insurrection", Barabbas (Mark 15:7). In this regard, Joanne Dewey is correct when describing Roman crucifixion as a "political execution" that had "no connection to a religious ritual" (Dewey 2011:71).

[18] An exception to this rule is found in Winn (2018), where Adam Winn interprets Mark's presentation of Jesus as the destroyer of the temple as propaganda directed toward Flavian in post-war Rome, which presented the new emperor, Vespasian, as the destroyer of Jerusalem's temple. In the end, this interpretation remains unconvincing, since it fails to incorporate Mark's main interpretative statements such as 14:24.

f. We will return to the role of the temple in Mark below and only note here that Jesus' mission peaks when he arrives in Jerusalem and immediately confronts the power of the temple (cf. Mark 11:1-26; 13:1-2; 14:58 and more). Of all the powers Jesus renegotiates, the role, status and position of the temple is right at the centre, as framed by the rending of the veil as the immediate response to his death (Mark 15:38), which in turn forms an intercalation, an overarching sandwich pattern with the rending of the skies in the prologue to Jesus' mission (Mark 1:10, cf. e.g. Caneday 2004).

Read in the light of Mark's Isaianic framework, the theological point of Jesus' intentional power confrontations becomes clear: Mark is retelling the promise of the new exodus of Isaiah, which in a comprehensive and robust way restores the creation by undoing evil and its consequences (cf. e.g. Isaiah 61:1-2). Put into reconciliation-terms, the gospel of "reconciliation" is a robust and broad story. It is a story that engages the entire cosmos and universe. Mark's gospel is a screenplay in "realtime" of what Paul meant with his statement of God "reconciling the world to himself in Christ" (2 Cor 5:19).

3.4 Isaianic proximity in Jerusalem – cross and resurrection (Mark 11:1-16:8)

A firm result of our survey above is the way in which Jesus' Galilean mission becomes an integral part of "the gospel" Mark intends to narrate. This does not mean, however, that we cannot speak of a centre and zenith in Mark's structure. Throughout, Jesus is on his way to Jerusalem – and actually the first hint or foreshadowing[19] of the pivotal role of Jerusalem is given in Mark 1:14, connecting Jesus' first public action with the "handing over" of John. This is the exact same word that is later used to describe Jesus' "handing over" in Jerusalem (Mark 8:31; 9:31; 10:32-34). Already in Mark 2:19-20, we are notified as readers that the groom will be taken from the bride and in Mark 3:6 the first plot against Jesus is formed.

---

[19] A number of researchers have pointed to Mark's intensive use of the literary device of foreshadowing later, pivotal events throughout his narrative. (Cf. e.g. Malbon 1993; Williams 2013).

This produces the central question of Mark's story: In which way does the death of Jesus advance his Messianic identity and bringing of the nearness of God's Isaianic kingdom and new exodus?[20]

Nowhere do the different understandings of "the gospel" collide more head-on than in this question, and the different understandings produce highly different answers:

    a.   As mentioned above, the anti-imperial readings focus on Mark 15:39 as the hermeneutical key to the cross-event. The centurion's confession of Jesus as "a son of a god",[21] is not only a confession regarding Jesus, but at the very same time a denouncement of his former "son of a god", the emperor in Rome. The cross-event epitomizes Jesus' mission against Rome. When releasing its most severe penalty on Jesus, the empire at the very same time handed Jesus the means to break its powers from within, in a process of reinterpretation (*catecresis*) transforming the cross from a symbol of fear to a symbol of honour for the disciples (Mark 8:34, cf. e.g. Leander 2013:139-44).

    b.   Contrary to this, an interpretation of "the gospel" from an Isaianic trajectory proposes Mark 15:38 and the rending of the temple veil as Mark's hermeneutical key. While Jesus dies by the hands of the Romans, the crucial point is Mark's interpretation hereof as a cultic death connected to the temple.[22]

In other words, when coming head to head, these two understandings are rooted side by side in Mark's narrative. Is there a way out of the deadlock that comes to grips with the obvious fact that the cultic and the imperial implication of Jesus' death, for the very reason of Mark 15:38 and 15:39, cannot be mutually exclusive in the theology of Mark?

The reading I am going to present will try to distinguish between three different (but connected) layers, through which Mark unfolds the theological meaning

---

[20] That Mark intends to answer this question is apparent from the disciples' reaction to Jesus' first prediction (Mark 8:32).

[21] The precise wording in Mark is indefinite. Still, it is possible to follow the traditional translation, "son of God," (cf. Collins 2007:766-8).

[22] For various interpretations along this line, see Collins (2007:760-4).

he is placing on the death of Jesus. First, Mark unapologetically reinterprets the cross as the very centre of Jesus' kingdom-mission. This is seen by the way in which there is an explosion of the kingly terms. Nowhere is the king-term used more often than exactly around the cross-event in chapter 15 (cf. 15:2, 9, 12, 18, 26, 32, 43). On a structural level, Mark specifically discusses the validity of the conflation of cross and king by having Jesus confirm it just before the cross-event (Mark 14:61-62) and the bystanders deny it just afterwards (Mark 15:32). The Isaianic vision of God as king lifted up and enthroned in Jerusalem (52:7-8) does, according to Mark, come to fulfilment in the cross-event. Mark has alerted his readers to this surprising conflation since Mark 1:14 with ever growing clarity (most evidently in the three predictions of Jesus' death in Mark 8:31; 9:31; 10:32-34), and when the event unfolds he uses all his available literary techniques to state his point: The fulfilment of the coming of the Kingdom happens *through* the cross. In the light of this, the centurion's confession, when he sees how Jesus dies in Mark 15:39, is not an identification of Mark's real enemy, but rather a confirmation of the surprising conflation. Who is better fit to confirm the crucified as king than the one serving the "king" in Rome? In Mark's theological outlook the cross-event is a kingly victory.

Secondly, *how* exactly is the merging of opposites, cross and king, a victory? The answer to this is found in two main theological ideas that Mark binds together to present his interpretation of the cross as a victory. Stage one concerns the way in which Jesus' death impacts the temple. As already noticed, this connection has been subjected to harsh criticism for some time now (cf. e.g. Dewey 2011). But from a straightforward reading I find it to be a very solid point of Mark to connect Jesus' death to the temple:[23]

a. Jesus' entry into Jerusalem is connected to the temple, just as the entire week before his crucifixion is linked with his critiques of the temple (cf. Mark 11:1-25; 12:1-12; 13:1-2; 14:58; 15:29).
b. In 14:24, we find the most important interpretative verse, in which Jesus labels the wine as "my blood of the covenant, which is poured out for many." This expression has only a single precedent in the Hebrew Bible, the inauguration of the covenant at Mt. Sinai in Exodus 24:8. After the reception of the ten commandments, a banquet is held on the slopes of Mt. Sinai

---

[23] For recent investigations pointing to the crucial importance of the temple in Mark's narrative, see Gray (2008), Joseph (2016) and Wardle (2016).

between 70 of the elders as representatives of the people and JHVH. The proximity and community they have here is cultic and in effect "a temple"-experience, since the very essence of the temple or tabernacle is to host the proximity of God to the people. The sacrifices offered in this connection are, however, not sin or guilt offerings, but fellowship offerings.[24]

c. This brings us to the question, if Mark interprets Jesus' death as an atonement for sin.[25] Since Mark does not directly refer to sin or atonement in his interpretation of Jesus' death, the case for this interpretation hinges on the notion "for many." While debated where exactly this statement has its location of origin in the Hebrew Bible, I find the classic interpretation to be the best option, namely Isaiah 53 speaking of the death of the servant as a guilt offering on behalf of "the many" (cf. Collins 1998; Watts 2007:230-2). This is highlighted also by the presentation of Jesus' death as a "ransom" (λύτρον, Mark 10:45), which may mean cultic atonement.[26]

d. This then brings us to Mark 15:38 and the rending of the veil. In the light of all said here, it should come as no surprise that I interpret this happening as the hermeneutical key to understanding the death of Jesus. While not enough information is provided by Mark to clarify whether he is thinking of the inner or the outer veil (cf. Collins 2007:759-60), the main point is clear enough: Jesus' death does something to the temple. With a divine passive, the veil is torn from top to bottom leaving open access and ending the need for further blood manipulation in order to provide proximity between God and the people (cf. the reinterpretation of the blood in Mark 14:24).

---

[24] This point is corroborated by the fundamental principle of the temple, namely to provide the means for God to reside among his people, as is evident in the temple nomenclature such as tent, house, palace (cf. Meyers 1992:351; Wassen 2013:58-9).

[25] For an in-depth investigation of this question specifically, see Jensen, Morten Hørning 2019, "Atonement Theology in the Gospel of Mark as Isaianic Proximity to the Divine", BIBLICA 100.1, pp. 84-104.

[26] E.g. Exodus 30:12-16. For a detailed discussion hereof, see Watts (2007:203-6). For an introduction to the vast research on this issue, see McKnight (2005:56-75).

Thirdly, the final way in which Mark makes sense of the cross is closely connected to the second and really just the flipside of the coin. The Siamese twin to Jesus' cultic temple death is his resurrection, which brings to full daylight the very nerve of what Mark wants to say and has been saying since the prologue: In Jesus, there is proximity to God through reconciliation. Actually, we could label this Mark's theology of rending:

a. In Mark 1:10 the heavens are rended above Jesus, and the term used in this connection forms an inclusion with Mark 15:38 and the rending of the temple veil. This emphasizes that an interpretative key to the death of Jesus is the drawing near of God as envisioned in Isaiah's second exodus.

b. Nowhere are the proximity theme and the rending of barriers more closely connected than in the resurrection of Jesus. It has been foreshadowed since Mark 8:31 and is enacted in chapter 16:the stone is rolled away and the way is cleared for a re-enactment of community, even for Peter (Mark 16:7).

c. The renewal of the community between Jesus and his disciples is emphasized twice by Mark (14:28; 16:7) highlighting it as a pivotal plot of the narrative. Jesus' death and resurrection in Jerusalem produces the means for a revival of the proximity in Galilee.

4 Conclusion: A Gospel of Reconciliation and Proximity

This investigation has been concerned with understanding what Mark wanted to communicate with his pointed *Stichwort*, "the gospel." Since the discovery of the Prine inscription in 1899, this issue has been vividly discussed in New Testament research with two interpretative strongholds focussed on the Roman Empire or an Isaianic trajectory respectively.

The reading I am offering here in light of the conference theme of "reconciliation" is that Mark, in effect, is presenting a "gospel of reconciliation" in the Pauline sense of 2 Corinthians, of a God taking the initiative to remove strongholds of power blocking the way for an encounter with the newness of his kingly rule. While Mark does not use the reconciliation nomenclature, the sense of "the gospel" as a relational category of nearness and union is embedded in the language of proximity (ἐγγίζω), rending (σχίζω), touching (ἅπτω), seing (ὁράω) and the like.

I arrive at this conclusion through the following main steps: Firstly, by asking for the content of Mark's "gospel," we should begin where he emphatically wants us to begin, i.e. with Isaiah. Mark is presenting Jesus as embodying the long-awaited "new exodus" bringing God and God's kingdom *near.*

Secondly, when trying to unfold what the nearness of God's Isaianic kingdom brings, we should step back from our well-trodden categories of a spiritual gospel of forgiveness or a social gospel of action, and observe the way in which the thematic thrust of the Isaianic vision concerns God's return to Jerusalem in his full, kingly glory. At its core level, the "gospel of Isaiah" concerns God's re-enacting of his presence in Jerusalem, which in the retelling of Mark translates into God's proximity in Jesus.

Thirdly, in defining Mark's "gospel" as a relational category of reconciliation, I am at the same time criticizing the two main competing interpretations. In his effort to describe the way in which Jesus proximates God's kingdom, Mark clearly uses power-language and power-renegotiation, including an attack on the powerbase of the Roman Empire. He likewise uses cultic language, as well as purity language. But in essence, Mark's gospel is neither a power language of rebellion nor a transactional language of cultic appeasement or placability. It is a relational language of bringing former separated parties together.

Fourthly, if we ask the question how Mark's "gospel" might inform a present day "gospel-life," I would suggest using the keywords "Galilee" and "Jerusalem" as basic guidelines. Jesus' Galilean ministry outlines a gospel-ministry engaged in comprehensive power negotiation, in which Jesus as a warrior attacks the powers of old and redistributes the hierarchy under the realm of the Kingdom. In this trajectory, something also happens to the Roman empire – which translates to us in a simple but profound way: The gospel always engages our world. A genuine church praxis informed by "the gospel" of the Gospel of Mark is necessarily bent on effecting reconciliation between people. Not in contrast but in fruitful tension to this, Jesus' ministry in Jerusalem has its overarching focal point on the temple and the grave. Jesus' death does something to the temple veil and the grave by rending both, reinterpreting the Roman cross-event as a gift "for many." Another way of phrasing this is that Mark's gospel-program of reconciliation works both vertically, establishing fellowship with God (*coram deo*), and horizontally, establishing fellowship between people (*coram hominibus*).

Finally, in my estimation, such a robust understanding of the biblical vision of reconciliation is not appreciated enough in recent trends within theological research and church practice. Some are unwilling to talk about the vertical dimension of reconciliation, since it smells too much of appeasement and the blood manipulation of, for example, Greek religion. Others are unwilling to talk about the horizontal dimension of reconciliation, since it smells too much of a liberal, social gospel. I suggest that both extremes fall short in coming to terms with Mark's vision of "the gospel." A much-needed reorientation towards a robust gospel begins with appreciating that the heart of the gospel spells "*relational reconciliation*" in and through Christ with God and with the world.

Bibliography

Abernethy, Andrew T. 2016. *The Book of Isaiah and God's Kingdom: A Thematic-Theological Approach*. New Studies in Biblical Theology. London: Apollos.

Bird, Michael F., and Joel Willits, eds. 2011. *Paul and the Gospels: Christologies, Conflicts, and Convergences*. London: T&T Clark.

Boring, M. Eugene. 1990. Mark 1:1-15 and the Beginning of the Gospel. *Semeia* 52, 43-81.

Büchsel, Friedrich. 1933. καταλλάσσω. Pages 254-8 in vol. I of *Theologisches Wörterbuch zum Neuen Testament*. Edited by Gerhard Kittel. IX vols. Stuttgart: Verlag von W. Kohlhammer.

Büchsel, Friedrich. 1964. καταλλάσσω. Pages 254-8 in vol. I of *New Testament Dictionary of New Testament Theology*. Edited by Gerhard Kittel, and Geoffrey W. Bromiley. X vols. Grand Rapids, Michigan: WM. B. Eerdmans Publishing Company.

Caneday, A.B. 2004. Christ's Baptism and Crucifixion. *Southern Baptist Journal of Theology* 8(3), 70-81.

Collins, Aela Yarbro. 1998. Finding Meaning in the Death of Jesus. *Journal of Religion* 78(2), 175-96.

Collins, Aela Yarbro. 2007. *Mark: A Commentary*. Hermeneia - A Critical and Historical Commentary on the Bible. Minneapolis: Fortress Press.

Croy, N. Clayton. 2001. Where the Gospel Text Begins: A Non-Theological Interpretation of Mark 1:1. *Novum Testamentum* 43(2), 105-27.

Dalman, Gustaf. 1930. *Die Worte Jesu*. Vol. 1. 1898. Reprint. Leipzig: J. C. Hinrichs'sche Buchhandlung.

Danker, Frederich W. 1982. *Benefactor: Epigraphic Study of a Greco-Roman and New Testament Semantic Field*. Missouri: Clayton Publishing House.

Dechow, Jon F. 2014. The 'Gospel' and the Emperor Cult: From Bultmann to Crossan. *Forum* 3(2), 63-88.

Dewey, Joanna. 2011. Sacrifice No More. *Biblical Theology Bulletin* 41(2), 68-75.

Dittenberger, Wilhelm, ed. 1905. Vol. 2. *Orientis Graeci Inscriptiones Selectae: Supplementum Syllogoges Inscriptionum Graecarum*. Leipzig: S. Hirzel.

Elliott, J. K. 2000. Mark 1.1-3 - A Later Addition to the Gospel? *New Testament Studies* 46, 584-8.

Evans, Craig A. 2006. The Beginning of the Good News and the Fulfillment of Scripture on the Gospel of Mark. Pages 83-103 in *Hearing the Old Testament in the New*. Edited by Stanley E. Porter. Grand Rapids, Michigan: Eerdmans.

Frankemölle, Hubert. 1984. Evangelium als theologischer Begriff und sein Bezug zur literarischen Gattung 'Evangelium' (Zweiter Teil). Pages 1635-704 in *Principat*. Edited by Wolfgang Haase. Vol. II.25.2 of *Aufstieg und Niedergang der römischen Welt*. Berlin: Walter de Gruyter.

Frankemölle, Hubert. 1988. *Evangelium - Begriff und Gattung: Ein Forschungbericht*. Stuttgarter biblische Beiträge. Stuttgart: Verlag katolisches Bibelwerk.

Friedrich, Gerhard. 1935. εὐαγγελίζω, εὐαγγέλιον, προευαγγελίζομαι, εὐαγγελιστής. Pages 705-35 in vol. II of *Theologisches Wörterbuch zum Neuen Testament*. Edited by Gerhard Kittel. IX vols. Stuttgart: Verlag von W. Kohlhammer.

Guelich, Robert A. 1982. "The Beginning of the Gospel" - Mark 1:1-15. *Biblical Research* 27, 5-15.

Gray, Timothy C. 2008. *The Temple in the Gospel of Mark: A Study in Its Narrative Role*. Wissenschaftliche Untersuchungen Zum Neuen Testament 2. Reihe. Tübingen: Mohr Siebeck.

Harnack, Adolf von. 1904. Als die Zeit erfüllet war. Pages 301-6 in *Reden und Aufsätze, erster Band*. Gieszen: J. Ricker'sche Verlagsbuchhandlung. Repr. 1899. *Christlichen Welt* 51

Horbury, William. 2005. 'Gospel' in Herodian Judaea. Pages 7-30 in *The Written Gospel*. Edited by Markus Bockmuehl, and Donald A. Hagner. Cambridge: Cambridge University Press.

Joseph, Simon J. 2016. *Jesus and the Temple: The Crucifixion in Its Jewish Context*. Society for New Testament Studies. Cambridge: Cambridge University Press.

Lim, Bo H. 2010. *The "Way of the Lord" in the Book of Isaiah*. New York: T & T Clark International.

Llewelyn, Stephen, and G. H. R. Horsley. 1978. *New Documents Illustrating Early Christianity*. Vol. 3 of G. H. R. Horsley. Grand Rapids, Michigan: Eerdmans.

Lund, Øystein. 2007. *Way Metaphors and Way Topics in Isaiah 40-55*. Forschungen zum Alten Testament 2. Reihe. Tübingen: Mohr Siebeck.

Heilig, Christopher. 2017. *Hidden Criticism? The Methodology and Plausibility of the Search for a Counter-Imperial Subtext in Mark.* Minneapolis: Fortress Press.

Horsley, Richard A. 2003. *Jesus and Empire: The Kingdom of God and the New World Disorder*. Minneapolis: Fortress Press.

Horsley, Richard A. 2008. Jesus and Empire. Pages 75-96 in *In the Shadow of the Temple: Reclaiming the Bible As a History of Faithful Resistance*. Edited by Richard A. Horsley. Luisville, Kentucky: Westminster John Knox Press.

Jensen, Morten Hørning. 2011. Conflicting Calls? Family and Discipleship in Mark & Matthew in the Light of First-Century Galilean Village Life. Pages 205-32 in *Mark and Matthew, Texts and Contexts I: Understanding the First Gospels in Their First Century Settings.* Edited by Eve-Marie Becker, and Anders Runesson. Tübingen: Mohr Siebeck.

Kähler, Martin. 1892. *Der sogenannte historische Jesus und der geschichtliche, biblische Christus.* Leipzig: A. Dieterich'sche Verlagsbuchh.

Kazen, Thomas. 2013. *Scripture, Interpretation, or Authority? Motives and Arguments in Jesus' Halakic Conflicts.* Wissenschaftliche Untersuchungen zum Neuen Testament. Tübingen: Mohr Siebeck.

Klauck Hans-Josef. 1997. *Vorspiel im Himmel? Erzähltechnik und Theologie im Markusprolog.* Biblisch-Theologische Studien. Germany: Neukirchener Verlag.

Larsen, Kevin W. 2004. The Structure of Mark's Gospel: Current Proposals. *Currents in Biblical Research* 3(1), 140-60.

Leander, Hans. 2013. *Discourses of Empire: The Gospel of Mark From a Postcolonial Perspective.* Semeia Studies. Atlanta: Society of Biblical Literature.

Malbon, Elizabeth Struthers. 1993. Echoes and Foreshadowing in Mark 4-8: Reading and Rereading. *Journal of Biblical Literature* 112(2):211-30.

Marcus, Joel. 2000. Mark - Interpreter of Paul. *New Testament Studies* 46, 473-87.

McKnight, S. 2005. *Jesus and His Death: Historiography, the Historical Jesus, and Atonement Theory.* Waco, Texas: Baylor University Press.

Meyers, Carol L. 1992. Temple, Jerusalem. Pages 350-69 in vol. 6 of *The Anchor Bible Dictionary.* Edited by David Noel Freedman. 6 vols. New York: Doubleday.

Mommsen, Theodor, and U. von Wilamowitz-Mollendorf. 1899. Die Einführung des asianischen Kalenders. *Mitteilungen des kaiserlich deutschen archaeologischen Instituts, athenische Abteilung* XXIV, 275-93.

Moore, Stephen D. 2006. Mark and Empire. Pages 70-90 in *Recognising the Margins: Developments in Biblical and Theological Studies.* Edited by Werner G. Jeanrond, and Andrew D. H. Mayes. Dublin: The Columba Press.

Peppard, Michael. 2011. *The Son of God in the Roman World: Divine Sonship in Its Social and Political Context.* Oxford: Oxford University Press.

Samuelsson, Gunnar. 2011. *Crucifixion in Antiquity: An Inquiry Into the Background and Significance of the New Testament Terminology of Crucifixion*. Wissenschaftliche Untersuchungen Zum Neun Testament. Tübingen: Mohr Siebeck.

Sherk, Robert K. 1969. *Roman Documents From the Greek East*. Baltimore, Maryland: The Johns Hopkins Press.

Silva, Moisés. 2014. ἀλλάσσω. Pages 242-50 in vol. 1 of *New International Dictionary of New Testament Theology and Exegesis*. Edited by Moisés Silva. 5 vols. Grand Rapids, Michigan: Zondervan.

Smith, Daniel Lynwood. 2016. The Uses of 'New Exodus' in New Testament Scholarship: Preparing a Way Through the Wilderness. *Currents in Biblical Research* 14(2):207-43.

Stanton, Graham. 2004. *Jesus and the Gospel*. Cambridge: Cambridge University Press.

Strecker, Georg. 1975. Das Evangelium Jesu Christi. Pages 503-48 in *Jesus Christus in Historie und Theologie*. Edited by Georg Strecker. Tübingen: J.C.B. Mohr.

Stuhlmacher, Peter. 1968. *Das paulinische Evangelium: Vorgeschichte*. Göttingen: Vandenhoeck & Ruprecht.

Wardle, Timothy. 2016. Mark, the Jerusalem Temple and Jewish Sectarianism: Why Geographical Proximity Matters in Determining the Provenance of Mark. *New Testament Studies* 62, 60-78.

Wassen, Cecilia. 2013. Do You Have to Be Pure in a Metaphorical Temple?. Pages 55-86 in *Purity, Holiness, and Identity in Judaism and Christianity: Essays in Memory of Susan Haber (Wissenschaftliche Untersuchungen zum Neuen Testament)*. Edited by Carl S. Ehrlich, Anders Runesson, and Eileen Schuller. Tübingen: Mohr Siebeck.

Watts, Rikki E. 1997. *Isaiah's New Exodus and Mark*. Wissenschaftliche Untersuchungen zum Neuen Testament. Reihe 2. Tübingen: Mohr Siebeck.

Watts, Rikki E. 2007. Mark. Pages 111-249 in *Commentary on the New Testament Use of the Old Testament*. Edited by G. K. Beale, and D. A. Carson. Grand Rapids, Michigan: Baker Academic.

Wikgren, Allen. 1942. Ἀρχὴ τοῦ εὐαγγελίου. *Journal of Biblical Literature* 61, 11-20.

Williams, Joel. 2006. Does Mark's Gospel Have an Outline? *Journal of the Evangelical Theological Society* 49(3), 505-25.

Williams, Joel. 2013. Foreshadowing, Echoes, and the Blasphemy At the Cross (Mark 15:29). *Journal of Biblical Literature* 132(4), 913-33.

Winn, Adam. 2008. *The Purpose of Mark's Gospel: An Early Christian Response to Imperial Propaganda.* Wissenschaftliche Untersuchungen zum Neuen Testament 2. Reihe. Tübingen: Mohr Siebeck.

Winn, Adam. 2018. *Reading Mark's Christology under Caesar: Jesus the Messiah and Roman Imperial Ideology.* Downers Grove, Illinois: IVP Academic.

"And there arose a sharp disagreement" (Acts 15:39): Inner-Christian Conflicts and their Resolution in Acts 6–15

Christoph Stenschke

Abstract

The current focus on conflict and violence in the popular and academic study of religious conflict must not detract from instances of de-escalation and resolution of conflict. While resolution of conflict and reconciliation must not be equated, the former in most cases provides the basis for the latter. In view of this, this article examines the de-escalation and resolution of the inner-Christian conflicts in the Book of Acts (6:1–7; 11:1–18; 15:1–41). How is reconciliation achieved and the unity of the community retained? What resources are available to the community for resolving its conflicts? A final section reflects on how this portrayal can be applied to today's inner-Christian and other conflicts.

1 Introduction

The Book of Acts contains conflicts of all sorts. It offers a multifactorial portrayal of religious conflict of different types, including a number of conflicts within Christian communites. Before turning to the conflict and resolution accounts of Acts, we consider issues raised by the survey of the current discussion of religious conflict by Mayer (2013). Mayer argues that religious conflict (2013:1f), encompasses not just the physical domain (violent acts), but also the discursive (violent, i.e., hostile/hate-filled speech), raising questions about the precise relationship between these two forms, how each should be addressed, and the degree to which each is harmful to society. The motivation for such violence, moreover, is often complex, leading to the conclusion that violent "religious" conflicts in late antiquity, for instance, were rarely purely religiously motivated. On careful examination they can be shown to owe as much, if not more, to political considerations, local conditions, and the personal motives of the chief protagonists.

Mayer emphasises the need for careful definition of the concept of religious conflict. According to her (2013:3), religious conflict is best understood as a complex phenomenon that involves a combination of contested domains, which include power, personality, space or place, and group identity. "These contested domains should not be confused with enabling factors or conditions, which ... can be political, social, economic, cultural and psychological". She argues for a distinction between "the root cause/s of the religious conflict (what is contested) and the way in which the conflict is discursively or narratively framed".

A further issue needs clarification in defining religious conflict, namely the agents involved. Mayer explains (2013:4):

> While individuals may be the chief protagonists, the coupling of religion with conflict implies that the agents involved are not individuals, but collective individuals, i.e., groups or communities. ... the agents in religious conflict are two or more groups that derive from identifiably separate religions, separate factions within the same religion (that result from splintering, i.e., sectarianism), the same faction within a religion (where splintering has not yet occurred – and may or may not, in fact, eventuate), and secular authority, the latter of which may also wield religious authority.

These observations are important for the inner-Christian conflicts of Acts. Their protagonists are groups of people or individuals. However, the individuals "self-identify and operate as part of a larger system", that is, the apostolic band and/or the Jerusalem Christian community. All figures are firmly set in the Christian community, although this community at large is involved in these conflicts to different extents.

Mayer also observes that in the recent discussion of religious conflict,

> the *focus on violence* (one extreme of religious conflict) obscures broader questions about what occurs *before or apart from violence*: the mechanisms at play in how conflict originates in the first instance, how it manifests in its early stages, the phenomenon of splintering into sub-groups (sectarianism) within a religion, and precisely what factors are operative in conflict escalation and de-escalation (2013:19, italics CS).

In contrast to other conflicts in Acts, the inner-community conflicts do not involve violence. While sharp disagreement is not passed over in silence, there is no violence. Therefore, we focus on the "broader questions" and examine the portrayal of "what occurs before or apart from *violence*", the origins of conflict and its manifestations in early stages, the contested domains and enabling conditions and the factors operative in de-escalation and resolution of conflict. The current focus on religious *conflict and violence* must not detract from instances of conflict *de-escalation* and conflict *resolution*, which also appear in Acts. Once the conflicts are resolved, Acts paints a portrait of peaceful *co-existence* and *co-operation* of the former conflict parties. This portrait suggests some measure of *transition* and *assimilation* to the consensus which was reached.[1] In short, we will apply a number of insights of recent theorising on religious conflict to Acts in order to shed fresh light on the inner-Christian conflicts. Some observations are in order:

- In this study, we concentrate on the *literary portrayal* of religious conflict. I do not discuss the historical validity of this portrayal or its contribution to the reconstruction of early Christian history.
- We focus only on conflicts involving the *whole community*, at least as *one* of the parties in conflict and resolution. While we include the conflict of Peter with a sub-group of the community of Jerusalem in Acts 11:1–18 ("the circumcision party", 11:2), we have *not* included the conflict of Peter with Ananias and Sapphira in Acts 5:1–11 and the conflict between Paul and Barnabas over John Mark in Acts 15:37–40. It is interesting to note that both of these inner-Christian conflicts between *individuals* are *not* resolved: There is neither de-escalation nor resolution to the conflict of Acts 5. Ananias and Sapphira remain in hypocrisy and lies; they do not repent and are not even given the opportunity to do so.[2] Paul and Barnabas are not "reconciled" to each other, part their ways and seek other co-workers for their further ministry. Paul is not reconciled to John Mark.[3] The decision not to include these conflicts obviously impinges on the conclusions. However,

---

[1] See Mayer (2013:17).

[2] The case could be argued that Peter does not act as a private person but as the leader of the group of the apostles or as leader of the community. He acts with their approval.

[3] While other passages in the NT suggest that there was some kind of rapprochement later on, Acts remains silent about it.

our focus in this paper is not on the conflicts as such but rather on their de-escalation and resolution.

- Our decision, not to speak of "reconciliation" but more modestly merely of the *de-escalation and resolution of conflict*, needs some explanation. According to R. W. Yarbrough, reconciliation "may be defined as the restoration of fellowship between estranged parties".[4] With reference to reconciliation among people in the New Testament, Yarbrough writes: "Paul underlines the social dimension of Christ's death; by it Jew and Gentile, paradigmatic for all humankind and the fractured creation, are made into 'one new man ... through the cross, by which he put to death their hostility' (Eph 2:15–16) ... Jesus points to the need to be reconciled ... 'to your brother' as a precondition of true worship (Matt 5:23–24)".[5] Yarbrough's definition raises several issues. While the "restoration of fellowship" well fits the context of inner-Christian disputes as the community is and should be characterised by fellowship, the question remains whether the cases of inner-community conflict in Acts are incidents of "estrangement", and if so, to what extent. Did the occasion of the conflicts lead to serious estrangement which needed "reconciliation"? Probably it boils down to a matter of definition. There is a certain danger that if we are looking for conflict and its de-escalation and resolution we are prone to identify conflict in incidents where the author of Acts or its first readers may not have seen conflict, as they lived in an agonistic culture different from ours.

In addition, as the language of reconciliation hardly occurs in Acts, we use more neutral terms and speak of the de-escalation and resolution of conflict. The one and only occurrence of the technical terminology of reconciliation in Acts appears in Stephen's survey of the history of Israel in Acts 7:26.[6] Stephen menti-

---

[4] For a survey see Yarbrough (2000:502).

[5] See also the use of reconciliation terms in 1 Cor 7:11.

[6] There is no occurrence of this terminology with regard to reconciliation between God and people, as in Pauline literature.

ons Moses' attempt of mediating between two quarrelling Israelites. This occurrence shows that the author of Acts is aware of this terminology, but for some reason has not employed it anywhere else, e.g. in the context of the solution of inner-community conflicts.[7]

2 Three Inner-Christian Conflicts in Acts and their Resolution

The beginning of Acts offers a portrayal of an ideal community of believers in Jesus in Jerusalem (2:42–47; 4:32–37). There is sharing of goods and great unity among the believers[8] in contrast to the various groups within Judaism and the inhabitants of Jerusalem. However, as the accounts of conflict in Acts 6:1–6; 11:1–18, and 15:1–35 indicate, this portrayal of the early Christian community of Jerusalem is not without challenges. In our study of each of these conflicts in the following, we will follow a pattern: After a brief summary of the occasion, we will examine the measures taken to initiate de-escalation and resolution of conflict. In closing, we ask whether the solution was persistent.

2.1 Acts 6:1–7

The *occasion* of the first inner-community conflict is a complaint by the "Hellenists", Jewish Christians with a diaspora background[9], against the "Hebrews" (Jewish Christians from Judea or Jerusalem) about the widows of the Hellenist faction being neglected in the daily distribution. As the distribution was the apostles' responsibility up to that point, the complaint should have been directed against them. Acts does not indicate why this was not the case,[10] neither is there indication whether the complaint was justified nor whether the neglect of the widows was more perceived than real fact. Compared to the conflict of the apostles with the religious leadership of Jerusalem in Acts 4–5, the account of this first inner-community conflict is short and its course "mild" (no threats of violence, no violence).

---

[7] Perhaps this was the case as the attempt of Moses failed.

[8] For a recent detailed analysis see Thompson (2012) and Hume (2011).

[9] For their identity see Zugmann (2009).

[10] Did this happen out of reverence for the apostles? Were people slow to criticise them after the Ananias and Sapphira incident or the stunning miracles of Acts 5? The apostles' conflict with the religious leaders of Jerusalem will have impacted their responsibilities within the Christian community.

The de-escalation of this conflict starts with the initiative of the apostles. They do not ignore the situation or the complaint but call *the whole community* together (6:2). They remind the community of the particular task given to them and insist that they cannot or can no longer "serve tables" instead. They trust the assembled community and propose that seven people be elected by the community for this task and indicate their qualification (6:3). The apostles will stick to their particular calling. "And what they said pleased *the whole gathering*". As a result the whole community chose seven men who had previously fulfilled the outlined criteria. All seven men bear Greek names. Presumably they come from the group of the Hellenists. Apparently, they were trusted to include the Hebrew widows as well. These men were brought to the apostles and ordained to this task. This was a public act. It was clear to the whole community who was now entrusted with "serving tables". Acts 6 does not report the consequences of this solution for the community.[11] Presumably the men fulfilled their task and the complaints stopped. The unity – which was emphasised previously – was restored.[12]

The solution to this conflict was persistent. Acts does not report further conflicts between these parties or along these lines. The accounts of further inner-community conflicts do not mention these groups again nor are there further instances of complaint.

2.2 Acts 11:1–18

On the surface, the *occasion* of this second round of conflict is the fact that Peter went to Gentiles in Caesarea and ate with them (11:3; the account of his activities is given in Acts 10:1–48). The events in Caesarea become known in Jerusalem: "Now the apostles and brothers who were throughout Judea heard that the Gentiles had received the word of God"). On his return to Jerusalem, Peter is challenged by the "circumcision party" (11:2). Their identity is difficult to define. Schnabel (2012:508) observes:

Since their critique does not mention the need to circumcise the converted Gentiles, they are evidently not identical with the "circumcision group" of Gal 2:12 …, nor are they identical with the minority group in the Jerusalem church con-

---

[11] See Acts 6:7.

[12] To what extent Hellenists and the Hebrews were "estranged" from each other and had to be (and now were) *reconciled* is difficult to determine (Yarbrough).

sisting of converted Pharisees who later demanded that Gentile converts be circumcised (Acts 15:5). The expression "the circumcised believers" describes Jewish believers who, as Jews, obviously were circumcised, in contrast to the
converted Gentiles (…, v. 1), who were not.

This group criticised Peter for going to Gentiles (presumably for entering their
ritually unclean houses) and for eating with them (presumably food which was
unclean and/or not properly tithed).

Like with the complaint against the Hebrews (when actually the apostles were
responsible, not the "Hebrews"), one may ask whether Peter's own transgres-
sion of Jewish purity laws was the real issue in this conflict. In doing so, Peter
relativized important aspects of Jewish identity. But was it not actually the
inclusion of Gentiles *as Gentiles* into the people of God? Perhaps this is suggested by the vague accusation of "going to Gentiles" and by the conclusion in
Acts 11:18: The critics do not explicitly agree that Peter was right in going to
Gentiles and eating with them, but conclude that God has granted to the Gentiles also repentance that leads to life.

Again the course of this second conflict is mild (in comparison to the previous
conflict of Stephen with some diaspora Jews and the ensuing persecution of
Christians, and with the fate suffered by Paul in Damascus and in Jerusalem).

The process of *de-escalation* is initiated by Peter's detailed account of the
events in good order, which preceded his disputed behaviour and which explains the reason for his change of attitude and behaviour (11:5–17). Peter summarises the events of chapter 10 and emphasises the *divine interventions* in the
process. He first mentions the vision which challenged his own attitude and that
of his critics (11:5–10): "What God has made clean, do not call common"
(11:9). He also refers to the divine command to go along with the envoys of
Cornelius ("And the Spirit told me to go with them, making no distinction"
(11:12). Only on that basis, did Peter enter a Gentile house. If he wanted to be
obedient (which is mandatory to do when the Spirit prompts, see 5:32), Peter
had no choice but to go to uncircumcised men, as he was charged (11:3).

Peter mentions six Christians who came with him and served as witnesses of
the event (12). Then Peter quotes verbatim the message which Cornelius received from an angel, who commanded him to summon Peter (13) and indicated
the significance of this encounter: "he will declare to you a message by which
you will be saved, you and all your household" (14). Peter next refers to the
supernatural coming of the Holy Spirit on the audience, apart from all concern

for purity regulations and circumcision: "As I began to speak, the Holy Spirit fell on them, just as on us at the beginning" (15).

Peter also shares with them how he, at that moment, remembered the words of Jesus, the undisputed authority accepted by Peter and his critics. The event recalls the annunciation of Jesus: "John baptized with water, but you will be baptized with the Holy Spirit" (16). That the announcement was actually given to the Jewish disciples and does not refer to Gentiles is apparently not an issue. In closing, Peter shares the conclusions which he drew from the vision, from the divine preparation of the encounter, and from the coming of the Spirit and which constitute the basis for his disputed behaviour, namely eating with Gentiles (11:3): "If then God gave the same gift to them as he gave to us when we believed in the Lord Jesus Christ, who was I that I should stand in God's way?". If God made no distinction, neither should people distinguish (any more).

The solution of conflict comes as Peter's critics accept his explanation for his disputed behaviour (going to Gentiles, eating with them): "And when they heard these things, they fell silent". They conclude: "And they glorified God, saying, 'Then to the Gentiles also God has granted repentance that leads to life" (11:18). The implication is that Gentiles need not become Jews first before they can participate in God's salvation for Israel. Therefore it was acceptable for Peter to go Gentiles (on divine instruction) and to have fellowship with them (on divine prompting). The critics were silenced and the conflict ends in joint glorifying of God.

Solution involved servient steps: Peter takes his critics seriously and explains to them the course of the events in detail (likely his speech in Acts 11 is a shortened summary of the events, the actual speech will have lasted longer than some 80 seconds). As had happened to him before, the critics come to realise the legitimacy of Peter's course of action and withdraw their criticism.

In the presentation of Acts, the solution to this conflict is persistent. Acts only now reports the systematic Gentile mission of Diaspora Jewish Christians from Jerusalem in Antioch. The next conflict in Acts 15 indicates that at least some Jewish Christians challenged the conclusion that Gentiles *as Gentiles* had been granted the repentance that leads to life.

2.3 Acts 15

Stage I: Conflict in Antioch. The *occasion* of this prolonged conflict is the legitimacy of the inclusion of Gentiles *as Gentiles* into the people of God as practiced by the nascent Gentile mission of the Hellenists in Antioch and by the missionaries from Antioch elsewhere. A number of Christians from Judea (v. 24, from Jerusalem?) come to Antioch and teach (*edidaskon*) the Gentile Christians: "Unless you are circumcised according to the custom of Moses [i.e., become full proselytes], you cannot be saved [i.e., fully participate in God's salvation for his people]" (15:1). This claim leads to major dissension and debate between these people and Paul and Barnabas, who were staying in Antioch after returning from the first missionary journey (13:1–14:25). As it stands, the critics address the Gentile Christians of Antioch, but their criticism also applies to the practice of Paul and Barnabas which was known in Antioch ("… they declare all that God had done"; 14:27).

Paul and Barnabas defend the progressive position by refuting the Judeans' claims. Acts does not indicate how they argued their case. Immediately prior to this conflict in Antioch, both men refer to the divine approval of their mission practice: "… they declared all that *God* had done with them, and how *he* had opened a door of faith to the Gentiles" (14:27). Acts 15:3 notes that their reports on the way to Jerusalem through both Phoenicia and Samaria regarding the first missionary journey ("describing in detail the conversion of *the Gentiles*") brought great joy to all the Christians. In this way, the Judean critics in Antioch appear as an isolated minority. Paul and Barnabas also receive recognition in Jerusalem ("they were welcomed by the church and the apostles and the elders", 15:4) and report "all that God had done with them". In this way, they give glory to God [an indication of their piety and character] and claim divine approval and prompting for their mission.

As it proves impossible to de-escalate and solve this conflict in Antioch and as the parties to this conflict are related to Jerusalem in one way or another (Judeans from Jerusalem?, Barnabas as a Jerusalem emissary to Antioch, Paul as a former member of the church in Jerusalem), the decision was taken that the matter should be decided by the apostles and the elders in Jerusalem (15:3). Apparently they are the acknowledged authority for both parties to this conflict. Paul and Barnabas and some others (perhaps to serve as impartial witnesses) are appointed to present the case in Jerusalem. It is noteworthy that despite major dissension, none of the parties resort to violent action. Paul and Barnabas do not use the supernatural powers (amply attested previously) in this conflict

54

(as Paul had done over against a Jewish adversary on Cyprus in Acts 13:6–11).[13]

Stage II: Conflict and solution in Jerusalem. The occasion for this second round of conflict are the warm welcome of the Antiochene delegation in Jerusalem by the church and the apostles and the elders and the reports of "all that God had done with" Paul and Barnabas (15:4, implying divine affirmation of this mission ad its practice). There is no mention of the conflict in Antioch and of the fact that these Christians had come up to Jerusalem as an official delegation to seek a solution to the conflict in Antioch. This acceptance and the reports move Christian critics in Jerusalem with a Pharisaic background to action. They make the same demand as the Judeans had made in Antioch: "It is necessary to circumcise them and order them to keep the Law of Moses" (15:5). The Greek word "saying" (like "teaching" in 15:1) does not imply a verbally forceful intervention.

De-escalation starts with a meeting of the apostles and elders who take the visitors from Antioch and the local Pharisaic Jewish Christians seriously (15:6). Acts 15:22 seems to suggest that more people were involved ("Then it seemed good to the apostles and the elders, with the whole church …"). As Paul and Barnabas got to speak as well (15:12), they must have been there, possibly also the Pharisaic Jewish Christians. The meeting was characterised by much debate. Of this debate, three contributions are singled out:

Peter again summarises the events in Caesarea (Acts 10; already reported in Jerusalem in Acts 11:1–18) with an *emphasis on his own divine appointment and God's actions*: "God made a choice among you … God, who knows the heart, bore witness to them, by giving them the Holy Spirit just as he did to us and he made no distinction between us and them, having cleansed their hearts by faith" (8–9). To act any different, that is demanding full observance of the law, would mean to put God to the test. In addition, Peter admits that Jews themselves have not been able to observe the law anyway. In closing he affirms that salvation is through the grace of the Lord Jesus, for Jews and Gentiles alike (11).

---

[13] That not all conflicts between Christians are solved also becomes clear from Acts 15:36–41. Paul and Barnabas do not reach agreement after their sharp disagreement over John Mark and separate. Neither of them attempts to transfer this case to Jerusalem for decision.

Barnabas and Paul (interestingly, Acts here returns to the initial order of the names) relate once more what signs and wonders God had done through them among the Gentiles. These signs and wonders indicate divine approval and affirmation (see 2:22: "Jesus of Nazareth, a man attested to you by God with mighty works and wonders and signs that God did through him in your midst …"). While some Christians questioned the mode of this mission, it had full *divine approval*.

James briefly summarises to Peter's account ("how God first visited the Gentiles, to take from them a people from his name", 14) and argues that these (admittedly surprising) events agree with Scripture. After a long quotation from the prophet Amos, he presents his conclusion that the Gentiles should not be troubled by the demand to become Jews and to keep the law of Moses. James suggests some practical stipulation which are aimed at enabling the fellowship of Jewish and Gentile Christians.[14] As the Law of Moses is well-known through proclamation and reading, those who live by it need to be respected.

The solution to stage II of this conflict occurs when all, the apostles, the elders, and the whole church agree on this proposal and see to its proper and efficient communication. The demands of the Pharisaic Jewish Christians were rejected.

Stage III: Solution in Antioch. At this point, the narrative returns to *stage I* of the conflict, that is to *Antioch*. Christians of Jerusalem are to come along with Paul and Barnabas to Antioch. Two named leading men are appointed.

In addition to the delegation sent to Antioch, the decision is communicated in the form of an official letter (quoted in 15:23–29, "will tell you the same things by word of mouth", 27). The letter clarifies that those who had come down from Jerusalem previously did so without authorisation (24). The letter affirms Paul and Barnabas as "our beloved Barnabas and Paul" and their authority (25). They are recommended as people who have risked their lives for the name of our Lord Jesus Christ (26). Judas and Silas are mentioned by name as official delegates (unlike those who had come to Antioch of their own accord). The letter then communicates the decisions agreed upon (28–29). At this juncture, the letter claims that the decision was not only a decision taken by humans, but that it also pleased the Holy Spirit. Thus it carries divine approval (as it agrees

---

[14] For discussion see Schnabel (2012).

with God's prior activities and the prophet Amos). This is an additional, transcendent enabling condition in this conflict.

The delegation is formally commissioned, arrives in Antioch, gathers the congregation together, and delivers the letter. All of this is unlike the previous unauthorised arrival of some Judeans, who initiated the conflict by their demands. The letter is read out and well received: "they rejoiced because of its encouragement" (15:31). Before their return to Jerusalem, Judas and Silas, themselves prophets, encourage and strengthen the Christians there with great intensity. Judas and Silas are sent off "in peace". The conflict is fully solved. As was the case before the conflict, Paul and Barnabas remain in Antioch and continue their ministry with many others also.

According to the portrayal of Acts, the solution to this conflict was lasting. The question of whether the Gentiles needed to become Jews and keep the Law of Moses is not raised again in Acts. The decision of the council is explicitly confirmed later in in Acts 21:25. The "conflict" of Acts 21 does not concern Gentiles but Paul's own observance of the law.

3 Summary and Reflection

The three conflicts which we analysed have different *occasions*: the distribution of material means and the neglect of some in the community, "going to Gentiles" and the behaviour of Jewish Christians and their adherence to Jewish traditions when confronted with Gentiles and finally the question under which conditions Gentiles may participate in God's salvation and how they should live.

The nature of the de-escalation and the respective solutions to these conflicts vary. They come by addressing the issues, presenting concrete proposals, giving clear instructions, creating new structures (6:1–6); by detailed reporting and explanations of the course of events which led to contested behaviour, including reference to divine guidance and activity and to the words of Jesus (11:1–18), and by generous discussion, reports of the course of events which led a certain position including divine affirmation of disputed domains, conclusions based on Scripture, God's word and the guidance of the Holy Spirit, proposal of a solution and course of action and clear and efficient communication (15:1–35). In the course of all three conflicts under consideration there is de-escalation and an eventual solution of conflict. In each case, the threatened unity of the community is restored.

In all these conflicts, the causes of conflict/dissension were recognised, taken seriously, and addressed and a solution was reached. In the portrayal of Acts, while not without conflicts regarding the distribution of material means (a typical contested domain in conflict) and the identity and maintenance of the own group, the followers of Jesus are people who manage to resolve conflicts and achieve solutions. In view of the other conflicts of Acts where conflict resolution is not possible, it is noteworthy that all three inner-Christian conflicts in the book can be resolved and the unity of the community is maintained.

With the exception of Antioch in Acts 15:1–2, all inner-community conflicts and their resolution involve Christians from Jerusalem, are located in the city, and occur between Jewish Christians (while the occasion in Acts 11 and 15 is the inclusion of Gentiles). The conflict in Antioch is resolved in Jerusalem. The circle of those involved in these conflicts and their resolution widens from the community and the apostles to the elders, the whole assembly and James.

The implications of the disputed issues are far-reaching (issues of Jewish identity, inclusion of Gentiles as Gentiles into the people of God and the authority to do so and the mode of this inclusion and all the repercussions which this may have for Jewish identity and the stance of the Christian community in Jerusalem under the critical eyes of other Jews!), the course of these conflicts is *mild* in comparison to other conflicts in Acts. There is murmuring, arguing, teaching, and saying, and eventually "no small dissension" and "much debate", but there is no stronger verbal interaction (no pressure is put on the opponents, there is no vilifying, no threats) or resort to violence by those whose position is rejected (in comparison, the defeated Jewish opponents of the Christian mission regularly resort to violence).

While for those involved, some contested domains and aspects of these conflicts are *superhuman* (for example, the significance of Jewish identity, the Law of Moses) and generous reference is made to divine activity and guidance in the course of de-escalation and seeking resolution (11:5–10, 12–15; 15:7, 9, 12), all three conflicts are solved and have to be solved by humans. In no case is conflict resolution simply achieved by the Holy Spirit or other divine intervention, of which there is a generous amount elsewhere in Acts. There is no reference to prayer in the context of these conflict solutions. Conflict solution takes time, wisdom and effort.

Only one of these conflicts involves Paul who dominates the second half of Acts. He is placed in a group of other Christians of Jerusalem, which includes

Barnabas and the Hellenist missionaries come from Antioch up to Jerusalem. While Paul was a highly disputed figure according to his letters, according to Acts, Paul was a disputed figure among non-Christian Jews and Gentiles, but not *within* the Christian community.

According to the portrayal of Acts, all three conflict solutions are persistent. Once the issues are solved, they do not come up again. The conflict between Judean and Diaspora Jews was resolved (6:1–6); the Christians of Jerusalem accepted Peter's controversial behaviour and the Gentiles as part of the people of God and did not demand that they become Jews and keep the Law of Moses.

The steps taken to achieve de-escalation and solution of conflict offer some inspiration for the resolution of present-day conflicts between Christians and also between other people. This is all the more so within the Church, where these accounts are part of canonical scripture and read regularly. In one way or another, they shape the self-understanding of the community and of its ideals. Where they are not read and reflected upon, something important is missing.

The steps taken in the de-escalation and resolution of these conflicts are timeless: time is granted to explain, people listen to each other, weigh arguments; there is room for ample discussion without verbal or physical violence (in marked contrast to the other conflicts of Acts!). People receive, recognise and respond to divine affirmation and guidance (where applicable); there is recourse to Scripture for guidance and the readiness to act, even though this may involve risks.

The conflict of Acts 6:1–6 could only occur because the number of the original 120 disciples, who had come with Jesus from Galilee, increased drastically and included people of different background (the Hellenists). The occasion of conflicts of Acts 10 and 15 were encounters of Jewish Christians with Gentiles, the mode of their inclusion into the community and the implications of this inclusion for Jewish believers. The conflict accounts of Acts remind us that communities, whose horizons are broadened, which encounter new situations and people, whose traditions and identities are challenged and modified, are likely to experience conflict. The question is *whether* they are willing and able to deal with such conflicts and *how* they do so. The events which generated these conflicts and their solution can broaden theological horizons. In our case, they brought in new people into leadership positions who play a significant role later on (including Philip, the first person to share the Gospel with an African!) and deepen understanding of God's intentions and of the identity of the community and its role.

Acts presents a Christian community that is not harmonious and ideal, but had its significant dissensions and conflicts. It allows for dissension (murmuring) and open discussion (even criticism), a community in which leaders can be questioned and are held accountable, and a community where those who disagree can take the initiative and also have a voice. That the church (and society at large) has not always followed this example is all too evident. The fact that the community managed to resolve these conflicts and how it went about doing it, is one of the abiding legacies of the portrayal of the early Christian community in Acts.

Bibliography

Hume, D. A. 2011. The Early Christian Community: A Narrative Analysis of Acts 2:41–47 and 4:32–35. Tübingen: Mohr Siebeck.

Mayer, W. 2013. Religious Conflict: Definitions, Problems and Theoretical Approaches, in W. Mayer, B. Neil (eds.), Religious Conflict from Early Christianity to the Rise of Islam. Berlin, Boston: Walter de Gruyter, 1–19.

Schnabel, E. J. 2012. *Acts. Zondervan Exegetical Commentary on the New Testament*. Grand Rapids: Zondervan.

Thompson, A. J. 2012. One Lord, One People: The Unity of the Church in Acts in Its Literary Setting. London: Bloomsbury T. & T Clark.

Yarbrough, R. W. 2000. Forgiveness and Reconciliation, in T. D. Alexander, B. S. Rosner (eds.), *New Dictionary of Biblical Theology*. Leicester: IVP, 498–503.

Zugmann, M. 2009. "Hellenisten" in der Apostelgeschichte: Historische und exegetische Untersuchungen zu Apg 6,1; 9,29, 11,20. Tübingen: Mohr Siebeck.

A Study of Ephesians: A New Identity Reshaped by the Gospel of Reconciliation[1]

Ester Petrenko

Abstract

This study attempts to show that in the Letter to the Ephesians the believers' new identity in Christ is shaped by the good news of Jesus Christ – i.e. Christ came to defeat the alienating evil powers and to reconcile Jews and Gentiles as a new humanity and both groups with God (the gospel of reconciliation). Accordingly, the believers' new identity involves the refashioning of the mind with the gospel of reconciliation and a new set of transforming relationships – i.e. the believers' interrelationship with God and Christ through the Spirit, and with other members of the Christian community. The new identity is characterised as unity and harmony, fellowship and love corresponding to the shape of the gospel of reconciliation.

1 Introduction

In general, scholarship in Ephesians recognises that the believers' new identity effected by the Christ-event has social and ethical implications. The relationship between *identity* and social/ethical behaviour has led scholars to analyse the connection between the theological statements of Ephesians 1-3 and its moral instructions in Ephesians 4-6,[2] and to resource to social-scientific models[3] in order to grasp the identity of the in-group (the Christian community) and its relation to the outside world.

---

[1] Petrenko's previous research on Ephesians (2011) is the basis for this study and its overall structure. The footnotes are from the previous research with an up to date bibliography, in accordance with its relevance for this study.

[2] The relationship between believers' *new identity* and ethical/moral practices has led scholarship to identify Ephesians 1-3 as dealing with believers' new identity in Christ and Ephesians 4-6 as the ethical/moral practices resulting from the new identity. For an overview on the relationship between Ephesians 1-3 and 4-6 see: Petrenko (2011:ch.1); Roitto (2011:157-171).

[3] E.g. MacDonald (1988; 2004:419-444; 2016:97-115); Darko (2008); Shkul (2009); Riotto (2011).

This paper attempts to show that the *new identity in Christ* expressed in social/ethical practices is embedded in the soteriology of Ephesians. *The new identity* is seen as the spiritual/ethical transformation of believers, which enables community-unity. The believers' new identity mediated by the Spirit reshapes the decision-making and desires with the gospel of reconciliation, so that their new orientation and social/moral practices are a manifestation of God's salvific goal of unity and reconciliation.

This study will first explore the content of the gospel of reconciliation and then how the gospel reshapes the believer and community – here we will show how humanity's former identity is presented within a theology of alienation (before the Christ-event) and the new identity within a theology of reconciliation (through the Christ-event).

2 The Content of the Gospel

In Ephesians 1:13 conversion-initiation takes place when believers "heard and believed" in the word of truth (i.e. "the gospel of your salvation"). This truth (or gospel of salvation) is described as God's purpose, good pleasure and will (Eph 1:5, 9-11; cf. 3:11; 5:10, 17) and is unfolded in his salvific plan "in summing up all things in Christ, things in heaven and things on earth" (Eph 1:9-10).[4]

The summing up of things in heaven is further expanded and clarified in relation to the spiritual powers — i.e. Christ's resurrection and exaltation in the heavenly places (Eph 1:20-22) represents a decisive victory over the spiritual powers (Eph 1:3, 10, 20; 2:6); however, the powers are still active in this world order (Eph 2:2; 4:27; 6:11-12).[5] The summing up of things on earth is revealed and epitomised in the reconciliation between Jews and Gentiles, and both groups with God (Eph 2:14-22; 3:5-6, 10; 4:9). This is further supported in Ephesians 3:6 (cf. Eph 3:7) where the Gentiles' new reality ("fellow heirs, members of the same body, and sharers in the promise") is based on the gospel of

---

[4] Most scholars subscribe the "summing up of all things" as the "climax" (Best 1998:137) or the "pivotal statement" of the whole letter (Moritz 1991:96).

[5] For a discussion on the eschatology of Eph 1:20-22, see Petrenko (2011:135-139).

reconciliation — i.e. the mystery *revealed* to Paul, to the apostles and prophets (Eph 3:2, 3, 5) *through the Spirit* (Eph 3:5).[6]

The disclosure of the mystery aims "to bring to light" (Eph 3:9)[7] that God's wisdom (i.e. the "eternal purpose in Christ to reconcile all things in Christ", Eph 1:8-10; 3:11) is displayed and made known through the church (the "one new humanity", cf. Eph 2:15) to the principalities and powers (Eph 3:10),[8] and to a darkened world (Eph 5:13-14; cf. 2:4-10). The church is the exponent model to all creation of God's/Christ's dominion over "all things" (cf. Eph 1:20-23; 3:9-11).[9]

Having outlined the content of the gospel of reconciliation, our particular interest is to analyse how the new identity shaped by the gospel enables social/moral transformation and the formation of a reconciling community. In this context, we need to understand humanity's identity/existence before and after the Christ-event within the framework of a theology of alienation and reconciliation, respectively.

3 A Theology of Alienation

In order to understand who they are in Christ, the readers of Ephesians need to understand who they were before they turned to Christ. Here we will show that the focal problem of humanity's former life is the mind (other terms used in Ephesians are "the heart" and "inner being"), which was tainted by humanity's rebellion against God and by the influence of evil powers. The corruption of

---

[6] Caragounis argues that the "summing up" is the central theme in the eulogy, and it is further developed in the rest of the epistle. It is the string that ties the letter together (1977:144-46). Cf. Turner (1995:139).

[7] "To bring to light" implies the existence of spiritual darkness, cf. Eph 5:8-14.

[8] This does not mean that the church has the task to evangelise the powers (*pace* Wink 1984:89) but, as Arnold (1989:63) affirms, the very existence of the church testifies to God's wisdom (Eph 3:9-10). Cf. Caragounis (1977:108).

[9] This seems to indicate that the "mystery" of chapters 1–3 does not only include the content of its immediate co-text (Eph 1:3-14) but effectively the bulk of all three chapters. The "mystery" involves God's eternal plan of cosmic unification, the creation of a new humanity as well as the outworking of that plan, and its proclamation by Paul and by the apostles and prophets (Eph 3:3-9).

the mind is then reflected in moral behaviour and social dislocation. The readers' former identities are described as corrupted selves with consequently corrupted moral/social behaviours.

3.1 Cosmic powers and human rebellion against God

Ephesians presupposes a cosmic rebellion against God whereby those *not* under God's dominion are under the dominion of the ruler of this world order and the evil powers (Eph 2:1-3; 4:27; 6:12).[10] This is then exposed at the level of a corrupted mind-set and of social dislocation/alienation.[11]

3.2 Corrupted structure of perception and knowledge

Ephesians 2:3 indicates that human "desires" and "impulses" have been tainted by the influence of evil powers; "the ruler who controls the realm of the air" (Eph 2:2b). The particular function of "the ruler of the power of the air" is to create an atmosphere of evil ('the spirit at work', Eph. 2:2c) to further alienate humanity from God ("being dead", Eph 2:1, 5), as seen in the Hebraistic expression "we all ... were by nature children of wrath" (Eph 2:3).[12] The realm of humanity, enthralled in a cosmic rebellion against God, is described as the dominion of the "flesh".[13] This state of affairs leads to an existence marked by corrupt behaviour ("dead in trespasses and sins" Eph 2:1, 5).[14]

---

[10] For a Jewish understanding on the antagonism between God and the [ruler of] evil spirits and its relevance for Eph. 2:1-3, see: Petrenko (2011:ch. 2; 99-105). Darko also points out that in the Greco-Roman world there was an understanding that spiritual beings have an influence in the earthly realm (2013:60-61).

[11] In this context, the readers' former existence is characterized as dead (meaning being alienated from God; Eph 2:1, 5), an old person/creation (Eph 4:22; cf. Eph 4:17-19), in darkness or belonging to darkness (Eph 5:8a) and folly (Eph 5:15a, 17a). In contrast, those under the dominion or power of God are characterized as alive (Eph 2:1, 5), a new person/creation (Eph 2:10, 15; 4:24), being light or belonging to the light (Eph 5:8-9), and wise or belonging to wisdom (Eph. 5:15b). For a further discussion on the dominion of God or evil powers in the life of the readers, see Petrenko (2011:ch.8).

[12] Roitto rightly points out that 'the Jews had no more control over their destructive desires than the gentiles had.' (2011:182).

[13] Lincoln (1990:98).

[14] Darko acknowledges the relationship between the spiritual human condition and social practice, however, he does not show how spiritual corruption affects social behaviour (2015:49). See Petrenko (2011:210-211 & section 4.2).

Ephesians 4:17-19, 22 further expands and substantiates Ephesians 2:1-3.[15] Human rebellion ("hardness of heart", Eph 4:18) and alienation from God corrupt the mind (seen in the expressions "futility of their minds", "darkened in the understanding", "the ignorance that is in them", Eph 4:17-18) and lead to the collapse of human conscience (they "have become callous", Eph 4:19a). This state of affairs is then mirrored in corrupt behaviour (they "have given themselves up to licentiousness, greedy to practise every kind of uncleanness", Eph 4:19b). The human existence is described as a life of deceit (Eph 4:22) — i.e. the realm of humanity embedded in a spiritual and moral fog and so an existence deficient of divine reality/truth.[16]

This context shows that alienation from God and a tainted mind-set lead to corrupt behaviour. In other words, corrupt behaviour is the visible mark of a humanity embedded in (a cosmic) rebellion against God.

3.3 Social dislocation & alienation

Humanity's former identity is further exemplified in the social dislocation/alienation between Jew and Gentile (Eph 2:11-12).[17] The reminder of the identity marks of the Jews vis-à-vis the Gentiles – the Gentiles were called the "the uncircumcision" by those who are called "the circumcision", "a physical circumcision made in the flesh by human hands", "separated" and "excluded" from the promise – mantained Jews and Gentiles apart, and point to a lack of peace amongst humanity (Eph 2:14-17). The reminder of the alienation between Jews and Gentiles reinforces the condition of humanity embedded in (a cosmic) rebellion against God (Eph 2:1-3).[18]

---

[15] We have pointed out in section 3.1 that the soteriological contrasts encapsulate the whole letter, which indicates that the soteriology of Ephesians is not confined to Eph 1-3. Furthermore, the ethical statements of Ephesians 4:17–5:21 revolve around two structural concepts: perception/knowledge and sphere(s) of influence, reinforcing the soteriological pattern already found in Eph 1-3. See Petrenko (2011:146-147, 159-160).

[16] Petrenko (2011:163-167, 211).

[17] Ephesians 2:11-22 continues to describe the readers' former existence. The conjunction "therefore" (Eph 2:11) links this pericope (Eph 2:11-22) with Ephesians 2:1-10, and the once/now scheme seen in Ephesians 2:1-10 'in which *once* you walked ... we all *once* lived ... *but God*' (Eph 2:2, 3, 4) is given continuity in Ephesians 2:11-13 ('therefore remember that *once* you Gentiles ... but *now* in Christ'). Cf. Darko (2015:52-53).

[18] Shkul opts for a social-scientific reading of Eph 2-3 and argues that the re-configu-

The nature of the enmity which mantained Jews and Gentiles apart has been an intense issue of debate with some scholars referring to the Law as the subject of enmity.[19] However, we tend to agree with Yee that the "enmity" involves the "human attitudes that perverted the gifts of God into signs of separation and exclusiveness".[20] Before the Christ-event, Jewish attitudes towards the Gentiles (Eph 2:11) were as much a theological/social problem as the Gentiles' state of affairs (Eph 2:1-3; 2:11-12) – this clarifies why both groups needed to be reconciled with God (Eph 2:14-18). In this context, it seems that the enmity between Jews and Gentiles stands for a fallen humanity embedded in a cosmic rebellion against God ("we all … were by nature children of wrath", Eph 2:3). Any attitude or behaviour that encourages segregation and exclusion characterizes the power(s) that control this world-age (Eph 2:2).[21]

In this context, it is no accident that the moral/social vices addressed in Ephesians 4:19, 25a, 26-27, 28a, 29a, 31; 5:3a, 4a, 5a, 6, 18a (described as the way of the Gentile but now applied to those who do not believe in Christ, Eph. 4:17) characterize those under the dominion of the devil (Eph 4:27,[22] cf. Eph 2:2-3), and epitomise social disruption. Such behaviour grieves the Holy Spirit not only because He is the creator of unity and dwells within the community (Eph 2:18, 22; 4:3) but also because He enables the spiritual transformation of believers

---

ration of Israel and the social inclusion of non-Israelites are shaped by the socio-ideological legitimation and social memory of Christ (Eph 2:11-22) and Paul (Eph 3:1-13). (2009:chs. 3-4).

[19] Darko follows Lincoln on this view (2015:54). See discussion, Petrenko (2011: 108-109).

[20] Yee (2005:160-161). Furthermore, it is doubtful the writer aims to affirm that the Law is the subject of enmity, this contradicts for example Ephesians 5:31; 6:3 where the writer quotes Genesis 2:24 and Exodus 20:12 respectively.

[21] See further on this issue in Petrenko (2011:116-129, 212-213).

[22] Roitto rightly points out that vices described in Eph 5:1-6 are similar to the description of the Gentiles in Eph 4:17-22, however, he limits spiritual influence to the level of emotions (Eph 4:26-27, 30-31) (2011:184, 237 respectively). Mel argues that the text is not against 'righteous anger' but 'self-centered' anger causing the grieving of the Holy Spirit (2015:49-54). Even though grammatically Eph 4:27 is directly related to Eph 4:26, the following vices can also be seen as giving room to the devil. Those who practise sinful deeds (Eph 5:3-6) are called "sons of disobedience" (Eph 5:6) and these are identified in Ephesians 2:2-3 as under the dominion of the "ruler of the realm of the air". See Petrenko (2011:169 n.551).

(Eph 1:8-10, 17-19; 3:17-19) which leads to righteous living. If the Spirit is not in the centre of the believers' hearts then his role is undermined.[23]

In sum, the nature of humanity's former identity shows that a corrupt mindset embedded in a cosmic rebellion against God inevitably leads to a human existence characterized by sinful practices (Eph 2:1; 4:17-19) and social alienation (Eph 2:11-22; 4:19, 25a, 26-27, 28a, 29a, 31; 5:3a, 4a, 5a, 6, 18a).

4 A Theology of Reconciliation

In contrast to the previous section, this section endeavours to demonstrate how the readers' new identity in Christ entails the reconstruction of the self through the gospel and through a new set of relationships leading to the unity of the community and reconciling relationships.

4.1 Cosmic & human reconciliation

The readers' salvation in Christ (Eph 2:4-10) is effected in Christ's cosmic unification (Eph 1:19-23).[24] Christ's decisive victory over the spiritual powers (Eph 1:21-22) brings the believers into a new realm of influence ('raised us up with him and made us sit with him in the heavenly places in Christ Jesus', Eph 2:6);[25] and the same power that raised and exalted Christ empowers the believers (Eph 1:19-20)[26] to a new resurrection-life (God 'made us alive together with Christ', 2:5b as opposed to being dead, 2:1, 5). This description points out

---

[23] *Pace* Riotto who argues "the recipients are thus indirectly told that there is a potential risk to lose the seal, or being excluded from the ingroup and the salvation, if they do not behave properly" (2011:238). However, there is no indication that the believers are at "risk to lose the seal" but rather the emphasis on the seal of their salvation reinforces the role of the Spirit as the enabler of existential renewal. Ephesians continues to present the eschatological tension that the Christian community lives in. Petrenko (2011:170).

[24] Gombis asserts that the narrative pattern of Eph 1:20-2:22 is best explained in "the narrative pattern of divine warfare found in ANE, developed in the Old Testament". (2004:404).

[25] In contrast to the old dominion under the influence of the evil powers (Eph 2:2). Lincoln (1981:144-50; 1983:621-22); Penner (1983:45); Harris (1991:77-78); Darko (2013:64-65; 2015:51).

[26] This is seen in the expressions *"dynamis"*, *"energeia"*, *"kratous tēs ischyos"* (Eph 1:19), in their union with Christ (emphasized in the prefix *syn* -; Eph 2:5-6).

a new spiritual orientation through the believers' fellowship with the risen Lord and God.

The new resurrection-life (Eph 2:4-6) seems to parallel the "new creation" in Christ explained as "we are his workmanship, created in Christ Jesus for good works" — this means that God's *creation* of a new identity is characterised by "good works".[27] The "good works" flow naturally from God's transforming/creative activity in the believers.[28] This contrasts with the past existence/identity characterised by corrupt behaviour – where the readers' "desires and impulses" were under the dominion of "the ruler of the power of the air" and led the readers to walk in 'the lusts of the flesh' (Eph 2:1-3).

4.2 Reconstruction of the self through the Gospel and a new set of relationships

The prayer reports (Eph 1:15-23; 3:14-21) elucidate how a corrupt mind is transformed through the gospel of reconciliation and a new set of relationships – the mind is the locus of salvific transformation.

In the thanksgiving prayer, the Holy Spirit (already received, Eph 1:13-14) mediates further wisdom and revelation of God's plan of reconciliation (Eph 1:18; cf. Eph 1:8-10)[29] to deepen the knowledge of and relationship with God (Eph 1:17),[30] in order to transform the centre of perception and decision ("the eyes

---

[27] In Eph 2:8 the connective particle *"gar"* and the article *"tē charity"* link with Eph 2:5, 7 and affirm that "this grace" (cf. Eph 1:6-7) is also seen in the re-creation of the human existence moving towards moral renewal ("created in Christ Jesus for good works"; Eph 2:10). God's *creation* of a new existence seems to enable ethical living. Petrenko (2011:115).

[28] This pool of ideas is also attested in the Old Testament and in Jewish texts. The existential renewal of Israel is seen as a "mass resurrection from dead bones" that leads to the re-recreation of the human heart in obedience to God (Ezek 36:24-27; 37; Jer 31:31-40) (Turner 1994:5; 1996:130-31). This renewal is also depicted in the *Book of Jubilees*, where God transforms rebellious hearts through the removal of the foreskin of the heart (*Jub* 1:7, 22-23; cf. Ps 51:10; Ezek 36:24-27). See further Petrenko (2011:Section 5.3).

[29] The great majority of commentators contend that *"pneuma"* refers to the Holy Spirit as the mediator of wisdom and revelation. Petrenko (2011:132 n.435).

[30] To know God is to know his plan of reconciliation. In other words, the more we understand (through the Spirit) God's plan of reconciliation, the deeper we understand God.

68

of your heart may be enlightened" Eph 1:18[31] and to reconstruct the believers' will and orientation.

The purpose of the enlightenment of the heart with the knowledge of God is that believers may know:[32] (1) their role and place in God's plan of cosmic reconciliation ('the hope of his calling', Eph 1:18b; cf. 1:3-14);[33] (2) they belong to God ('the riches of his glorious inheritance in the saints', Eph 1:18c);[34] and (3) God's power is available to them ('the immeasurable greatness of his power in us who believe', Eph 1:19). This new reality aims to have a profound effect on their decisions ("the eyes of your heart enlightened") and consequently on their behaviour – whereby their behaviour reflects God's reconciling plan.

In the intercessory prayer (Eph 3:14-21), the Holy Spirit strengthens the believers with Christ's love and they experience this love in the fellowship of the church so that believers will be able to reveal the fullness of God. The first prayer request (two coordinated requests, Eph. 3:16-17), Paul prays that the believers will be strengthened with power in the inner being (the centre of decision and motivation, Eph 3:16; cf. Eph 1:17)[35]. The strengthening of the Holy Spirit deepens Christ's transforming presence ("Christ may dwell in your hearts through faith", Eph 3:17a) as the indwelling Christ *roots and founds* believers in love (Eph 3:17b). Thus, Christ's love is the hallmark of his presence in the

[31] For a syntax analysis, see discussion in Lincoln, *Ephesians*, 47. The "heart" is used to refer to the centre of the human will, thinking and feeling. See Baumgärtel and Behm ('Kardi,a', *TDNT*, 3:605-14).

[32] This is expanded in the parallel clauses introduced by *"tis"*, *"tis"*, *"ti"*.

[33] The language of "calling" brings to mind the believers' role in God's plan "to sum up all things in Christ" (Eph 1:10). In the present context, the emphasis of the noun "hope" and its cognate verb "to hope" does not lie primarily on the activity of hoping but on the content of what is hoped for, which refers to the content of salvation in Ephesians 1:3-14. Lincoln (1990:59); Lincoln and Wedderburn (1993:118).

[34] The possessive pronoun *"autou"* indicates that the readers are *God's* inheritance. The writer stresses that it is *his* (God's) inheritance and this is best understood as the inheritance which belongs to him. In the OT God's inheritance usually denotes the people of Israel (e.g. Deut 4:20; 9:26, 29; 1Kgs 8:51, 53; 2 Kgs 21:14; Isa 19: 25; 47:6; 63:17; Jer 10:16).

[35] There is a parallel between the Spirit strengthening the "inner man" and Christ dwelling "in your hearts" (Eph 3:17). The "inner man" seems to be the place where the Spirit strengthens the believers (cf. Rom 7:22-25; 12:2).

believers. Ephesians 3:18-19b expresses two interrelated purposes to the requests of Ephesians 3:16-17. Believers need to strengthen their inner being so that together with other believers ('with all the saints") they will be able to grasp "what is the breadth and length and height and depth" (Eph 3:18) of Christ's love ("and to know the love of Christ that surpasses knowledge", Eph. 3:19a).[36] Thus, to comprehend these four dimensions (Eph 3:18) is to understand the love of Christ, which surpasses all knowledge (Eph 3:19a). In other words, Christ's love is fully known in the fellowship of all believers. The final purpose is "that you may be filled [towards] all the fullness of God" (Eph 3:19b, i.e. God's presence and power). God's fullness dwells in Christ (cf. Col. 1:29-2:10) and this fullness is displayed in the Church (Eph. 1:22-23). In this context, "Christ's and God's fullness are revealed and achieved through the continuous actualisation of loving relationships in the church (Eph 3:19, cf. Eph 1:23)."[37] Therefore, Paul prays that the believers' mind be transformed with the knowledge of God's plan of reconciliation and empowered to live in conformity with God's plan of reconciliation. He also prays that Christ's love mediated by the Spirit will empower the believers to actualise Christ's love in the fellowship of the Church so to display the fullness of God.

In this context, it is no coincidence that the exhortations of Ephesians 4:1–6:9 reinforce moral/social practices that promote the unity and harmony of the Christian community.[38] Ephesians 4:1-6:9 further explains how the gospel of

---

[36] The absence of an object in Eph 3:18 has led to some dispute as to what these four measurements relate to: some of the recent views suggest that the writer wants believers to understand "all mysteries, even the dimensions of the universe" (Dahl 2000:365-88; this view is also followed by van Kooten 2003:179-83). Arnold, based on the magical papyri, argues that it refers to the dynamic of the powers (1989:89-95). Goulder explains the dimensions against the background of Jewish-Christian visionaries who had heavenly visions of the heavenly dimensions, breath and length and height and depth (1991:21-22). Usami proposes that the four dimensions concern the comprehension of the Christian community itself (1983:176-77). See further discussion on this issue in Lincoln (1990:209-213); Best (1998:344-46). For a summary of earlier views see Hoehner (2002:486-87). Whatever view we take on the background to these four dimensions, the writer seems to apply them to the love of Christ 'and to know the love of Christ which surpasses knowledge' (Eph 3:19a).

[37] Petrenko (2011:214-215; see further 141-142).

[38] Ephesians 1–3 describes the content and nature of salvation and the need to continually reinforce the spiritual understanding of God's purposes. It does not, however, fully clarify how

reconciliation and the believers' relationship with God and Christ through the Holy Spirit refashion the believers' mind and enable the unity and harmony of the Christian community: through the ministries of the Church, through the interrelationships amongst believers and in the household.

Believers are called to live out God's plan of reconciliation: "I therefore, the prisoner in the Lord, beg you to lead a life worthy of the calling to which you have been called" (Eph 4:1, 3a; cf. Eph 1:4-10, 18).[39] And God's plan is to be worked out in the interrelationships in the Christian community.

> i.e. in the corporate 'humility and meekness, with patience, forbearing one another in love' (Eph 4:2). These moral qualities are part of the 'work of the Spirit' ('eager to maintain the unity of the Spirit in the bond of peace'; Eph 4:3b).[40] Ephesians 4:3 recalls Ephesians 2:14-18 where the universal outpouring of the Holy Spirit facilitates the unity and harmony of the corporate community. Here the writer spells out how that unity takes place as the Spirit assists in the 'kind' of behaviour that *maintains* the unity and harmony brought into effect in Christ's salvific act. The triadic *formulae* (Eph 4:4-6), which remind the readers of the new reality in Christ (Eph 1–3),[41] intend to bring a conscious awareness as to why the believers need to *continue* to 'walk worthily of their calling' by *maintaining* 'the unity of the

the soteriological transformation is actualized and maintained in the life of the Christian community as the visible manifestation of the cosmic reconciliation. It is here that Ephesians 4–6 makes its contribution by explaining and expanding on the soteriological pattern of Ephesians 1–3 — i.e. how the reconstruction of the self is effected and sustained in order to facilitate the moral renewal and reconciling relationships in the Christian community and household.

[39] See above the reference to the prayer of thanksgiving where "The hope of his calling" (Eph 1:18b; cf. 1:3-14) is connected to God's plan of reconciliation.

[40] Verses 2 and 3 are parallel clauses. Cf. Lincoln (1990:237).

[41] "The "one body" not only recalls the corporate renewal of God's people (Jews and Gentiles) but also emphasizes the "quality" of their unity as "one body" (i.e. mutual recognition and harmonious attitudes; cf. Eph 2:14-18). The "one Spirit" reminds us of the transforming power of the Spirit in bringing the unity and harmony of believers (Eph 1:16-23; 2:16-18; 2:19-22; 3:16-19). The "one hope that belongs to your call" (which functions as an *inclusio* with the calling of v. 1) is spelt out earlier in terms of being 'holy and blameless in love', in a filial relationship with God and the believers' role in the 'summing up all things in Christ' (Eph 1:4-7, 9-10; cf. 1:18) as the goal of God's salvific plan." Petrenko (2011:150-151).

spirit in the bond of peace' (cf. Eph 2:14-18, 22). The more these truths (Eph 4:4-6) are reinforced, the more they become ingrained in the believers' lives.[42]

Furthermore, the renewal of the mind with the knowledge of the truth embodied in Jesus ("as truth is in Jesus" Eph 4:20-21, 23 cf. 1:7-8, 13; 2:20; 3:3-7; 4:11)[43] brings into effect God's creative act of spiritual renewal (i.e. "created according to the likeness of God in righteousness and holiness, which comes from the truth", Eph 4:24). The believers' transformation with the truth is further reinforced in the phrases "discovering what is pleasing to the Lord" (Eph 5:10) and "understand what the will of the Lord is" (Eph 5:17) – these phrases "chime back to God's will and good pleasure revealed and embodied in Christ (Eph 1:7-8, 13) and to what the believers had already learned, heard and were taught in the gospel of truth (Eph 4:20-21; cf. Eph 1:3; 3:5, 7; 2:20; 4:11) — i.e. a gospel of reconciliation".[44] In this context, believers are characterized as belonging to the light[45] and wisdom (Eph 5:8-10, 15b, 17b, 18b; in contrast to their former characterization of their minds being futile and in darkness, Eph 4:17-19; cf. Eph 2:1-3). Therefore, "the ongoing reminder of the gospel reinforces the new frame of mind — i.e. believers are not isolated selves but created to be in fellowship with others — this enables the community to follow a pattern of life which promotes unity and reconciliation (cf. Eph 4:25-5:21)."[46]

4.3 The Unity of the Christian Community & Reconciling Relationships

If alienation from God and social dislocation is the characterization of humanity's existence embedded in a cosmic rebellion against God (Eph 2:1-3; 2:11-

---

[42] Petrenko (2011:215-216).

[43] The "truth" chimes back to the gospel of reconciliation. See section 2.

[44] Petrenko (2011:216).

[45] "The outcome of light ("*karpos tou photos*" – i.e. all goodness, righteousness and truth) – manifests the truth (i.e. the sphere of divine reality and light, in contrast with deceit, Eph 4:24, 22) and the transforming power of life which is operative in the believer (Eph 5:8)." Petrenko (2011:216).

[46] Petrenko (2011:216).

13), reconciliation between the nations and with God implies a transformation on an existential level, which enables this restoration. Therefore, we contend that the Christ-event brought into effect the spiritual renewal of humanity (depicted in the metaphors of "one new humanity", "one body", "in one Spirit", and a "holy temple") in the dynamic of the Spirit, which enables and facilitates the unity and harmony of a *new corporate community* (i.e. Jewish and Gentile Christians).

Some of the evidence is shown in the way "peace" and a [new] "creation" are worked out in both Jews and Gentiles to form a *new humanity*. The reference to "peace" in Ephesians 2:14-17(18) evokes Isaiah 52:7 and 57:19.[47] In the context of Isaiah, "peace" involves the eschatological restoration and spiritual/moral renewal of Israel and the nations (Isa 52; 57; cf. Isa 32:15-18; 44:3; 58-66).[48] Furthermore, in some texts in the Old Testament the concept of (new) *creation* denotes a new eschatological age where there will be the re-creation of the righteous in terms of a social/ethical transformation (cf. Ezek 36-37; Jer 31:31-34; Isa 65-66).[49] The corporate restoration of God's people is sustained and enabled by the Spirit of the Lord (or of truth/holiness) who purifies and transforms them (Isa 32:15-18; 43:14-18; 44:3; Ezek 36:26-27; 37:14). This eschatological renewal is seen as an act of creation and cosmic renewal (new heavens and new earth, evoking Isa 65-66).

In this context, Christ's "peace" effecting the creation of "one new humanity" (Eph 2:15, cf. Eph 2:10; 4:24; Gal 6:15; 2 Cor 5:17) strongly suggests that the

---

[47] Yee contends that the inclusiveness and universal scope of Isaiah 52:7 and 57:19 used in Ephesians 2:17 aim to "turn the tables on the practice of Jewish ethnocentrism" and to reinforce the inclusive ministry of Christ. According to Yee, vertical reconciliation is "secondary" in the sense that God is not seen, in the context of Ephesians 2:11-18, as the "injured" party (2005:135-36). However, Yee misses a key point in his analysis of Isaiah 52, 57 and Ephesians 2:14-16. The *restoration of the nations requires repentance before God* (including Israel, cf. Isa 58-59); Moritz (1996:33). The focus of our analysis is how 'peace' is understood in Isa 52:7; 57:19 and Eph 2 for an understanding of the *nature* of salvation in Ephesians.

[48] Isa 57:20 also mentioned that the "wicked" (those inside and outside of Israel) shall not find "peace", which implies that not *all* will recognize and repent before the Lord.

[49] Hence, the idea that the "new person" refers to individual Jews and Gentiles who are becoming part of a new humanity seems inadequate. This view ignores the fundamental corporate focus of the concept of "new creation". *Pace* Best (1955:153; 1998:261-63).

"new humanity" is an act of eschatological renewal and spiritual transformation. This is further confirmed in Ephesians 2:18: "both of us [together] have access *in one Spirit* to the Father". This verse indicates that the Holy Spirit has a soteriological role in the unity of Jews and Gentiles. The Holy Spirit's role in the unity of Jews and Gentiles depicts the Jewish concept that in the eschatological age the Holy Spirit will be given *universally* (Joel 2:28-29) and will enable the transformation and purity of God's people. The Holy Spirit will re-create the human heart and enable it to obey God and live in holiness (Jer 31:31-40; Ezek 36:24-29; 37:14; Isa 32:15-18; 43:14-18; 44:3;[50] cf. Ps 51:10-14).

Ephesians 2:19-22 further clarifies the spiritual/existential transformation of the new corporate community. The emphatic inferential connective *"ara oun"* links Christ's reconciling work on the cross (Eph 2:14-18) with what follows (Eph 2:19-22). Whereas the expressions "no longer aliens" and "resident aliens" (Eph 2:19a) de-constructs previous perception (the former social dislocation, Eph 2:11-12), the prefix *sun-* (meaning "with") reinforces the inclusiveness of the community in terms of a reconstruction of relationships — "fellow citizens with the saints", "members of the household of God" (Eph 2:19), and similarly "fellow heirs, members of the same body and partakers of the promise in Christ Jesus through the gospel" (Eph 3:6). This terminology intensifies the dynamic interrelatedness of each member of the new community.[51]

Within this frame of reference, Ephesians 4:7-16 further demonstrates how the transformation of believers enables the unity and growth of the corporate community. The dynamic unity and growth of the church (as a corporate community) are a reality through Christ's exaltation and authority (Eph 4:8-10) to bestow grace and gifts upon *all* believers (Eph 4:7)[52] and church leaders (Eph

---

[50] For further connections between Ephesians and Ezekiel see Suh (2007:715-33).

[51] Petrenko (2011:124-128).

[52] There has been some dispute as to whether Christ's grace was given to all Christians (Eph 4:7 "to each one of us..." cf. Eph 4:16) or whether that grace was especially given to church leaders (Eph 4:11) to the building up of the body (Eph 4:12) (this latter view argued by Schlier 1971[2] [1957]:191 and Merklein 1973:59, 60). Schnackenburg's revised position indicates that the transition from the 'all' of 4:6 to the 'we' of 4:7 is too great; rather the shift is from the second person plural of 4:1-6 to the more inclusive first person plural (Eph 4:7; cf. Eph 4:16); moreover the linguistic parallels between *"Heni de hekastō"* and Rom 12:4-6 (where all Christians are included; cf. 1 Cor 12:7, 11) are so close that all Christians must be included.

4:11-12). The grace and gifts given "to each one of us" (i.e. to all believers, Eph 4:7, 16), and to Christian leaders (apostles, prophets,[53] evangelists, pastors and teachers, Eph 4:11) aim to promote the growth of the body (Eph 4:12) and to bring "the unity of the faith and of the knowledge of the Son of God" (Eph 4:13a). The "unity of faith" is closely related to "the knowledge of the Son of God" and, as in verse 5, it refers to the believers' appropriation (by faith) of what Christ *has begun* to accomplish for them. The "knowledge of the Son of God" is not an intellectual knowledge (i.e. to know *about* Christ) but the (experiential) knowledge of the gospel of truth (i.e. "as the truth is in Jesus", Eph 4:20-21; cf. Eph 1:8-10, 13; 1:17-19; 3:2-10) which transforms the believers into the character of Christ (i.e. love, cf. Eph 3:16-19). This is further supported in Ephesians 4:13b-16. The meaning of the two metaphors 'to mature manhood'[54] (Eph 4:13b) and "to the measure of the stature of the fullness of Christ" (Eph 4:13c) seem to be clarified in the correlated metaphors 'to grow up in every way into him [Christ] who is the head' (Eph 4:15b) and "from whom the whole body ... grow[s] and up build[s] itself in love" (Eph 4:16). The relationship between these metaphors suggests that to achieve "mature manhood" and "the stature of the fullness of Christ" is to be a church/body in complete unity and harmony,[55] and wholly transformed into Christ's character (i.e.

Schnackenburg (1991 [1982]:174-178 n. 410). Cf. Lincoln (1990:241-242, 248-249); Gosnell (1992:30-33).

[53] Some scholars (e.g. Schnackenburg 1991 [1982]:180-181; Lincoln 1990:248-252; Best 1993:157-158) affirm that the ministries of 'apostles and prophets' were the foundation of the church and the inaugurated revelation of the gospel (Eph 2:20 and 3:5) but now are figures of the past. However, there is no reference in the context that the description of these ministries was cited on a historical sequence. Additionally, the other ministries (evangelists, pastors and teachers) already existed during and, subsequently, after Paul's time (e.g. Acts 20:17, 28; 1 Cor 12:28-29; Gal 6:6). Turner (1994[4]:1238).

[54] Barth translates *"andra teleion"* ('the perfect man', Eph 4:13) as being Christ whom the church (his Bride) will meet at the end – 'until we meet the Perfect Man' (1974:484-496). However, if Barth is right we would probably expect *"ton anthrōpon teleion"* (cf. Eph 2:15) rather than *"andra"*, the choice of the latter aims to contrast with *"nēpioi"* (Eph 4:14) which characterizes the immature person. Furthermore, the third statement of the goal to be attained (*"eis andra teleion, eis metron hēlikias tou plērōmatos tou Christou"*) – the measure of the full stature of Christ – the genitive *hēlikias* is in apposition to *"metron andra tou plērōmatos"* as an adjectival genitive.

[55] Best (1955:148-49); (1998:402-03); Merklein (1973:103-104); Barth (1974:493-94); Gnilka (1971:215).

love).[56] This suggests that the gifts bestowed upon each believer and upon the Christian leaders aim to deepen the (experiential) knowledge of Christ (through the gospel of truth) and to bring the church into complete unity/harmony, reflecting the character of Christ.

> Those whose minds are refashioned by the reality of the new creation treat their fellow neighbours as one unified body in Christ (Eph 4:25; cf. Eph 1:23; 2:16; 4:4, 12) and build up one another in love (Eph 4:2, 15a, 16b). Every time believers speak the truth (Eph 4:25; cf. Eph 4:15a), 'give to those in need' (Eph 4:27), edify one another (Eph 4:29b) and look for the well-being of others (Eph. 4:29c), the corporate unity of the community is manifested. In this way, the divisive work of the devil (Eph 4:27) and of sinful outsiders (Eph 5:3-7) have no ground to influence or alter the unity of the community.[57]

The unity and harmony of the Christian community is also reshaped through transforming relationships. The Holy Spirit dwells in the community (Eph 2:18, 22; 4:3) and purifies the believers ("the Holy spirit of God" Eph 4:30, emphasizing his ethical role; cf. Eph. 1:8-10; 17-19; 3:17-19). In contrast to evil speech (Eph. 4:29, 31; 5:4), the Holy Spirit also inspires praise and worship,[58]

---

[56] Mbennah argues that spiritual maturity is a "bridge" between believers' new identity (Eph 1-3) and its corresponding moral code (Eph 4:17-6:20) – he concludes: "Maturity refers to a specific final and discernible destination of all Christians who increasingly become 'one' as they approach that destination" (2016:110-132). However, we argued elsewhere "What the writer says here is that the Christ-event was a transforming-event which has still to be realized — in the double sense of 'grasped mentally' and 'made effective in practice'. That is why Christ bestowed gifts and grace upon each member and Christian leaders so that the church could grasp mentally (through teaching) and make it effective in practice. The task of believers, as seen in Ephesians 2:19-22, is not to bring the unity of the church into completion, but to allow the teaching-ministries and the loving relationships to assist and to actualize the unity and growth of the church." (Petrenko 2011:quote 157, 154-157, 124-128).

[57] Petrenko (2011:216). Darko's study of Ephesians 4:17-6:9 (2008) argues that the behaviour patterns described in the text are not a call for believers to isolate from or integrate into society but to live and function in society. The behaviour patterns aim to promote group identity and unity of the in-group. However, we will see below that the role of the Christian community is not simply to know how to live in the world. Rather, its reconciling nature and identity is *missional* – it aims to impact the world.

[58] "The songs which believers sing to each other are spiritual songs because they are inspired by the Spirit and manifest the light of the Spirit" Lincoln (1990:346). For a dif-

and enables the believers to recognise God, the Father, as the creator of all things and the source of salvation[59] through the Lord Jesus Christ (Eph 5:20b; cf. Eph 1:3-14). The presence of the Holy Spirit continues to bring a sense of belonging amongst the members of the community.

Furthermore, the intimate relationship of the community with God and Christ empower the unity and ethical living of the community. The believers' relationship with God, the Father (as 'beloved children', Eph 5:1, cf. Eph 1:17, 3:14, 19b), aims to reorientate the believers to live in conformity with God's character (Eph. 5:1)[60]– 'to be kind to one another' 'compassionate' and 'forgiving one another' (Eph. 4:32-5:1)[61] – the believers experienced the same qualities of God's character when they turned to Him (Eph 1:5, 7; 2:4, 7; 3:14, 19b).[62] As seen before, this relationship is deepened through an understanding of God's plan of reconciliation (mediated by the Spirit, Eph 1:17, 3:14, 19b) which empowers the heart/inner being (the centre of perception and decision, Eph 1:19-20; 3:20) to live in conformity with God's plan. Moreover, the exhortation for believers to "walk in love" (Eph 5:2) reinforces the believers' experience of Christ's sacrificial love in bringing reconciliation between Jew and Gentile (Eph 2:16-18).[63] The transforming power of Christ's love is mediated by the Holy Spirit as he *roots* and *founds* the believers *in love*, so to enable them to realize that love in the fellowship with the community (Eph 3:16-19).

---

ferent view see Gombis who argues that the five participles in Eph 5:19-21 should be interpreted as "participles of means" (2002:268-71).

[59] Lincoln (1990:348).

[60] N. A. Dahl affirms that Eph 4:32 and 5:2 (cf. Eph 5:25, 29) follow a "conformity pattern". This means that "Christ is not seen simply as a model to be imitated; his conduct is prototypical precisely to the degree that it is of saving significance. What is important is Christ's surrender for us, his incarnation and his death, which imply salvation. Therefore, it would be better to speak of *conformitas* and not *imitatio* because of later connotations of the term" (1976:30-36).

[61] Cf. *T. Sim.* 3:4-6; *T. Benj.* 3:1-4; 1QS 2:24-26; 4:2-7.

[62] Cf. *T. Sim.* 4:4; *T. Zeb.* 5:1; 7:2; 8:1; *T. Gad* 6:3, 7; *T. Benj.* 4:1-41; QH 4:9-15, 17-26; 8:24-27; 12:37; 14:9; 15:18, 29b-31, 35; 17:7-8, 13-14; 18:21.

[63] A. J. Hultgren asserts that "the sacrificial death of Christ was an expression of his love, and it is in that respect that it was 'a fragrant offering and sacrifice to God' (RSV). The idea lying behind the phrase is that acts of devotion to God are sacrifices pleasing to him" (1987:104).

The believers' transforming relationship with Christ is further depicted in the phrase "you are light in the Lord' (Eph. 5:8) – denoting that through the believers' union with Christ, they are under his sphere of influence (cf. Eph 2:4-6, instead of living in darkness Eph 4:17-18), and therefore under his transforming power (Christ is the source of light and the transforming power of divine life, Eph 5:14b). Accordingly, the believers' transforming experience *in the Lord* produces light (*"karpos tou photos"*, "found in all that is good and right and true" Eph 5:9)[64] and they are called children of light (Eph 5:8). This reflects believers' moral renewal and spiritual transformation (Eph 2:10; 4:15, 24, 25) in contrast with the 'unfruitful works of darkness' (Eph 5:11).[65]

> Ephesians 5:14: 'Awake, O sleeper, and arise from the dead and Christ shall give you light' expresses perfectly the new creation in Christ and the role of the community as a reflection of the fullness of God/Christ (cf. Eph 1:23; 3:19) and the beginning of the reconciliation of all things in Christ (cf. Eph 1:10; 3:8-10). The time which was marked by a religious and spiritual lethargy (sleep) and alienation from God (death, cf. Eph 2:1) is now marked by the transforming light of Christ and by the awakening of the Christian community ('the sons of light'), which exposes the works of darkness and demonstrates the fruit (*karpos*) of light that flows from Christ (Eph 5:9; cf. Eph 2:7-10; 4:24). This reinforces, once again, that the call of the community (as a new creation) has a transforming effect inside and outside the community. The Christian community is not isolated from the world but its reconciling nature and identity impacts the world.[66]

---

[64] A literal translation of 5:9 is "the fruit of light consists in all goodness, righteousness and truth". This indicates that the fruit is found in the sphere of goodness, righteousness and truth.

[65] The "fruit of light" (5:9) and the works of the darkness (5:11) are closely related with the "fruit of the spirit" and the works of the flesh in Gal 5:19, 22.

[66] Petrenko (2011:217-218). Roitto is more nuanced than MacDonald in the distinction of the ingroup and outgroup (MacDonald points for a strong 'introversionist sectarian response that the other Pauline epistles...' quoted from Roitto 2011:187). Roitto asserts that lack of overt reference to evangelism simply indicates that it was not the primary purpose of the letter, but it does not necessarily mean that the author was an introversionist

The relationships in the household (between husband/wife, children/parents and slaves/masters) are included in the transforming work taking place in the Christian community.[67] In all relationships in the household, there is a redefinition of one's self-perception, task and purpose based on the new reality in Christ.

> The role of the wife, namely 'submit to [their] husbands as to the Lord' (Eph 5:22), is seen in terms of her new identity in Christ as a new creation (Eph 5:18, 5:21). The wife's subordinating response to her husband is embedded in the way she serves the Lord (Eph 5:22; cf. Col 3:23). The husband being the 'head' of the wife is grounded in Christ — 'as Christ is the head of the church' (Eph 5:23, cf. Eph 1:22-23). The husband's position of authority is qualified and defined in the clause 'and gave himself up for her' (Eph 5:25) — Christ's power and authority is revealed in the servant attitude of his death (cf. Eph 5:1-2). Thus, to love his wife 'just as Christ loved the church and gave himself up for her' would imply a redefinition of the husband's self-perception.[68] Furthermore, the spiritual transformation that is taking place in the church is to be reflected in marriage. And in turn, the marriage union (two in one flesh) should reflect the eschatological union between Christ and the church.[69]

In the relationship between children and parents (Eph 6:1-4), the childrens' role to 'obey your parents' (Eph 6:1) is seen in terms of both their own and their parents' new reality and understanding of the Lord (Eph. 6:1, 4). The children can only obey the parents if they are reminded that their obedience to the parents 'in the Lord' ultimately shows obedience to the Lord (Eph 6:1) and to God (Eph 6:2-3;

(2011:187). The articles of Van Aarde point to the missional nuance of the term "*oikonomia*" (Eph 3:10 and 1:3-14) in the church's role in carrying out God's plan whereby the *missio Dei* is implied (37:1 a1489; 2015:45-62).

[67] More recently, Keown asserts that the main focus of the household code is to define *paterfamilias* (husband, father and master) in early Christianity – a husband who loves his wife, the father who raises his children and the master who serves his slaves (2016:47-60).

[68] Moulton argues that the household code in Eph 5:21-33 "aims to resist any form of exploitative power in contemporary as well as ancient empire" (2014:163-185).

[69] Petrenko (2011:quote 217-218, 198-200).

cf. Ex 20:12; Deut 5:16). Similarly, parents ought not to provoke anger in their children (seen in Eph 4:26-27 to give ground to the devil and leading to disharmony) but to instruct their children with the right knowledge in the 'discipline and instruction of the Lord' (Eph 6:4) so that their social relations are changed and indeed reflect obedience to Christ and God (Eph 6:1-3).[70]

In terms of the relationship between slaves and masters, there is also a redefinition and reinforcement of the slave/master relationship shaped by the new understanding of Christ's lordship (the Master in heaven). The slaves' obedience and service to their earthly masters are redefined as an act of obedience to '[do] the will of God from the heart' (Eph 6:6c; cf. Eph 6:4; 5:10, 17) and as a task of service to Christ (Eph 6:6b). Slaves and masters only have the right attitude towards one another if both know ("*eidotes*" Eph 6:8-9) that 'whatever good any one does' he/she will be rewarded by the heavenly Master (Eph 6:8), and that both the slaves and masters are ultimately servants of Christ (Eph 6:9). This knowledge re-orientates and determines their actions and attitudes.[71]

5 Conclusion

The readers' *new identity* entails the refashioning of the mind with the gospel of reconciliation and a new set of transforming relationships – i.e. the believers' interrelationship with God and Christ through the Spirit, and with other members of the community. The new identity is characterised as unity, fellowship and love corresponding to the shape of the gospel.

Any attitude or behaviour that encourages segregation or unity reflects this world age or the reconciling power of the gospel, respectively. The appeal of Ephesians continues to chime in our ears today: 'Awake, o sleeper, and arise from the dead and Christ shall give you light' (Eph 5:14). As a Christian community, we are called to expose exclusion and segregation and be partakers in the *missio Dei* of reconciliation and unity.

---

[70] Petrenko (2011:217-218).

[71] Petrenko (2011:219).

Bibliography

Arnold, C.E. 1989. *Ephesians: Power and Magic. The Concept of Power in Ephesians in Light of its Historical Setting* (SNTSMS 63). Cambridge: CUP.

Barth, M. 1974. *Ephesians 4–6* (AB34b). New York: Doubleday.

Baumgärtel, F., and J. Behm, 'Kardi,a'. *TDNT*, 3:605-14.

Best, E. 1955. *One Body in Christ*. London: SPCK.

Best, E. 1993. 'Ministry in Ephesians', *IBS* 15 (1993), 146-66.

Best, E. 1998. *Ephesians* (ICC). Edinburgh: T & T Clark.

Caragounis, C. 1977. *The Ephesian Mysterion: Meaning and Content* (ConBNT 8). Lund: Gleerup.

Dahl, N. A. 1976. 'Form-Critical Observations on Early Christian Preaching' in his *Jesus in the Memory of the Early Church*. Minneapolis: Augsburg.

Dahl, N. A. 2000. 'Cosmic Dimensions and Religious Knowledge (Eph. 3:18)' in D. Hellholm, V. Blomkvist and T. Fornberg (eds.), *Studies in Ephesians: Introductory Questions, Text- & Edition-Critical Issues, Interpretation of Texts and Themes*. Tübingen: Mohr, 365-88.

Darko, D.K. 2008. *No Longer Living as the Gentiles: Differentiation and Shared Ethical Values in Ephesians 4:17-6:9* (LNTS 375). London: T & T Clark.

Darko, D.K. 2013. 'Spirit-Cosmology in the Identity and Community Construction of Ephesians 1–3', *Plērōma anul XV* 1 (2013), 59-71.

Darko, D.K. 2015. 'What does it mean to be saved?', *JPT* 24 (2015), 44-56.

Goulder, M. 1991. 'The Visionaries of Laodicea', *JSNT* 43 (1991), 15-39.

Gnilka, J. 1971. *Der Epheserbrief* (HTKNT 2). Freiburg: Herder.

Gombis, T. G. 2002. 'Being the Fullness of God in Christ by the Spirit: Ephesians 5:18 in Its Epistolary Setting', *TynBul* (2002), 259-271.

Gombis, T.G. 2004. 'Ephesians 2 as a Narrative of Divine Warfare', *JSNT* 26 (2004), 403-418.

Gosnell, P.W. 1992. 'Behaving as a Convert: Moral Teaching in Ephesians Against Traditional and Social Backgrounds' Unpublished PhD thesis, University of Sheffield.

Harris, W.H. 1991. '"The Heavenlies" Reconsidered: Ouvrano,j and 'vEpoura,nioj in Ephesians', *BSac* (1991), 73-78.

Hoehner, H. W. 2002. *Ephesians: An Exegetical Commentary*. Grand Rapids: Baker.

Hultgren, A. J. 1987. *Christ and His Benefits: Christology and Redemption in the New Testament*. Philadelphia: Fortress.

Keown, M.J. 2016. Paul's Vision of a New Masculinity (Eph 5. 21-6:9)', *Colloquium*, 48:1 (2016), 47-60.

Kooten, G. H van. 2003. *Cosmic Christology in Paul and the Pauline School. Colossians and Ephesians in the Context of Graeco-Roman Cosmology, with a New Synopsis of the Greek Texts* (WUNT 2.171). Tübingen: Mohr.

Lincoln, A.T. 1981. Paradise Now and Not Yet. Studies in the Role of the Heavenly Dimension in Paul's Thought with Special Reference to His Eschatology (SNTSMS 43). Grand Rapids: Baker.

Lincoln, A.T. 1983. 'Ephesians 2:8-10: A Summary of Paul's Gospel?', *CBQ* 45 (1983), 617-30.

Lincoln, A.T. 1990. *Ephesians* (WBC 42). Dallas: Word.

Lincoln, A.T. and A. J. M. Wedderburn 1993. *The Theology of the Later Pauline Letters*. Cambridge: CUP.

Lona, H.E. 1984 *Die Eschatologie im Kolosser- und Epheserbrief* (FB 48). Würzburg: Echter Vlg.

Penner, E. 1983. 'The Enthronement Motif in Ephesians'. Unpublished PhD thesis, Fuller Theological Seminary.

Petrenko, E.A.G.D. 2011. 'Created in Christ Jesus for good works': The Integration of Soteriology and Ethics in Ephesians (PBM). Milton Keynes, Colorado Spring, Hyderabad: Paternoster.

MacDonald, Margaret Y. 1988. *The Pauline Churches: A Socio-Historical Study of Institutionalization in the Pauline and Deutero-Pauline Writings* (Society for New Testament Studies Monograph Series 60). Cambridge: Cambridge University Press

MacDonald, Margaret Y. 2004. 'The Politics of Identity in Ephesians', *JSNT* 26 (2004), 419-444.

MacDonald, Margaret Y. 2016. 'The Problem of Christian identities in Ephesians: inspiration from the work of Nils Alstrup Dahl', *Studia Theologica* 70:1 (2016), 97-115.

Mbennah, E.D. 2016. 'The Goal of Maturity in Ephesians 4:13-16', *Acta Theologica* 35:1 (2016), 110-132.

Mel, D.B. 2015. 'Perspectives on anger from Ephesians 4', *Africanus Journal* 7:2 (2015), 49-54.

Merklein, H. 1973. *Das Kirchliche Amt nach dem Epheserbrief* (SANT 33). München: Kösel Vlg.

Moritz, T. 1991. '"Summing Up All Things": Religious Pluralism and Universalism in Ephesians' in A. D. Clarke and B. M. Winter (eds.), *One God, One Lord in a World of Religious Pluralism*. Cambridge/Grand Rapids: Tyndale

Moritz, T. 1996. *A Profound Mystery. The Use of the Old Testament in Ephesians* (SNovT 85). Leiden: Brill.

Moulton, E. 2014. 'Reimagining Ancient Household Ethos? On the implied Rhetorical Effect of Ephesians 5:21-33', *Neotestamentica* 48:1 (2014), 163-185.

Roitto, R. 2011. *Behaving as a Christ-Believer: A Cognitive Perspective on Identity and Behavior Norms in Ephesians* (CBNT 46). Winona Lake, IN: Eisenbrauns.

Schlier, H. 1971[2] (1957). *Der Brief an die Epheser: Ein Kommentar*. Dusseldorf: Patmos Vlg.

Schnackenburg, R. 1991 (1982). *The Epistle to the Ephesians*. Edinburgh: T & T Clark .

Shkul, M. 2009. *Reading Ephesians: Exploring Social Entrepreneurship in the Text* (Library of New Testament studies 408). London: T & T Clark.

Suh, R.H. 2007. 'The Use of Ezekiel 37 in Ephesians 2', *JETS* 50 (2007), 715-33.

Turner, M. 1994. 'The Spirit of Prophecy and the Ethical/Religious Life of the Christian Community' in M. Wilson (ed.), *Spirit and Renewal. Essays in Honor of J. Rodman Williams*. Sheffield: SAP, 166-190.

Turner, M. 1994[4]. 'Ephesians' in D. A. Carson et al. (eds.), *New Bible Commentary*. Leicester: IVP.

Turner, M. 1995. 'Mission and Meaning in Terms of "Unity" in Ephesians' in A. Billington, A. Lane and M. Turner (eds.), *Mission and Meaning: Essays Presented to Peter Cotterell*. Exeter: Paternoster.

Turner, M. 1996. *Power from on High. The Spirit in Israel's Restoration and Witness in Luke—Acts* (JPTSup 9). Sheffield: SAP.

Usami, K. 1983. *Somatic Comprehension of Unity: The Church in Ephesus* (AnBib 101). Rome: PBI

Van Aarde, T.A. "The Use of oivkonomi, a for Missions in Ephesians', *Verbum et Ecclesia*, 37:1 a1489.

Van Aarde, T.A. 2015. 'The Use of oivkonomi, a for the Missional Plan and Purpose of God in Ephesians 1:3-14', *Missionalia,* 43:1 (2015), 45-62.

Yee, T.-L.N. 2005. *Jews, Gentiles and Ethnic Reconciliation: Paul's Jewish Identity and Ephesians* (SNTS 130). Cambridge: CUP.

Wink, W. 1984. *Naming the Powers: The Language of Power in the New Testament*. Philadelphia: Fortress.

Shalom without Recompense? Some Notions on the Hebrew Term "Shalom"

Hans-Georg Wünch

Abstract

This paper tries to shed some light on the concept of "Shalom" in the Old Testament. Of special interest is the basic meaning of the verb "sh-l-m". Traditionally, the Hebrew term "Shalom", as well as the verb "sh-l-m", are understood in light of the concepts of "wholeness" or "completeness". Gerleman and others have questioned this understanding. According to them, the basic meaning of the verb "sh-l-m" is much more concrete. It rather means "to repay" or "to recompense". This understanding sheds light on the question of how the state of "Shalom" can be reached. Is there peace without retribution? Can there be reconciliation without the double action: to repay the evil deeds on the one hand and to compensate the evil, which has been done, on the other?

1 Introduction – The Meaning of the Root sh-l-m

A search in Google for the word "peace" generates some 925 million results! Peace seems to be one of the most important topics of today. However, the theological publications of the last 20 to 30 years do not reflect this importance. There are many books on the topic itself, discussing the relevance of peace in an un-peaceful world. What is missing though is thorough research on the basic understanding of peace and its theological meaning in the Old and New Testament.

This becomes evident when we look at works like the *Theologisches Wörterbuch zum Alten Testament*, the *Theologische Realenzyklopädie*, the *New International Dictionary of Old Testament & Exegesis* or the *Religion in Geschichte und Gegenwart*. They all build on the discussion on the OT understanding of the Hebrew root *sh-l-m* between Walter Eisenbeis and Gillis Gerleman in the early seventies of the last century. It seems that the theological discussion has not really developed further since these years.

Walter Eisenbeis (1969) started his research with an analysis of the Hebrew noun *Shalom*. He looks at the understanding of this root in other Semitic languages and then states: "Der Wurzel liegt die Vorstellung der Ganzheit zugrunde." (Eisenbeis 1969:50). According to him, it is not possible to decide definitively if the noun derives from the verbal root or vice versa (:52). He nevertheless proceeds to define the whole concept from his understanding of the noun *Shalom*. He uses about 140 pages to discuss the various aspects of *Shalom*, while there are only about 35 pages for discussing the verb. According to Eisenbeis the noun refers to "Ganzheit als etwas Umfassendes" (:81), while the verb either denotes a "Zustand der Ganzheit", or a "Geschehen, welches zur Ganzheit führt" (:297). This understanding of *Shalom* builds on the works of theologians like Wilhelm Caspari and especially Johannes Pedersen, who defined *Shalom* as a state of friendship and harmony in family, kinship and nation (Pedersen 1946:285, 311). It has become the majority view among most Old Testament theologians.

Gillis Gerleman challenges this majority view in his book on the meaning of the root *sh-l-m* (Gerleman 1973). He explicitly argues against Eisenbeis. According to Gerleman, the "Begriff 'Ganzheit' ist zu unscharf und allgemein." (:3). Instead, he wants to understand the root *sh-l-m* from the verb, especially in its *Piel* form. There are only eight verses where the *Qal* is used, while the *Piel* has 89 occurrences in the Old Testament (and five with the *Pual*). Gerleman justifies his decision not on the basis that he thinks the noun to be derived from the verbal root (he does not discuss this question at all). Instead, he argues:

> "Die Wahl dieser Verbform zum Ausgangspunkt einer Untersuchung des Sinnbereiches von שלם hat pädagogische Gründe. Grundsätzlich wäre es natürlich ebensogut möglich, von einer beliebigen Wortform der Wurzel auszugehen. Aber mit seinen 90 Belegen ist das Piel weitaus die häufigste Verbform." (Gerleman 1973:3-4)

In addition to this, the *Piel* of *sh-l-m* has a clearly defined meaning. "Es meint durchweg 'bezahlen, vergelten'." (Gerleman 1973:4). This meaning "liegt … allen Bildungen der Wurzel … zugrunde" (Gerleman 1984:923), as Gerleman states in his article on the root *sh-l-m* in the *Theologisches Handwörterbuch zum Alten Testament* (Jenni und Westermann 1984). He goes on and writes:

> "Auch das Subst. *šālōm*, das gewöhnlich als 'Ganzheit, Unversehrtheit' bzw. als 'Friede' aufgefaßt wird, hängt mit der Grundvorstellung des Bezahlens und Vergeltens eng zusammen, und wie bei den übrigen Wortformen ist die 'Vergeltung' auch hier ambivalent: sie kann positiv … oder negativ … sein." (Gerleman 1984:927)

Of special interest are the cases where Gerleman considers the noun *Shalom* to have a negative connotation (Gerleman 1984:931). He first cites Micah 5:4, where the coming ruler from Bethlehem is called "our peace". Micah then explicates this "peace" with the retribution of the Assyrians for their invasion of Israel. The second instance he cites is Isaiah 53:5, where the *ebed Yahweh* bears the "punishment of our peace", the *musar shelomenu*, upon himself. Then Gerleman mentions Isaiah 9:5, where he translates the phrase *sar Shalom* as "Fürst der Vergeltung", which in my view is very doubtful. Finally, he comes to Psalm 37:37, where the NAB reads: "Observe the person of integrity and mark the upright; Because there is a future for a man of peace." Gerleman understands the phrase *ki acharit leïsch Shalom* as "because at the end he will be a man, who receives retribution". As with Isaiah 9:5, I think he overstretches his argument here. In my view, this verse should be read as "because in the end he will be a man, who lives in peace." (comp. Gerleman 1984:931).

Gerleman also speaks about the peace offering (*shelamim*). In this special offering (mainly explained in Leviticus 7), only the fat of the animal was to be brought as a sacrifice. The priests and the man who brought the offering should eat the meat as a fellowship meal. Gerleman argues:

> "Die nächstliegende Annahme scheint dann zu sein, daß die Jahwe dargebrachten Fettstücke als Ersatz des ganzen, Jahwe grundsätzlich zugehörigen Opfertieres betrachtet wurden, durch welche das bei dem gesamten Mahl zu verzehrende Fleisch 'bezahlt' und zugleich freigekauft wurde." (Gerleman 1984:932)

This discussion between Eisenbeis and Gerleman still is an open one. In his article on the verb *sh-l-m,* Karl-Johann Illman in the *Theologisches Wörterbuch zum Alten Testament* (Botterweck und Fabry 1995) states that most theologians understand the basic meaning of the root *sh-l-m* as "Friede" or "Ganzheit" (:93), but he also mentions Gerleman and his view (:94). In his article on *Shalom* in the same volume, Franz Stendebach argues for a more holistic view. He does not follow either Eisenbeis and his definition of "wholeness" (which he thinks is too broad) nor Gerleman and his derivation of *Shalom* from the *Piel* of *sh-l-m* (which he thinks is too "forced") (Stendebach 1995:17). Instead, he writes:

> "Wir kommen ... wohl nicht an der Feststellung vorbei, daß *šālôm* eine Bedeutungsbreite hat, die durch kein deutsches Wort adäquat wiederzugeben ist. ... *šālôm* ist zusammenfassender Ausdruck all

dessen, was der alte Orientale als Inhalt des Segens begehrt."
(Stendebach 1995:18)

Then, he tries to combine the two positions of Eisenbeis and Gerleman stating:

> "šālôm ist ein zutiefst positiver Begriff, der mit den Vorstellungen
> von Unversehrtheit, Ganzheit, Heilsein von Welt und Mensch zu tun
> hat. Dem muß Genüge geleistet, das muß wiederhergestellt werden,
> wenn es gestört oder verletzt ist." (Stendebach 1995:18-19)

This understanding of *Shalom* leads to a more holistic understanding of the
concept of "peace" in the Old Testament.

If we follow Stendebach in his combination of the two aspects, "wholeness"
and "retribution", we can define *Shalom* as a status, where everything is as it
should be. The verb *sh-l-m* in its *Piel* stem then shows what is necessary to
achieve such status when something belonging to that wholeness is missing.
This is the place where recompense and retribution as well as payment or pay-
back become important elements of restoring peace. This is also in accordance
with one of the basic meanings of the stem *Piel*, namely its factitive function.
The *Piel* often expresses the way to achieve the things stated in the *Qal*.

I therefore argue for an understanding of *Shalom*, which is in line with the *Qal*
of *sh-l-m*. In this stem the verb is used for the completion of a particular work
in three different passages (1 Ki 7:51; 2 Chr 5:2; Neh 6:15). Isaiah further uses
it in 60:20, where he speaks about the completion of the days of sorrow, and in
9:4, where Job asks who can resist God and come out unscathed or complete.
From here, we come to the understanding of *Shalom* (which seems to be derived
from the Inf. abs. *Qal*) as a status in which everything is complete. The *Theological Wordbook of the Old Testament* defines *Shalom* as "completeness,
wholeness, harmony, fulfillment", while "the idea of unimpaired relationships
with others and fulfillment in one's undertakings" is implicit (Harris et al.
1980:931)[1].

2 The Noun Shalom

Gerleman thinks this understanding is too broad (Gerleman 1984:922). But this
cannot be used as an argument against it. When we look through the verses in

---

[1] Comp. also Hempel (1961:59) and Otto (2008:359-360).

which *Shalom* occurs in the Old Testament, we indeed find such a broad sense. When classifying the verses, we can find the following uses:

In 89 verses, the term *Shalom* is used without any special meaning that could be deduced from the context (e.g. Gen 26:29; Dt 20:10; Ps 4:9; Is 9:5). Then there are about 43 verses in which *Shalom* occurs in the sense of health, wealth or welfare. Very interesting is Gen 37:14, where Jacob sends his son Joseph to ask for the *Shalom* of his brothers and the *Shalom* of the sheep and goats! In 2 Sam 11:7, David asks Uriah, who just returned from the war against the Ammonites, about the *Shalom* of Joab, the *Shalom* of the people (meaning the army of Israel) and about the *Shalom* of the war! This very clearly shows that the traditional translation of *Shalom* as "peace" is not a good one. There are only seven passages where *Shalom* definitely means the opposite of war: 1 Ki 2:5; 5:4; 20:18; Ps 120:7; Eccl 3:8; Jer 4:10; Mi 3:5; Zec 9:10. There are other passages which can be understood in this sense, but are not definitively so. They are classified here as passages without a clear special meaning.

Quite a few passages use the word *Shalom* to denote something that is good, without further classification. There are six passages though, where the context clarifies it (Gen 41:16; 1 Sam 16:4.5; 1 Chr 12:19; Is 29:7 and Jer 29:7). Jer 29:7 is especially interesting. Through the prophet, God admonishes his people to seek the *Shalom* of the city of Babylon, where they have been brought to, because in its *Shalom* there would also be the *Shalom* of the Israelites. 18 times, we read about someone coming or going in *Shalom* (eg. Gen 26:31; Jos 10:21; Jdg 18:6; 2 Ki 5:19), without specifying this further. Four times we read about someone dying in *Shalom* (Gen 15:15; 2 Ki 22:20; 2 Chr 34:28 and Jer 34:5). In one instance (1 Ki 2:6), David admonishes his son Solomon not to let Joab die in *Shalom*.

The general understanding of *Shalom* as something, which is good, can also be found in the 8 instances in which *Shalom* is used in the sense of a greeting (Gen 43:23; Jdg 19:20; 2 Sam 18:28; 2 Ki 4:23; 5:22; 10:13; 1 Chr 18:10; Dan 10:19) and in three passages where it is used as a blessing. These are Num 6:26 (in the famous Aaronic blessing), Jdg 6:23, where God promises Joshua peace instead of death. This then leads Joshua to building an altar, which he calls *Yahweh Shalom* (V. 24). The third passage in this regard is Ps 29:11, where the Lord is asked to give *Shalom* to his people.

In three passages, *Shalom* is used in opposition to something being evil (1 Sam 20:7.21; Is 45:7), and in another seven passages as a synonym for security and quietness (2 Chr 15:5; Ps 55:19; 122:7; Is 32:17.18; Jer 12:5; 25;37).

Besides these passages, there are a few instances where *Shalom* takes a special meaning. Amongst these are five times in which we read about the covenant of peace (Num 25:12; Jos 9:15; Is 54:10 Ez 34,25 and 37:26). Pedersen even argues that *Shalom* and *berit* "do not designate a different kind of relationship. *shālōm* means the state prevailing in those united: the growth and full harmony of the soul, *berīth* the community with all the privileges and duties implied in it." (Pedersen 1946:285) Although this seems to be an overstatement, the connection of the two terms is nevertheless noteworthy.

To find *Shalom* can mean to find favor in someone's eyes (So 8:10), to go ahead in *Shalom* can mean to go safe and sound (Is 41:3). In Zec 8:16, God asks his people to speak the truth to each other and to judge *Shalom* in the gates of the city. In this context, *Shalom* is used as a synonym for justice, *zedekiah*.

In three verses, we read about someone speaking in *Shalom* with someone else (Gen 37:4; Dt 2:26 and Ps 28:3); meaning to speak friendly with each other (or in the case of Joseph and his brothers not being able to do so). In four instances, the "man of *Shalom*" designates someone's friend (Ps 41:10; Jer 20:10; 38:22 and Obd 1:7). Not very clear is Ps 55:21, where the plural of *Shalom* is used. Someone stretches out his hands against his *Shelomim*. This could mean either his friends or the ones, with whom he has made a covenant of *Shalom*. A similar problem is found in Ps 69:23. The first part of the verse reads: "Their table shall become a trap for them". Then follows the second part of the verse saying: *welishlomim lemokesh*. If this forms a parallel synonym, *lishlomim* should be parallel to "table", while *mokesh* is parallel to the "trap". Some translations understand the word *lishlomim* as coming from the peace offering, others think it is the plural form of *Shalom*, designating the "people of *Shalom*", the friends. The same plural form is also used in Jer 13:19, where it means the "completeness" of Judah.

Another plural form, which is clearly connected to the *Piel* of *sh-l-m* is the word *schellumim*. In Is 34:8, it functions as a synonym for *n-k-m*, which means "vengeance" or "retribution". The same word also occurs in Hos 9:7 and Mi 7:3.

This brief overview of the use of the noun *Shalom* in the OT shows that this word indeed covers a wide range of meanings. Rainer Albertz writes: "Shalom meint umfassend das Heil-Sein einer Gemeinschaft, umgreift damit auch Gerechtigkeit und Gesundheit" (Albertz 1983:17, Fn 6). The *Theological Wordbook of the Old Testament* formulates: "The general meaning behind the root *sh-l-m* is of completion and fulfillment – of entering into a state of wholeness and unity, a restored relationship." (Harris et al. 1980:930). Von Rad emphasizes that "selbstverständlich" everything connected with the term *Shalom* in the OT was automatically related to Yahweh and expected from him, the giver of all that is good (von Rad 1950:401).

One of the aspects of this state of *Shalom* is that it is marked by justice (as we can clearly see in Zec 8:16 (see above)). The *Theological Wordbook of the OT* states:

> "*shālōm* is the result of God's activity in covenant (*bᵉrît*), and is the result of righteousness (Isa 32:17). In nearly two-thirds of its occurrences, *shālōm* describes the state of fulfillment which is the result of God's presence." (Harris et al. 1980:931)

This presence of God guaranties the *Shalom*. Philip Nel writes:

> "Peace (*šālōm*) according to the prophetic preaching is the result of restored righteousness and cannot be achieved while one is persisting in sin and evil (Isa 32:17; 48:18; 54:13; 60:17)." (Nel 1997:132)

The prophets, especially Isaiah[2], envision a coming kingdom of *Shalom*, where God rules and his *mishpat* is acknowledged everywhere (Is 52:7; 54:10-15; 55:3-5; 57:19). Therefore, there will be no injustice and no need to fight anymore. The reason for this *Shalom* will not be that all those who wrongly fight their conflicts in the name of God are now renouncing their power, as Albertz thinks (Albertz 1991:707), but because God guaranties the righteousness (*zedekiah*) for everyone through his universal rule (*mishpat*). We will come back to this again later.

3 The Verb *Sh-l-m*

We will now turn to the verb *sh-l-m* and its meaning. As with the noun, I have tried to classify the different uses of the verb to get an overview of its meaning in the OT. While the noun *Shalom* describes a status, the verb (especially in its

---

[2] I am using the term "Isaiah" to speak about the book in the final stage of its editorial process, as it is represented in the OT.

Piel stem) tells us how to reach this status. There are eight verses in the OT in which the *Qal* is used. As already stated, three of them speak about the completion of a work (1 Ki 7:51; 2 Chr 5:1; Neh 6:15) and in Is 60:20 the days of sorrow are fulfilled. Job 9:4 asks if anyone who ever resisted God, was still in *sh-l-m*. In two other verses (Job 22:21 and Ps 7:5), the *Qal* is used to denote a state of friendship or peace that someone keeps. The same can be said about the one occurrence of a participle passive *Qal* in 2Sam 20:19.

From this understanding of the *Qal,* we can also understand the *Hifil* form, which is used in another 13 verses, and the one verse with a *Hofal*. The *Hifil* usually represents a *causative* clause to *Qal*. There are eight verses in which this form is used with the meaning "to make peace" (Dt 20:12; Jos 10:1.4; 2 Sam 10:19; 1 Ki 22:45; 1 Chr 19:19; Pr 16:7 – compare also the *Hofal* in Job 5:23). The other five verses speak about completing something (Job 23:14; Is 44:26.28). In Is 38:12.13, Hezekiah complains that his life has come to an end.

The main use of the verb *sh-l-m* is in the *Piel* (89 times in 80 verses). There are some instances in which the meaning of the *Piel* is quite near to the *Hifil*. As already stated, the *Piel* can denote the *factitive* of the *Qal*. This of course is not very far from the *causative* of the *Hifil*. We can see this in 1 Ki 9:25, where we read that the house of God was completed. This idea of completing something can also be seen in the 19 verses *sh-l-m* in *Piel* is used in the sense of fulfilling a vow (eg Dt 23:22; Ps 22:26; Is 19:21).

In numerous instances (38 verses) the *Piel* is used to denote some kind of "repayment". This can be very general as in Gen 44:4 in the sense of repaying good with evil (comp. Ps 35:12; 38:21 and also Jer 18:20, where the *Pual* is used in the same sense). In Ruth 2:12, Boaz blesses Ruth and asks God to repay her good deeds, so that her wages would be full (using the adverb *shelemah*). In Is 57:18, God promises to "make full" the comfort of Israel and in 2 Ki 4:7 the *Piel* is used to repay one's debts. This leads to the use of the *Piel* in the Torah, where the law speaks about compensating someone for his losses. If for example someone dug a pit and did not cover it correctly, so that the ox or donkey of a fellow Israelite fell into it and died, the one who opened the pit had to pay the owner for the loss of his animal (Ex 21:34). In the Torah, the *Piel* of *sh-l-m* is quite often used in this sense (18 times in Exodus and Leviticus).

The idea of repaying someone for something is also behind the use of *sh-l-m* in 26 verses, where it denotes the recompense for evil deeds. Twice, this form is used within a rhetorical question (Job 21:31 and Joel 4:4). In Ps 41:11, God is

92

asked to help repay evil and Ps 137:8 prays for the recompense of the evil Babylon has done to Jerusalem. In all other instances, the verb refers to God and his deeds. This understanding of *sh-l-m* is often found in the Psalms (31:24; 62:13; 137:8), Isaiah (59:18; 65:6; 66:6) and especially Jeremiah (16:18; 25:14; 32:18; 51:6.24.56). God will compensate evil and he will repay the evildoer. In a classical way, this is formulated for example in Dt 7:10, where the *Piel* of *sh-l-m* is used twice:

> "… but who repays with destruction those who hate him; he does not delay with those who hate him, but makes them pay for it."

Recompensing evil deeds therefore is not the task of humans in the OT; this is God's responsibility. Prov 20:22 explicitly admonishes:

> "Do not say, 'I will repay evil!' Wait for the LORD, who will help you."

We can therefore say that the *Piel* of *sh-l-m* is mostly used in the sense of repaying a debt when it refers to human beings and their behavior, while its understanding as a recompense of evil is almost completely reserved for God. Psalm 62:13 even declares that this recompensing is a sign of God's *chäsäd*, his covenantal loyalty.[3]

3.1 How can there be shalom?

If *Shalom* indeed means a status of wholeness, in which everything is as it should be (as shown above), any component that is missing must be replaced, before that status can be fully reached. This refers to material as well as immaterial things. It means that every debt must be payed, every illness healed, every shortage filled and every evil recompensed. We can easily see that such a status is impossible on this earth, but this does not mean that we should not strive towards it.

There are things that could and should be done. This is the lesson to learn from the different laws concerning the repayment of debts and the replacement of goods that were taken away from someone wrongfully. Striving for peace surely also means striving for the equal rights of everyone. There is a lot of

---

[3] Comp. Hans Heinrich Schmid (1993:606): "Tatsächlich steht im Hintergrund von *šlm* auch und gerade da, wo wir uns mit Übersetzungen wie ,bezahlen', ,vergelten' behelfen müssen, der Gedanke des (Wieder-)Herstellens eines *šalôm*-Zustandes".

injustice to address in the name of God, from the personal and individual level up to the realm of global economics. There are many people living on this earth whose status is far from being one of wholeness. They are missing even the essentials of everyday life. Striving for "peace" therefore means striving for all those people in the name of God!

3.2 Striving for peace

The Bible shows that it is at the heart of God to bring peace to an un-peaceful world. In this context, it is important to realize that it is God himself, who will care for peace in the end. The Old and New Testament speak of a day of judgement, when God recompenses every injustice. The Bible explicitly speaks about the wrath of God in this regard. Walter Groß has shown that this wrath of God does not function as the counterpart of his love or the result of his holiness, but that it belongs to his justice: "He is just in his wrath. His wrath is a product of his righteousness."[4] (Groß 1999:233). Bernd Janowski argues that justice is a central term in the cultures of the Ancient Near East (Janowski 2014:40). He specifically looks at Ps 82, where God as Judge brings together judgement and salvation. This he calls the "Doppelgesicht der Gerechtigkeit" (:48). It not only has a social, but also a cosmic and a theological dimension (:48-50).

Henrik Peels argues that the term vengeance must not be understood from a Western perspective, where it almost completely has a negative connotation. The "negative connotations of the word vengeance hinder a proper understanding of the intention and meaning of the theologoumenon of God's vengeance." (Peels 1995:2-3). Peels formulates:

> "The vengeance of God marks the transition from injustice to peace, from demise to restoration." (Peels 1995:207-208)

Nel thinks that Is 57:18 is very important in this regard:

> "In this eschatological vision, Yahweh will restore (*šlm*) comfort to the contrite in contrast with his issuing of accusations against the wicked (56:9-57:13). It is used here in parallel with *rp'*, heal .... The result of this *šlm*-action of Yahweh will be peace (v. 19 ...) for the

---

[4] "Er ist in seinem Zorn gerecht, bzw. sein Zorn ist ein Ausfluß seiner Gerechtigkeit...".

94

nation, but the wicked will experience no peace (v. 21)." (Nel 1997:131)

It is God who will bring about justice in the end. This is important to realize[5]. However, this does not mean that one should refrain from working towards justice in this world. If it is at the heart of God to care for justice and peace, it should be on our agenda as one of the most important goals also. Nevertheless, the knowledge that justice in its complete and final stage will only be achieved by God himself, sets us free to do what we can to establish as much justice as possible. In this regard, it is interesting to note that the OT does not understand the term "justice" in the sense of a social equality, as it was used for example in the French revolution. Leonhard Rost shows that it is more a term meaning that everyone receives that which he or she deserves. It describes the ideal condition of a community, in which God's *mishpat* is in force and therefore his justice dominates every aspect of life. (Rost 1971:41) Schmid calls this "eine lebensermöglichende Geordnetheit"[6] (Schmid 1993:605). It should be obvious that it is not possible to reach such a status *fully* through human activity.

Let me make clear what I mean by an example from my family. My grandfather worked as a guardian in one of the concentration camps of Nazi Germany. He was not able to go to war because of health issues. Therefore, they forced him to enter Nazi SS and work at the concentration camp. After the end of World War II, everyone who worked for Nazi Germany was put to trial. In the trial of my grandfather, many prisoners of the concentration camp where he worked, vowed for him and testified that he did a lot of good for the prisoners. As a result, they released him after the trial.

These trials were important for coping with the grand injustices done during World War II. On the other hand, some serious offenders managed to escape before going to trial. Others, who deserved to be acquitted, may not have had – for various reasons – anyone to vouch for them. Some were certainly condemned to death, although they were no more guilty than my grandfather.

What we can see here is that there will never be *perfect* justice in this world. Nevertheless, it does not mean that we should not try to work for it. Evil deeds

---

[5] Comp. Nel 1997:132: "Peace (*šālōm*) according to the prophetic preaching is the result of restored righteousness and cannot be achieved while one is persisting in sin and evil (Isa 32:17; 48:18; 54:13; 60:17)".

[6] "eine lebensermöglichende Geordnetheit".

need retribution, so that there can be justice and peace. The knowledge that God will ensure that there will be complete and total justice in the end, frees us to do as much as we can to strive towards such justice in this world. Moreover, it assures us that it is indeed God's will to do so.

3.3 Abandoning personal revenge

The knowledge that God will take care of justice in the end can also free us from the need to make sure to get revenge for every evil deed done against us personally. This is what Paul explicitly says in Rom 12:19, when he cites Dt 32:25:

> "Beloved, do not look for revenge but leave room for the wrath; for it is written, 'Vengeance is mine, I will repay, says the Lord.'"

Abandoning one's own personal revenge therefore is a motif found in the Old and New Testament alike (Lev 19:18; Prov 20:22; 24:29; Luk 6:28; Rom 12:17-19; 1 Thess 5:15; 1 Petr 2:21). It is based upon the knowledge of God's recompensing justice, both for evil and good deeds. To know this sets people free to work towards justice and peace in this world.

3.4 Peace in the political arena

There is another aspect of *Shalom* which can only be touched upon here. It is the question of how the government of a given state can establish this "peace" in the political arena and in legislation. To unfold such a topic is beyond the scope of this article.

A government is responsible for resisting and punishing offenders, as Paul writes in Rom 13:3-4. In the Old Testament, Israel's rulers were compelled to judge according to the principle "an eye for an eye", meaning that the sentence should equal the offence. The Old Testament law builds on this principle. On the other hand, there was also room for mercy should an evildoer repent.

There is no easy answer to the question of how a government can work towards a status of *Shalom* for its people. Should there be recompense for every evil deed? Should there be room for forgiveness, which might encourage the evildoer to repent? Germany struggled with this question after World War II; South Africa experienced the same after apartheid. As already said, there is no place to answer this question here. Nevertheless, this article might also have some significance for the political sphere.

The title of this presentation reads "Shalom without recompense?". It should be clear by now that it is not possible to reach a status of wholeness unless there is a total and just recompense of all injustice done. One can easily see that such a status is impossible on this side of heaven. It is therefore important to realize that this recompense is something God will bring about[7]. As already said, this does not mean that we should not work for *Shalom* on all levels of society, but we should do so with the knowledge of the coming Kingdom of God, where *Zädäk* and *Shalom*, justice and peace will kiss each other, as Psalm 85:11 states.

4 A Brief Look at the NT

This understanding of the topic of *Shalom* has a clear resonance within the New Testament. It speaks about God's way of making peace, of bringing about this status of wholeness, to which the Hebrew term *Shalom* refers. Paul speaks about Jesus in Col 1:19-20 when he says:

> "For in him all the fullness was pleased to dwell, and through him to reconcile all things for him, making peace by the blood of his cross [through him], whether those on earth or those in heaven."

Although the Greek term *eirene* does not have the same meaning as the Hebrew word *Shalom*, Paul seems to use it here in such a comprehensive sense. The peace God made through Christ encompasses not only human beings, but also "those on earth" and "those in heaven". There is a universal or cosmic aspect to it – peace, wholeness and fullness in the complete sense of the word is going to encompass every aspect of creation[8].

God brings about this peace through the "blood of his cross". Without going into the whole discussion of the meaning of the cross and its connection to the OT sacrifices, it seems clear that the cross is about recompensing the evil done by human beings. In this way, God brings together his righteousness and mercy, his forgiveness and retribution.

---

[7] Klaus Koch strongly argues against the idea of a direct link between doing and result (Tun-Ergehen). This is often understood as if Koch argues against the idea of recompense or retaliation itself, which is not the case. Koch thinks that God supervises the connection of doing and result and – if necessary – strengthens and even leads this connection to an end (Koch 1955:9).

[8] Comp. Murray 1992, *The Cosmic Covenant*, who argues that there are remnants of a cosmic covenant to be found in the OT.

However, this is not an automatic process. It is indeed an offer made to all humankind, but it waits for an answer and it is definitely clear from the NT that not every human being will give this answer, not even most of them. Therefore, it is only one part of what the NT has to say to the question of peace. The other part lies in God's final judgement. In a very detailed way, we see this in the book of Revelation. The kingdom of God can only come in its full and final nature when God has recompensed every evil. Again, I will not go deeper into all the theological aspects related to this, but only show that we find here also a direct line between the OT and NT in this regard. God will take care of all injustice and recompense, every good or bad deed. To know this makes us free from the need to care for this on our own.

Bibliography

Albertz, Rainer 1983. Shalom und Versöhnung. Alttestamentliche Kriegs- und Friedenstraditionen. *Theologia Practica* 18 (1/2), 16–29.

Albertz, Rainer 1991. Friede. AT, in Manfred Görg & Bernhard Lang (eds): *Neues Bibel-Lexikon. A–G*, vol 1. 3 volumes. Zürich: Benziger, 706–707.

Botterweck, Gerhard Johannes & Fabry, Heinz-Josef (eds) 1995. *Theologisches Wörterbuch zum Alten Testament*. Stuttgart: Kohlhammer.

Eisenbeis, Walter 1969. *Die Wurzel שלם im Alten Testament*. Berlin: de Gruyter.

Gerleman, Gillis 1973. Die Wurzel šlm. *Zeitschrift für die alttestamentliche Wissenschaft* 85 (1), 1–14.

Gerleman, Gillis 1984. שלם *šlm* genug haben, in Jenni & Westermann 1984, 919–935.

Groß, Walter 1999. Zorn Gottes – ein biblisches Theologumenon, in Walter Groß (ed): *Studien zur Priesterschrift und zu alttestamentlichen Gottesbildern*. Stuttgart: Verl. Kath. Bibelwerk (Stuttgarter biblische Aufsatzbände, 30), 199–238.

Harris, R. Laird, Archer, Gleason L. & Waltke, Bruce Kenneth 1980. *Theological Wordbook of the Old Testament*. 2 volumes. Chicago: Moody press.

Hempel, Johannes 1961. *Apoxysmata. Vorarbeiten zu einer Religionsgeschichte und Theologie des Alten Testaments*. Berlin: Verlag Alfred Töpelmann.

Janowski, Bernd 2014. *Ein Gott, der straft und tötet? Zwölf Fragen zum Gottesbild des Alten Testaments*. 2., durchges. und um einen Literaturnachtr. erw. Aufl. Neukirchen-Vluyn: Neukirchener Verl.-Ges (Neukirchener Theologie).

Jenni, Ernst & Westermann, Claus (eds) 1984. *Theologisches Handwörterbuch zum Alten Testament*. Zwei Bände; THAT. 3., durchges. Aufl. München: Kaiser (2).

Koch, Klaus 1955. Gibt es ein Vergeltungsdogma im Alten Testament? *Zeitschrift für Theologie und Kirche* 52, 1–42.

Murray, Robert 1992. *The cosmic covenant. Biblical themes of justice, peace and the integrity of creation*. London: Sheed & Ward (Heythrop monographs, 7).

Nel, Philip J. 1997. שלם, in Willem VanGemeren (ed): *New international dictionary of Old Testament theology & exegesis*. 5 volumes. Carlisle, Cumbria: Paternoster Press (Theology, 4), 130–135.

Otto, Eckart 2008. Frieden III. Altes Testament, in Hans Dieter Betz (ed): *Religion in Geschichte und Gegenwart. Handwörterbuch für Theologie und Religionswissenschaft*, vol 3. 4., völlig neu bearb. Aufl., ungekürzte Studienausg. Tübingen: Mohr Siebeck (UTB, 8401), 359–360.

Pedersen, Johannes 1946. *Israel. Its Life and Culture*. Reprint of the first edition from 1926. London: Geoffrey Cumberlege (I–II).

Peels, Hendrik G. L. 1995. The vengeance of God. The meaning of the root NQM and the function of the NQM-texts in the context of divine revelation in the Old Testament. Available at Theol. Univ. van de Christelijke Gereformeerde Kerken in Nederland, Diss., 1992. Leiden: Brill (Oudtestamentische studiën, 31).

Rad, Gerhard von 1950: שָׁלוֹם im AT, in Gerhard Kittel (ed): *Theologisches Wörterbuch zum Neuen Testament*. Zweiter Band: Δ–H, vol 2. Reprint of the first edition from 1935, 400–405.

Rost, Leonhard 1971. Erwägungen zum Begriff šālôm, in Karl-Heinz Bernhardt (ed): *Shalom. Studien zu Glaube und Geschichte Israels. Alfed Jepsen zum 70. Geburtstag dargebracht von Freunden, Schülern und Kollegen*. Stuttgart: Calwer Verlag (Arbeiten zur Theologie, 1. Reihe, Heft 46), 41–44.

Schmid, Hans Heinrich 1993. Frieden. II. Altes Testament, in Gerhard Müller & Horst Robert Balz (eds): *Theologische Realenzyklopädie*, vol 11. Studienausg. Berlin, New York: de Gruyter, 605–610.

Stendebach, Franz J. 1995. שָׁלוֹם šālōm, in Gerhard Johannes Botterweck & Heinz-Josef Fabry (eds): *Theologisches Wörterbuch zum Alten Testament*, vol 8. Stuttgart: Kohlhammer, 13–46.

Reconciliation as Healing of Memory – A Missionary Task of the Church

Johannes Reimer

Abstract

Reconciliation is part and parcel of God mission to the world, the missio Dei. It defines God's aim of mission. God sends Christ to the world to reconcile the world with Himself. Consequently, the mission of the Church will aim towards reconciliation. The instruments of her mission might vary, but the aim does not. In this paper we will explore the theological validity of God's Mission as reconciliation and focus on the concept of Healing of Memories (HoM) from a missiological perspective as a valid tool for the reconciling ministry of the Church in mission.

1 Mission as Reconciliation in a World of Destructive Conflicts

David J. Bosch (1991:368-510) named 12 elements of an upcoming Ecumenical paradigm of mission in his epochal work on transforming mission. The elements mentioned did not include reconciliation. But the issue as such is present, even if Bosch does not lift the theme to a missionary task on its own, which to some extant reflects the missiological debate of his days. Reconciliation was viewed as a possible fruit of mission, not as mission in its best meaning, and covering rather the reconciling act between God and sinners.

It is fascinating to see that the issue has become one of the central themes in mission circles since the beginning of the 1990s (Schreiter 2013:13) and has developed rapidly to a vividly discussed model of mission (see for instance an overview of the debate in Matthey 2005:174-191). Some authors even postulate that solving the disturbing factors and eliminating sources of societal conflict in society, aiming for a meaningful convivance will determine the future of Christian mission (Sundermeier 1986:86ff; Reimer 2011:19-35). Robert Schreiter speaks of reconciliation as paradigm of mission (2005). The Lausanne Movement on the one hand (LOP 51) and the mainline churches (Rice 2005:18-19), the Ecumenical Movement (WCC 2005) and the RCC (Pope Benedict XVI 2011) on the other – all reclaim mission as reconciliation for their future operations.

The changes that have occurred after the turn of the century regarding reconciliation as mission are best depicted by looking at the fundamental difference
in how the Lausanne Movement regards reconciliation. In 1974 Lausanne emphasized that "reconciliation with God is not reconciliation with other people".
Here reconciliation was viewed as a fruit of evangelism. In 2010 a different
note is struck: "Reconciliation to God is inseparable from reconciliation to one
another" (Rice 2013:2) and it is a model of mission.

What is reconciliation and how is the term integrated into the concept of mission? The Merriam-Webster dictionary defines reconciliation as "the act of
causing two people or groups to become friendly again after an argument or
disagreement".[1] Theologically speaking such conflicting parties may be seen
as God and his creation, humans among themselves and the physical vs. spiritual world, as Tormod Engelsviken (2013:79) points out. This obviously includes spiritual and social, ecclesial and societal matters. The question is, however, whether such a wide concept is biblically justified and missiologically
relevant.

2 Reconciliation – Biblical Mandate

Mission is first and foremost God's mission, *missio Dei* (Vicedom 2002:32).
Whatever we might think and say about the mission of the Church, it must be
rooted in God's mission, "the heart of all mission" (Escobar 2006:86). The
Church exists for God's mission, she is, as Emil Brunner (1951:17) puts it,
"eine verkündigende Existenz", a proclaiming existence. She proclaims God's
redemptive heart and act. Craig Ott (2010:155) consequently defines mission
as "…the sending activity of God with the purpose of reconciling to himself
and bringing into his kingdom fallen men and women from every people and
nation to his glory." Together with other authors, he bases his conviction in
Pauline theology (see in this regard, Breytenbach 1989). Apostle Paul states in
2 Cor. 5:18-21:

> "All this is from God, who reconciled us to himself through
> Christ and gave us the ministry of reconciliation: that God was rec-
> onciling the world to himself in Christ, not counting people's sins
> against them. And he has committed to us the message of reconcili-
> ation. We are therefore Christ's ambassadors, as though God were

---

[1] http://www.merriam-webster.com/dictionary/reconciliatio1, accessed 19.02.17.

making his appeal through us. We implore you on Christ's behalf: Be reconciled to God. God made him who had no sin to be sin for us, so that in him we might become the righteousness of God."

The text underlines three basic propositions: (a) reconciliation is God's work in Christ, (b) reconciliation aims towards restoration of God's relationship with the world; (c) reconciliation is a core ministry of the church.

It is the current condition of the world in relationship to God, which brings reconciliation to the table (Bieringer 1987:295-326). The world has become godless by having forsaken and forgotten what God's plan for the world originally was. Dishonoring God, humans have fallen into a self-destructive life mode. And as a result, says Paul, "they were filled with all manner of unrighteousness, evil, covetousness, malice. They are full of envy, murder, strife, deceit, maliciousness. They are gossipers, slanderers, haters of God, insolent, haughty, boastful, inventors of evil, disobedient to parents, foolish, faithless, heartless, ruthless" (Rom. 1:29-31). This all is produced by a corrupted mind, by the futility of godless thinking. The apostle warns the church in Ephesus:

"So I tell you this, and insist on it in the Lord, that you must no longer live as the Gentiles do, in the futility of their thinking. They are darkened in their understanding and separated from the life of God because of the ignorance that is in them due to the hardening of their hearts." (Eph. 4:17-18).

Ignorance is the problem. Humans have lost their vision. They have turned blind and walk in darkness. Their leaders are blind; leading blind (Matt. 15:14). And they do what is wrong in the sight of God following their own thoughts and desires and cause His wrath (Eph. 2:1-3). The result is peacelessness and broken relationship between God and man as well as humans among themselves.

The loving heart of God, however, seeks renewal and restoration. God does not want sinners to perish (Ez. 33:11) and, therefore, He sent His only begotten Son to save and reconcile the world with himself (2 Cor. 5:18). To reconcile means to bring God's plan back to memory, ignite the original vision. This is the message of God's revelation in Scripture. "From Genesis to Revelation, Scripture witnesses to God's total mission "to reconcile to himself all things, whether things on earth or things in heaven" (Col. 1:15-20). The fullness of reconciliation is friendship with God in Jesus Christ ..." (Rice 2005:11).

The reconciled are new in Christ (2 Cor. 5:17) and follow Christ's mind (Phil. 2:5). Reconciliation means restoration of memory, renewal of mind and the ability to understand what the will of God for our life is (Rom. 12.1-3). Leaving our godless past behind and striving towards a future designed by God for those who accept Christ as their Lord and Saviour – this is what reconciliation does to people. God desires peace with his creation and, therefore peace is at the heart of his mission (Reimer 2017:69). Pope Benedict XVI writes: "Reconciliation then, is not limited to God's plan to draw estranged and sinful humanity to himself in Christ through the forgiveness of sins and out of love. It is also the restoration of relationships between people through the settlement of differences and the removal of obstacles to their relationships in their experience of God's love" (Pope Benedict XVI 2011:8). And Robert Schreiter (2013:14) summarizes properly:

> "What we see in these Pauline passages is how reconciliation is a central way of explaining God's work in the world. Through the Son and the Spirit, God is making peace – between God and the world, and thus also within all of creation itself. When this insight is brought together with the concept of the *missio Dei* developed a few decades earlier in missiology, we see the biblical foundations for reconciliation as a paradigm of mission, a paradigm that began taking on a particular poignancy and urgency in the last decade of the twentieth century."

To say this does not, however, eliminate the other elements of God's mission in the world. To the contrary, reconciliation works as a frame of reference for evangelism, diakonia, dialogue and so on. In words of Schreiter:

> "Reconciliation as a paradigm of mission does not replace the other paradigms, but can bring them into closer connection with one another within the larger frame of God's intentions for the world. So this two-fold contribution – to the larger questions of reconciliation in the world today and to the dialogue between paradigms of mission within the churches – assures a continuing role for this paradigm of reconciliation on missionary thinking for the coming decades." (Schreiter 2013:29).

3 Bringing the Alienated to the Table

God works peace through His Son Jesus Christ. But how does the praxis of reconciliation look like? How do we leave our past? How do we capture future? How do we become free for a life in God? Jesus says: "You will see the truth and the truth will set you free" (John 8:32). The answer to our questions is that we will be set free by realizing the truth for both, our past as well as our future. Using a biblical image we may say: restoration is a process of redressing. We undress our old man made according to flesh and put on the new made in the Spirit (Col. 3:5-15). Thus restoration is a two step process: (a) we realize what is old in us and leave it, (b) we understand what Gods new creation for us is and put it on.

3.1 Recovering our sinful memory

"Every conflict has its story." (Baumberger 2012:114). Restoration of God's vision for us begins with a critical recovery of our own past. The blind will only see if their sight is recovered. But to recover sight presupposes recognition of one's blindness. How will a blind person ever know what a healthy sight even means? Those born blind know nothing about seeing. They may only know by believing those who see. God, however, is not blind. He knows us *in toto*. He will reveal what is right and/or wrong in our lives. Jesus promises to send His Spirit, who reveals to the world her sin and God's judgement (John 16:8-9). The Holy Spirit leads people in all the truth (John 14:26). To see our own life story, our own biography from God's perspective, to read the pages of our past together with God's Spirit will uncover our sinful ways and set us on His paths. Reconciliation starts with recovering our memories about our own sinful life. Apostle John states:

> "If we say we have fellowship with him while we walk in darkness, we lie and do not practice the truth. But if we walk in the light, as he is in the light, we have fellowship with one another, and the blood of Jesus his Son cleanses us from all sin." (1 John 1:6-7).

Realizing our own sin and confessing sin to God, opens the chance of forgiveness. Forgiveness, then, breaks the chain of bad memory and inferiority complexes.

3.2 Recovering God's vision.

Restoration of God's vision, secondly, presupposes an understanding of what His new creation implies, since the new creation follows God's original idea of creating men and women into His own image (Gen. 1:27). We leave the "demonic cycle" and enter "God's cycle" in reconciliation (Baumberger 2012:116). What does it mean to be newly born? How different are children of God and in what way? Apostle Paul promises that God reveals to his children who they are in Christ and what gifts and power they are given (Eph. 1:3-23). There is a whole theology behind the new identity in Christ described to us in His word. Reconciled people will find their orientation for their every-day-life here. They will accentuate the mind of Christ and steadily build up a recovered memory of God's plan for their life. Thus, memories are healed and the past no longer influences the present and future.

Nina, a young lady, is an example. She came from a broken family and her own life story was marked by violence and abuse. Not only once did she attempt to commit suicide. Life did not make much sense to her. Friends introduced her to Jesus and she decided to follow Him. "No, I did not become all new as some Christians claim", says Nina. "Memories of abuse hunted me down time after time, again and again. I needed deep counselling. The church I attended offered me help. Years later, I can truly say that Jesus restored me completely. I still do remember the bad days of my life, but they have no influence on me any longer. I am truly new in Christ."

The Church is God's ambassador of reconciliation. Walter Freitag (1950:11-12) rightly pointed to the fact that a Church, accepting God's mission as her source of being, will less preoccupy herself with internal matters, but seek engagement towards reconciliation of the world. She has been entrusted with the "word of reconciliation". In reality she will speak prophetically into the lives of people, societies and even nations (Reimer 2017:53-62). She will uncover the personal and collective sins of humans calling them to confession. And she will present to the world an alternative way of life, inviting everybody to join a process of transformation. A process, which may, according to Robert Schreiter (2013:19), include four practices: healing, truth-telling, pursuit of justice and forgiveness.

The first practice is healing. "[...] reconciliation is about healing wounds, rebuilding trust, and restoring right relationships," states Schreiter. He divides healing into three dimensions: healing of memories, healing of victims and healing of wrongdoers (:Ibid).

The second practice is truth-telling. "Truth-telling involves testimony to what really happened in the past, and a common effort to reconstruct a public truth" (:Ibid).

The third practice is the pursuit of justice. Punitive justice is the punishment of the wrongdoers. Restorative justice "may involve restitution and reparation, as well as opportunities to explore how to rebuild a just and meaningful society" (Schreiter 2013:20). And lastly, structural justice, such as changing social structures.

The fourth and final practice is forgiveness, which is a process for both individuals and societies. Schreiter also warns us against cheap forgiveness or a forgiveness that is forced upon the victims. He emphasizes that forgiveness is directed at the wrongdoers themselves and not their actions. (:Ibid).

Schreiters missiological practice is greatly reflected in the process called Healing of Memories (HoM).

4 Healing of Memories – Methodology of Reconciliation

Healing of Memories (HoM) is a method to reconcile the broken relationship between victims and offenders. The concept was developed and employed for the first time in post-apartheid South Africa (Botman 1996) and is now broadly used worldwide in ministries of conflict resolution and reconciliation (see an overview in Garzon 2002).

The method was introduced to the European context in the second half of the 1990s (Guitierrez 1999:152-156), tested in the context of politically unstable North-Ireland (McEvoy 2008:144-155) and then employed in a number of other European countries. Reconciliation processes conducted by using HoM as tool were realized in Serbia, Ukraine, Slovakia and Finland (Brandes 2008). In 2004, the Conference of European Churches (CEC)[2] and the Community of Protestant Churches in Europe (CPCE)[3] decided to establish a joint project in „Healing of Memories". The project was placed in Romania, a bridging country between Western and Eastern European cultures. Dieter Brandes, the former

---

[2] https://www.ceceurope.org (1.12.2017).

[3] http://www.leuenberg.net/de (1.12.2017).

Secretary General of the Lutheran Gustav-Adolf-Werk (GAW), was appointed to the leadership of the project (see Brandes 2009).

HoM as developed in South Africa focused on reconciliation of individuals. In Europe, however, the concept expanded through the work of the „Irish School of Ecumenics"[4] to reconciliation between groups and cultures, using the basic ecumenic document relating European churches to one another, the *charta ecumenica*[5] as its foundation. The articles three, six and eight, addressing dialogue and reconciliation between churches, are of particular importance.

The third Conference of European Churches gathered in Sibiu, Romania, from 4.-9. September 2007, and called all European Christian Churches to cooperation in matters of peace and reconciliation.[6] One year later, the foundation „Reconciliation in South East Europe" (RSEE)[7] and the „Ecumenical Institute of Healing of Memories" was established in Sibiu, Romania. The programs developed here have been used in many conflict settings including the countries in Central Africa, such as Burundi, Rwanda and Congo. They follow a three-step approach (Brandes 2011:179-186; Bauer 2013:92f).[8]

a) *Joint recovery of history.* In this phase the parties interdisciplinarily work through the socio-cultural and religious backgrounds of the evolution of conflicts together. The aim is to understand how conflicts arise and develop and what influences them. It is crucial that all conflict parties work in this together. (RSEE 2017)

b) *Joint participation in the pain and sufferings of each other.* In this phase of the process the parties hear each other's stories of pain and suffering and develop a sense of understanding why the common history causes so much pain on the one hand,

---

[4] See: https://www.tcd.ie/ise/ (12.07.2017).

[5] Full text: http://www.oekumene-ack.de/fileadmin/user_upload/Charta_Oecumenica/Charta_Oecumenica.pdf, accessed 9.09.2017.

[6] See the text of the congress appeal in: https://www.domradio.de/sites/default/files/pdf/Sibiu.pdf, accesed 9.9.2017.

[7] http://www.healingofmemories.ro/preocess-healing-of-memories, accesed 9.09.2017.

[8] Ibid.

but also a sense for understanding why the offense happened. The aim is to open ways for apology and forgiveness, understanding and acceptance. (RSEE 2017)

c) *Joint working together on building future.* Solving the problems of the past opens ways to work for a common peaceful future. In order to work together, the parties will have to discover the richness of the other, gifts and competences of each other. Active and peaceful participation in the life of each other is the aim of this step. The result is an expected reconciled community. (RSEE 2017)

It is easy to see the correlation between the Pauline concept of reconciliation as developed above and HoM. The steps are similar: recover sinful past, ask for forgiveness and start a new and changed life. Bringing God, the reconciler, with all the creative power of the Holy Spirit into the process, HoM will win an impressive momentum. The Spirit reveals the truth, brings people to the table of the prince of peace, grants gifts and abilities and establishes patterns of a renewed life.

Reconciliation leads to healing of memories. The conflict-loaded past is not excused, but rather forgiven due to a clear confession of sin and a plea for forgiveness. At the same time, an alternative future is brought to the table – God's vision. This and only this is the common base for peaceful convivance. Healing of our memories leads to a common future.

5 Reconciliation among Christians

In recent years a number of Christian denominations have started conversations towards reconciliation between churches, driven by the idea that only reconciled churches may work for peace and reconciliation in the world (Ahrens 2005:162-173). Such conversations begin where we realize that unity is not optional. Jesus sets the agenda: unity is a precondition for effective mission (John 17:21). Unity is not a natural human condition. In fact, the opposite is the case. But unity is achieved in Christ. He is the peacemaker *per se* (Eph. 2:14) because he serves a God of Peace (Rom. 15:33) und proclaims a gospel of peace (Eph. 6:15). To serve God as Jesus did means to get involved in peacemaking.

Mennonites, for instance, are involved in a number of Ecumenical conversations driven by the dream that healing memories offers great chances for a common peaceful co-existence even where theological stands may still place stumbling blocks ahead of them (see examples in Enns 2008:29-132). Between 1998-2003, for instance, they met – for the first time in their own history – with Roman-Catholic Leaders to discuss each other's faith convictions and sort out conflicts developed in centuries of disconnect.

In their conversation on healing of memories Mennonites and Catholics named the controversial issues of the past, which had created the difficult relationship between the two, and their own unchristian approach to solve them as sin and asked for forgiveness (Enns/Jaschke 2008:95). This required a joint reading of history in the spirit of prayer and contemplation. Conflicting parties typically develop their own reading of historical events. These may not always be accurate. Historical treatments are always interpretations. Humans interpret from particular perspectives. As a result polemics dominate relationships and hinder parties to see their own portion of guilt in the basket. Reading history together helps to discover alternative views, relativize predefined positions and open a road for mutual understanding. It is crucial to name wrongdoing as sin regardless what the motivation may have been. Sin can never be excused. The only way to overcome sin is forgiveness. This was successfully achieved between the two denominations. Other conversations with Lutherans, Reformed, Baptist and Seventh-Day-Adventist followed (Enns 2012). Other Churches have undergone similar conversations.[9]

6 Reconciliation in Multi-Optional Communities

We live in a multi-optional world, a world in which different and at times totally divergent life concepts stand side by side. Globalization has created a world mixed by cultures, religions and orientations. In such a world, tensions and conflicts are unavoidable. Consequently, reconciliation becomes the central issue in community development (Haspel 2003:472-490). Community mediation is a newly established discipline in university departments of social work and enjoys an unprecedented growth. Faculties of practical theology and missiology respond to the new trend. Some even argue that convivance is the central challenge for the Christian Church of the future. Christian mission of the future will

---

[9] See reports in: http://www.osservatoreromano.va/en/news/reconciliation-begins-listening, accessed 1.12.2017.

work for a meaningful convivance and the ministry of reconciliation is her core competence (Reimer 2011:19-35).

But how does reconciliation work in multi-optional societies where the parties in conflict may not automatically accept a common base for reconciliation found in the Holy Scriptures? Theological meaning as such will be irrelevant to many people. De Gruchy (2002:26) says:

> "For them, reconciliation refers to the overcoming of enmity between people whether we speak of interpersonal relations, or the broader social and political situation, without reference to God or divine activity."

On the other hand, reconciliation as practiced by Christians cannot avoid religious concepts. Do we have to evangelize first in order to lay foundations and only as a second step offer restoration of relationships? This has been the approach in Evangelical circles for centuries. Reconciliation with God precedes reconciliation among people. And in many instances this approach proved to be very successful.

Today, however, the majority of Christian missiologists follow a different approach. Reconciliation is understood integrally. Mission is, in fact, reconciliation, as we have seen above, and it always presupposes contextualization. Consequently, De Gruchy suggests using slightly different words and concepts for practicing reconciliation in secular or non-Christian contexts. He calls this the primary and secondary expression of reconciliation. Whereas the primary expression can only be verified through scripture and faith-based experience, secondary expressions "[...] are visible in social and political reality." (2002:18).

HoM offers an ideal tool for this. To work on bringing our difficult past experiences with one another together, on trying to understand the hurts and feelings of each other, on forgiving each other and working for a common future without referring to our religious convictions verbally, is an active way to live out the gospel. This is evangelism through being and doing. Words may follow in time being.

This works perfectly, as the recent experience of the Peace and Reconciliation Network (PRN) of the World Evangelical Alliance (WEA) proves. The program for peacebuilding capacities among conflicting parties of Muslims and

Christians applied here is called „Building Leaders 4 Peace" (BLP).[10] BLP invites Christians and Muslims on a weeklong peace camp in which the participants work on the troublesome relations between Christians and Muslims in countries with a Muslim majority. The parties express their frustration and anger with the other side, name the issues without any political correctness. And then they ask each other for forgiveness. Slowly the atmosphere in the camp changes. The first signs of growing trust appear and suggestions for a better future are made.

It is here where the Muslim representatives start asking questions about the religious power behind peace. As a rule, they will point to Isa the Messiah, to Jesus Christ who brings peace to the nations. Now the conversation is open. Questions about Jesus, the reconciler of victims and offenders are asked and answers waited for. A process starts: from the reality of Jesus' offer to potentially a conversation about Him and His kingdom. This is mission!

Bibliography

Ahrens, Theodor 2005. Versöhnung in der ökumenischen Diskussion. *Zeitschrift für Mission* 3, 2005, 162–173.

Baumberger, Marianne 2012. Lasst es uns noch mal versuchen. Mediation als Weg, Beziehungen wieder zu ordnen, in Sommer 2012, 114–122.

Bieringer, R. 1987. 2 Kor 5,19a und die Versöhnung der Welt. *Ephemerides theologicae lovanienses* 63 (1987), 295–326.

Bohler, Frieder 2012. Begegnung wagen. Eine Kultur des Friedens entwickeln, in Sommer 2012, 123–127.

Bosch, David J. 1991. *Transforming Mission. Paradigm Shifts in Theology of Mission.* American Society of Missiology Series, 16. Maryknoll, New York: Orbis Books.

Botman, Russel H. & Petersen, Robin M. (eds) 1996. *To remember and to heal*: *Theological and psychological reflections on truth and reconciliation.* Cape Town, Pretoria, Johannesburg: Human & Rousseau.

---

[10] http://wea.peaceandreconciliation.net/projects/building-leaders-4-peace/ (1.08.2017).

Brandes, Dieter (ed) 2008. *Healing of Memories in Europe. A Study of Reconciliation between Churches, Cultures and Religion.* Leipzig: Evangelische Verlagsanstalt.

Brandes, Dieter 2011. Heilende Erinnerung, in Bettina von Clausewitz (ed): *Jahrbuch Mission / Gerechtigkeit: Visionen vom Reich Gottes.* Hamburg: Missionshilfe Verlag, 179–186.

Brandes, Dieter & Lukács, Olga (eds) 2009. *Die Geschichte der christlichen Kirchen aufarbeiten. Healing of Memories zwischen Kirchen, Kulturen und Religionen. Ein Versöhnungsprojekt der Kirchen in Rumänien.* Leipzig: Evangelische Verlagsanstalt.

Breytenbach, Cilliers 1989. *Versöhnung. Eine Studie zur paulinischen Soteriologie.* Wissenschaftliche Monographien zum Alten und Neuen Testament, 60. Neukirchen-Vluyn: Neukirchener Verlag.

Brunner, Emil 1951. *Vom Missverständnis der Kirche.* Stuttgart: Evangelisches Verlagshaus.

De Gruchy, John W. 2002. *Reconciliation, Restoring Justice.* Minneapolis: Fortress Press.

Escobar, Samuel 2006. *La Palabra – Vida de la Iglesia.* Atlanta: Editorial Mundo Hispano.

Engelsviken, Tormod 2013. Reconciliation with God – Its Meaning and its Significance for Mission, in Robert Schreiter & Knud Jørgensen (eds): *Mission as Ministry of Reconciliation.* Oxford: Regnum Books, 79–89.

Enns, Fernando (ed) 2008. *Heilung der Erinnerungen – befreit zur gemeinsamen Zukunft. Mennoniten im Dialog. Berichte und Texte ökumenischer Gespräche auf nationaler und internationaler Ebene.* Frankfurt a. M: Lembeck; Paderborn: Bonifatius.

Enns, Fernando & Jaschke, Hans Joachim (eds) 2008. *Gemeinsam berufen Friedensstifter zu sein. Zum Dialog zwischen Katholiken und Mennoniten.* Schwarzenfeld: Neufeld Verlag; Paderborn: Bonifatius Verlag.

Enns, Fernando & Seiling, Jonathan 2012. *Mennonites in Dialog. Official Reports from International and National Ecumenical Encounters.* Eugene: Pickwick.

Garzon, Fernando L. & Burke, Lori 2002. Healing of Memories: Models, Research, Future Directions. Faculty Publications and Presentations. Paper 37. URL: http://digitalcommons.liberty.edu/ccfs_fac_pubs/37 [Accessed 1.12.2017].

Gutierrez, Juan 1999. Friedens- und Versöhnungsarbeit. Konzepte und Praxis, Unterwegs zu einer dauerhaften, friedensschaffenden Versöhnung, in Calließ, Jörg (ed): *Agenda for Peace: Reconciliation*. Loccumer Protokolle 55/98. Loccum: Evang. Akademie, 152–196.

Haspel, Michael 2003. Rechtfertigung, Versöhnung und Gerechtigkeit. Die Globalisierung als Herausforderung christlicher Sozialethik. *ÖR* 52, 2003, 472–490.

LOP 51. Reconciliation as the Mission of God: Faithful Christian Witness in a World of Destructive Conflicts and Divisions. URL: https://www.lausanne.org/wp-content/uploads/2007/06/LOP51_IG22.pdf [Accessed 1.1.2017].

McEvoy, Kieran 2008. Making Peace with the Past. Healing through remembering. Options for truth recovery regarding the conflict in and about Northern Ireland, in Brandes 2008:144–155.

Matthey, Jacques 2005. Versöhnung im ökumenischen missionstheologischen Dialog. *ZfM* 3, 2005, 174–191.

Ott, Craig 2010. *Encountering Theology of Mission. Biblical Foundations, Historical Developments, and Contemporary Issues.* Grand Rapids, MI: Baker.

Pope Benedict XVI 2011. Post-Synodal Apostolic Exhortation *Africae Munus*. URL: http://w2.vatican.va/content/benedict-xvi/en/apost_exhortations/documents/hf_ben-xvi_exh_20111119_africae-munus.html [Accessed 1.12.2017].

Reimer, Johannes 2011. Der Dienst der Versöhnung – bei der Kernkompetenz ansetzen. Zur Korrelation von Gemeinwesenmediation und multikulturellem Gemeindebau. *Theologisches Gespräch* 1/2011, 19–35.

Reimer, Johannes 2017. *Missio Politica. The Mission of the Church and Politics.* Caliste: Langham.

Rice, Chris (ed) 2005. *Reconciliation as the Mission of God. Christian Witness in the World of Destructive Conflicts.* Durham, NC: Duke Divinity School.

Rice, Chris 2013. Cape Town 2010: Reconciliation, Discipleship, Mission, and the Renewal of the Church in 21. Century, in Robert Schreiter & Knud Jørgensen (eds): *Mission as Ministry of Reconciliation.* Oxford: Regnum Books, 9-29.

Schreiter, Robert 2005. Reconciliation and Healing as a Paradigm for Mission. *International Review of Mission*, January 2005. Volume 94, issue 372, 74–83.

Sommer, Tom (ed) 2012. *Das Buch vom Frieden.* Witten: SCM R. Brockhaus.

Sundermeier, Theo 1986. Konvivenz als Grundstruktur ökumenischer Existenz heute. *Ökumenische Existenz Heute* 1/1986, xx–xx.

Vicedom, Georg 2002. *Missio Dei – Actio Dei.* Neu herausgegeben von Klaus W. Müller. Mit Beiträgen von Bernd Brandl und Herwig Wagner. Edition AfeM. Mission Classics, Bd. 4 Nürnberg: VTR.

WCC 2005. Participating in God's Mission of Reconciliation – A Resource for Churches in Situations of Conflict. Faith and Order document 201. Geneva: WCC. URL: https://www.oikoumene.org/en/resources/documents/commissions/faith-and-order/vi-church-and-world/Faith-and-Order-201?set_language=en [Accessed 1.12.2017].

Knowing the Other: A First Step Towards Unity in Christ in a Post-Western Christianity

Matthias Ehmann

Abstract

The chapter examines phenomena of migration and marginalization of migrants in the context of European societies. It refers to discourses on the role of Christianity in these social debates, based on an artwork from the "documenta art exhibition" in Kassel. The article first points out six major problems in the relationship of existing European churches to new international churches and then shows possible ways of mutual encounter and enrichment. In particular, the role of hospitality on a path of inner-Christian reconciliation is worked out.

1 Art as a Seismograph of Society

photo: private

At the world-famous art exhibition Documenta (14) in Kassel, Germany, this artwork could be seen. Every five years, artists from around the world gather in this not very important German city to make it the hotspot of the international art world for one summer. And this Obelisk – traditionally a symbol of power, standing in the big squares of European capitals of former colonial empires – is not placed far away on the outer borders of the exhibition area. It stands on the "Königsplatz", one of the major squares of the city. The Nigerian-born American artist, Olu Oguibe, has set up this symbol of power together with words from the book of Matthew. It is written on the stone in German, English, Turkish and Arabic. The context of the artwork is, obviously, the big discussion concerning the phenomenon of mass migration. The artist's aim with the inscription is, per the artist himself, to provoke those Evangelicals in the US who are strongly against hosting refugees. Oguibe himself, according to his testimony, is not a Christian but his father had been a preacher (Hessenschau 2017). The artwork is printed on the front cover of the main exhibition magazine, setting the tone of 2017 Documenta.

From my point of view, the extraordinary attention drawn to this piece of art reflects the big debates in society of today. Migration, with its political, social, economic as well as ethical implications, sets the agenda for the big debates of today. Maybe, the world of art is always ahead of the discussions and therefore a good seismograph for feelings, issues and debates of the future.

An artist, although not Christian by his confession but strongly familiar with Christian traditions and with this specific Jesus logion, directs this heritage against a group in society – the Evangelicals – that strongly claims to hold Christian tradition high.

So, the question of migration, of marginalisation of migrants, the question of power in a postcolonial context is, consequently, a question of the relation of different religious formations within Christianity. And that is the connection to the topic of this conference volume on the topic of: "Reconciliation: Christian Perspectives – Interdisciplinary Approaches". This article will not deal with the topic of "art and the so-called migrant crisis". It puts the spotlight on the need of reconciliation within Christianity in context of this so-called "migrant crisis". Many years before the summer of 2015, which put great attention to the phenomenon of migration in mass media, migration to European countries had become a quite normal thing. And with migration, many different congregations, churches, new denominations and religious groups with their own Christian heritage were formed. Although this received some attention in the international missiological community (Hanciles 2008), the whole phenomenon of new international churches in the context of migration still is a strongly underrated topic in academic theology as well as in ecumenical working groups or the ecumenical partnerships in local churches. Even in academic theology, ecumenism is mostly attached to the field of the World Council of Churches. In a headline of a chapter in his missiological textbook the German missiologist Henning Wrogemann demands: "Intercultural Theology: Ecumenism in full, please, not just in part!" (Wrogemann 2016:17). He insists that academic theology tends to negotiate expressions of church outside the horizon published in academic literature. New international churches are forming transnational networks with other churches outside the traditional bodies of ecumenism. Moreover, there are stereotypes on the side of western churches and traditional bodies of ecumenism as well as on the side of new international churches in the west. Therefore, real dialogue is needed for a better understanding, for overcoming stereotypes and for real reconciliation within Christianity (2006:17-18).

In the last years, several researchers picked up the topic; researchers from western origin – for example, Claudia Währisch-Oblau (2005), Benjamin Simon (2010) and Bianca Dümling (2011) – who focused on topics of migration churches in Germany. But there are researchers as well who are related to migration theology through their own biographies, like Afe Adogame (2013), now a professor at Princeton Theological Seminary, and Harvey C. Kwiyani (2014), director of "Missio Africanus" and, since spring 2017, part of the faculty of Liverpool Hope University. Both can probably be counted to the most influential researchers with personal migration experience in the German context. Besides academia, there are some approaches in the Lausanne Movement as well as the World Council of Churches that give more attention to migration churches and the Christian diaspora. Both bodies have installed working groups on the subject (WCC 2015). Although the complex phenomenon of migration, diaspora and church is starting to gain attention in the sphere of intercultural theology as well as in ecumenical bodies, there are still major problems in the relations between western traditional churches and the new international churches in European countries.

So, first, this article outlines the burden hindering a real unity of the one body of Christ in a context of migration and church relations. Second, I will name the goals of restoration in a process of reconciliation and, in the following, give ideas for a first step that could be done. The need for this step is underscored by the seismograph of art, which shows that this is no longer a side-issue that only gains attention by some specialists. It is a topic right in the middle of church and society.

2 Burdens on the One Body of Christ

There is a basic understanding within the traditional European churches of the importance to accept and include the new European Christians who migrated into Europe. On the one hand, there is a deep theological understanding of the "other" as brother and sister. Biblical texts like Deuteronomy 10:19 ("Love the sojourner, therefore, for you were sojourners in the land of Egypt.") or Matthew 25:35b ("I was a stranger and you welcomed me") are well known in European churches. On the other hand, churches have been and still are major advocates concerning migration issues in public discussions and key players in many integration programs (Heinemann 2016:78-81 and Sekretariat der Deutschen Bischofskonferenz 2016). However, although goodwill is present in European churches, there are major burdens in the relations between the new European Christians and their churches and the traditional ones. Therefore, reconciliation within this changing body of Christ in Europe is needed. Some of these burdens are outlined in the following.

First, the mission history of Europe and the countries of origin of many migrants is controversial. There has been a deep impact of the Western Mission Movement on World Christianity. Paradigmatically, this could be seen in the education of later key figures of the church in Africa, like Samuel Adjai Crowther, the first Bishop of Nigeria (Walls 2002:155-164). But the merits of the Western Mission Movement were accompanied by problematic links between mission and political and economic power. Over time, some missionaries' tendencies to work for European rule in the mission areas increased in the 19th century (Ward 2017:478-480). In many cases, the Western Mission Movement went hand in hand with imperialism (Sievernich 2009:91-93). The credibility of the Christian community was fundamentally disrupted by these relationships of mission and power.

Second, besides the history of western mission, the Western Mission Movement today is also linked to the history of western colonialism and the global system in place today that it has shaped. This is another burden from the past. And there are moments of power imbalances until today. Jehu J. Hanciles, in his book "Beyond Christendom: Globalization, African Migration, and the

Transformation of the West" in a chapter called "White Man's Burden" (Hanciles 2008:48-51), outlines how this imbalance of power is shaping today's world and African culture and identity in a way economic interests want them to.

Third, there are stereotypes that must be overcome by the church. Harvey Kwiyani notes: "For most people in the West, even well-wishing Christian leaders, to be black is still suspicious. […] Unfortunately, a typical African Christian in a Western church is also greeted with suspicion, perceived as a potential criminal, refugee, or a beggar, and more often than not, he or she cannot prove otherwise. Many African Christians in the West have to face this reality every day in their lives and ministries" (Kwiyani 2014:175-176). These hostilities could be one reason for the increased construction of distinctive African identities as Adogame (2006:67-68) shows in his study. But also, the members and leadership bodies of new international churches have to overcome the reflex of building a monoethnic diaspora church (Kwiyani 2014:150-152).

This tendency to build up an ethnocentric community is the fourth burden to overcome. Diaspora Churches are important actors in the construction of an identity in diaspora. These churches must decide whether they want to be a space gathering around a cultural heritage or a space gathering around their spiritual center, Jesus Christ. Through the example of churches of the African diaspora in Hamburg, Ekué describes that there is the possibility that these churches "are able to create space for a transcultural Christian conversation, because they serve as bridge-builders" (Ekué 2007:454) between the country of origin of their members and the country they now live in.

The fifth burden is that of conceptualizing national and cultural borders between churches and, in some cases, the racial exclusivism of western churches. Migrants are seen first as migrants and not as belonging to the same ecclesial tradition. This becomes clear, for example, when migrant communities are assigned according to their nationality and not according to their denomination (Währisch-Oblau 2012:323-326) in the context of German churches. In some cases, migrant pastors reported being mobbed, ignored and bullied from western pastors out of the same congregation (Kwiyani 2014:176).

The sixth burden is the marginalisation of migrant Christianity in the ecumenical context. On regional conferences, migrant Christians are typically invited to participate in the band, singing songs which the non-migrant regional leader selected beforehand. There are few conferences to which preachers from migrant congregations are invited to preach or even plan and lead the event. The same marginalisation takes place on church boards and conferences. Tent-maker pastors, which form the main part of migration church clergy, are often not invited, or the conferences and meetings take place at a time only a fulltime pastor can attend. This observation is made in my own church, the German Bund Freier evangelischer Gemeinden (Ferderer, Rose and Theis 2016:40-41).

3 Unity as the Goal of Inner Christian Reconciliation

In the beginning, the spread of African Christianity, as well as other non-western Christianities, was not a planned event, a strategy or something likewise. It was mainly formed out of geopolitical and economic circumstances (Kwiyani 2014:133). But once the differently shaped social and cultural structures of church grew in Europe, these different problems that I tried to point out became clear. All of them are symptoms of one central problem. There is a lack of real unity; to be the one body of Christ amid these differently shaped social and cultural structures of church[1]. I want to point out that unity must be the main goal of a process of reconciliation within Christianity. In my opinion, there are three perspectives in which the call for unity can be seen.

First, theologically, unity as the one church of the Triune God is a key aim of a sound theology. The prayer of Jesus in John 17:21 ("that they may all be one, just as you, Father, are in me, and I in you, that they also may be in us, so that the world may believe that you have sent me.") is a central guiding principle for church unity. The theological dialogue of the World Council of Churches strongly affirms the unity in the diverse streams of Christianity as a key goal of the universal church. "Christians, as pilgrims on the way to the Messianic ban-quet, view identity and otherness in the light of the kingdom that is to come. Our identity is determined by our communion with Christ and being part of the kingdom-community. This identity embraces diversity as much as it celebrates unity" (WCC 2015:12).

Second, there is a wish and even some pressure in society on the churches to be a place of integration as well as a moderator of the interests of Christians from a diverse background. There is a discussion about the role of religious commu-nities in the process of integration and segregation. Migration Churches can help the integration but can also reinforce the segregation of their members

---

[1] German: Sozialgestalten von Kirche.

(Lehmann 2015:104). Often society strongly affirms ecumenical collaboration, for example when looking at prison chaplaincy or religious education in schools (Reiss 2015:161-169). Ecumenism is just a simple way for society to get along with an increasing diversity within Christianity. At the same time, society requests "capital engineering", as Pierre Bourdieu put it. The New European Churches are important players in the engineering of social and cultural capital (Adogame 2013:101-111). Society could benefit from these effects if the integration of these communities is successful.

The third call for unity comes from mission strategists and missiologists within Traditional European Churches (Reimer 2011:55-56) as well as missiologists with a background in New European Churches (Kwiyani 2014:168-171). In a more and more multicultural society, a multicultural church is needed to start a multicultural missionary movement. This unity is crucial to mission in both ways. A joint mission praxis will have the experience for cross-cultural communication and the unity of a diverse group of people will be a witness to the world, as the prayer of Jesus in John 17 states.

According to these three perspectives, there is a real need for unity. And this unity – looking at the six outlined burdens – has to become reality in a process of inner Christian reconciliation. In western theology, there is a tendency to neglect those streams of Christianity which are not part of the World Council of Churches or the Roman-Catholic Church. The western view on World Christianity is dominated by those theologies, which are represented in academia and are accessible by books and papers. Alone for accounting for the number of Christians of lesser known streams of Christianity, a new approach of intercultural theology is needed (Wrogemann 2016:17-20). So besides big visions of a multicultural missionary movement in Europe, the integration through a multicultural church in a new society and the full unity in one church, there is the simple need of the pure knowledge of the other. This simple step seems to be a needed first. One needs to know who to talk to. A second step is also needed: to be able to talk about the burdens that we bring into this one body of Christ. And the pure knowledge of the other could be the start of a deeper understanding and lead to further steps into unity through reconciliation. Beside some specialists in faculties, mission agencies and ecumenical offices (Theologische Kommission 2011), there is few information, contacts, and relations to the new Christians in Europe and their churches. So, the biblical image of hospitality could be a paradigm for the future phase of getting to know each other (Kwiyani 2012:265). The biblical understanding of the household of God could serve as a framework for further reflection on common flourishing. In the narration of the disciples on the way to Emmaus, the banquet with the stranger becomes a metaphorical image for the arrival in the encounter with God. The missionary concept of conviviality developed by Theo Sundermeier (1995) creates the theoretical framework for a theology of encounter with the stranger. Benjamin Simon applies the concept in his Festschrift on the occasion of the 70th birthday of Sundermeier to the idea of hospitality as a way of Christian integration. For him, five elements are central to a path of hospitality: First, giving space to the stranger. Second, protecting the stranger. Third, that being together is done together. Fourth, that there is a mutual interest, and fifth, eating and drinking together. The most intense form of the last is the Lord's Supper (Simon 2005:202-207). This theological approach has been further developed as a theological model named convivenzia by Regina Polak. It is understood as spiritual partnership, learning environment and celebratory community with the possibility for churches to contribute to a peaceful and just coexistence. The perspective for the fundamental qualification of this community is always the kingdom of God (Polak 2015:211-212).

At the end of this article small but pragmatic and practical steps for the future will be outlined as a conclusion.

4 The Church in the Process of Reconciliation through Hospitality

The following suggestions come from my perspective as a German free-church pastor and a researcher on the interdependence of migration and mission and are shaped by my own context. Most of these suggestions are not completely new and some experts might have given similar advice on parts of the topic.

First, a basic knowledge about contemporary World Christianity should be taught at bible colleges, seminaries, and faculties. This could be part of denominational studies, mostly part of Systematic Theology, or of Intercultural Theology and Missiology. But a basic knowledge about World Christianity, Migration Churches, and the New European Churches are needed. Although many denominations in Europe do have migrant communities within their denomination, often the young people from these communities do not attend the denominational seminary. While the German Church of Pentecost, for example, consciously promotes the theological education of leaders from new international Churches, Bianca Dümling states in her study that upon request the German

Bund Freier evangelischer Gemeinden and the Mühlheimer Verband Freikirch-lich-Evangelischer Gemeinden had no program for these communities (Düm-ling 2011:199-200). So, besides pure knowledge, a place of community, of di-alogue, and for the building of relationships is needed. Such a place could be established through internships, as is the case in other areas of application (Werner 2011:140-143).

Second, tentmakers should be admitted in formal and non-formal networks. Most of the pastors in the new European local churches are tentmakers; some with ordination and a theological education and some of them without. They should be indexed in the lists of pastors, if not ordained, a special status could be invented. Plus, they should be invited to gatherings of pastors and to ecu-menical bible studies. In my opinion, they are often excluded in an ecumenical context, like female pastors. In my denomination, the incorporation of mission-aries from the US into the community of pastors has a long tradition, while this praxis is not fully applied to migration church pastors.

My third point is connected closely to the second. Many conferences for pastors are held during the week. In my denomination, most of them start on Monday and last till Thursday. Regional pastors' conferences and local pastors' break-fasts are held on a weekday morning. For most of the pastors in the new inter-national congregations, these are the worst times to attend such meetings. While these meeting spaces are strongly needed to build relationships, to start dialogue and to get to know each other, the meetings can hardly be attended by non-full-timers. Conferences and meetings on the weekends or the evenings are needed. This will cost the German full-time pastor an evening with his or her family, but it is the only way to enable the non-full-timers to participate in the commu-nity.

Fourthly, real community is often established while working together. Besides meeting spaces that are needed, collective efforts in projects and institutions are also needed. Many know their fellow pastors from collective efforts, from a youth camp, from the board of the denominational mission or diacona l agency or elsewhere. Members of the new churches are often asked to participate with music or with food at a regional conference. But real participation from sermon to event management is needed. Only through these actions, it will be possible to know the other beyond stereotypes. Why are there no Christians with migra-tion background participating as bishops or in the denomination's leadership or in the free-church mission agencies? Especially in the mission agencies, being transcultural enterprises by their very nature, this is an issue to be raised. Models of participation in mission agencies, like the United Evangelical Mission, which considers itself as a "communion of Protestant churches in three continents, who work together with equal rights and on a partnership basis" (UEM 2018) point in the right direction.

My fifth point is, that there should be planned and moderated conversations about this process. The process needs to be planned together. The new European Christians within denominations and the educational and leadership bodies of the denominations should plan and evaluate this process from time to time. This needs special meetings and cannot be done on the run. The same is needed for ecumenical organisations as the "Arbeitsgemeinschaft Christlicher Kirchen" and the "Evangelical Alliance". Reconciliation is a gift by the Spirit of God, but it also needs will power, good planning and hard work.

At the end of such a process, maybe there is no obelisk needed for Christians to know that they are all strangers and sojourners on a pilgrimage towards the heavenly banquet.

Bibliography

Adogame, A., 2006, Dinge auf Erden um Himmels Willen tun: Aushandlungsprozesse pfingstlicher Identität und die afrikanische religiöse Diaspora in Deutschland, in Bergunder, M. & Haustein, J. (Hg.): *Migration und Identität: Pfingstlich-charismatische Migrationsgemeinden in Deutschland*. Frankfurt am Main: Lembeck. (Beiheft der Zeitschrift für Mission 8), 60-82.

Adogame, A., 2013, *The African Christian Diaspora: New Currents and Emerging Trends in World Christianity*. London: Bloomsbury.

Dümling, B., 2011, *Migrationskirchen in Deutschland: Orte der Integration*. Frankfurt am Main: Lembeck.

Ekué, A.A., 2017, Migration, in Ross, K.R., Asamoah-Gyadu, J.K. & Johnson, T.M. (eds): *Christianity in Sub-Sahara Africa*. (Edinburgh Companions to Global Christianity). Edinburgh: Edinburgh University Press. (Edinburgh Companions to Global Christianity), 445-457.

EMW (Hg.) 2011, *Zusammen wachsen: Weltweite Ökumene in Deutschland gestalten*. Hamburg: EMW. (Weltmission heute 73).

Ferderer, W., Rose, D., & Theis, B., 2016, Migranten und Migranten-Pastoren stellen Fragen an Deutsche, in Bund Freier evangelischer Gemeinden (Hg.): *Fragen und Antworten zum Thema Migration und Integration: Handreichung AK IGAD Internationale Gemeinde in Deutschland.* Witten: Bund Freier evangelischer Gemeinden, 38-41.

Hanciles, J.J., 2008, *Beyond Christendom: Globalization, African Migration, and the Transformation of the West.* Maryknoll: Orbis.

Heinemann, S., 2016, Flüchtlinge – eine Herausforderung für Gesellschaft und Kirche Teil 2: Was die Kirchen daraus machen könnten. *Deutsches Pfarrerblatt* 116, 78-81.

Hessenschau (Hg.) 2017, Documenta Obelisk: Arnold Preis für Olu Oguibe. [Online] http://hessenschau.de/kultur/documenta/documenta-obelisk-arnold-bode-preis-fuer-olu-oguibe,bode-preis-100.html [Accessed: 2018-10-01].

Kwiyani, H.C., 2012, Pneumatology, Mission, and African Christians in Multicultural Congregations in North America. PhD Dissertation. Luther Seminary, St. Paul.

Kwiyani, H.C., 2014, *Sent Forth: African Missionary Work in the West.* Maryknoll: Orbis Books. (American Society of Missiology Series 51).

Lehmann, K., 2015, Complex Processes of Integration and Segregation: The Local Role of Christian Communites in Berlin, in Polak & Reiss 2015, 97-142.

Ludwig, F. & Asamoah-Gyadu, J. (eds), 2011, *African Christian Presence in the West: New Immigrant Congregations and Transnational Networks in North America and Europe.* Trenton: African World Press.

Polak, R., 2015, Flucht und Migration als Chance? *ZMR* 99, 202-212.

Polak, R. & Reiss, W. (Hg.), 2015. *Religion im Wandel: Transformation religiöser Gemeinschaften in Europa durch Migration – Interdisziplinäre Perspektiven.* Göttingen: V&R.

Reimer, J., 2011, *Multikultureller Gemeindebau: Versöhnung leben.* Marburg: Franke.

Reiss, W., 2015, Auswirkungen der religiösen Pluralität auf staatliche Institutionen und die Anstaltsseelsorge, in Polak & Reiss 2015, 143-182.

Sekretariat der Deutschen Bischofskonferenz (Hg.), 2016, *Leitsätze des kirchlichen Engagements für Flüchtlinge*. Bonn: DBK. (Arbeitshilfen Nr. 282).

Sievernich, M., 2009, *Die christliche Mission: Geschichte und Gegenwart*. Darmstadt: WBG.

Simon, B., 2005, Gastfreundschaft: ein Weg christlicher Integration, in: Simon, B. & Wrogemann, H. (Hg.): *Konvivale Theologie: Festgabe für Theo Sundermeier zum 70. Geburtstag*. Frankfurt am Main: Lembeck, 199-210.

Simon, Benjamin 2010. *From Migrants to Missionaries: Christians of African Origin in Germany*. New York: Peter Lang. (Studies in the Intercultural History of Christianity 151).

Sundermeier, Theo 1995. *Konvivenz und Differenz: Studien zu einer verstehenden Missionswissenschaft*. Erlangen: Verlag der Evangelisch-Lutherischen Mission. (Missionswissenschaftliche Forschungen NF 3).

Theologische Kommission des Evangelischen Missionswerks in Deutschland 2011. Migrationskirchen als Chance und Herausforderung für die gemeinsame Mission, in EMW 2011, 15-19.

Tira, Sadiri Joy 2015. Diasporas: From Cape Town 2010 to Manila 2015 and beyond – The Lausanne Movement and Scattered Peoples. *Lausanne Global Analysis* 4(2), 11-15.

UEM 2018. About UEM. Online im Internet: URL: https://www.vemission.org/en/about-uem.html [Stand: 2018-10-01].

Währisch-Oblau, Claudia 2005. Migrationskirchen in Deutschland: Überlegungen zur strukturierten Beschreibung eines komplexen Phänomens. *ZMiss* 31, 19-39.

Währisch-Oblau, Claudia 2012. *The Missionary Self-Perception of Pentecostal/Charismatic Church Leaders from the Global South in Europe: Bringing Back the Gospel*. Leiden: Brill.

Walls, Andrew F. 2002. *The Cross-Cultural Process in Christian History: Studies in the Transmission and Appropriation of Faith*. Maryknoll: Orbis.

Ward, Kevin 2017. Das Christentum in Afrika vom späten 18. Jahrhundert bis 1914, in Schjørring, Jens Holger & Hjelm, Norman A. (Hg.): *Geschichte des globalen Chritentums: 2. Teil. 19. Jahrhundert.* (Die Religionen der Menschheit 33). Stuttgart: Kohlhammer. (Die Religionen der Menschheit 33), 451-488.

WCC 2015. *The "Other" is my neighbour. Developing an Ecumenical Response to Migration.* Geneva: WCC Publications.

Werner, Dietrich 2011. Theologische Ausbildung bei Migrationschristen: Aspekte aus der Perspektive des Ökumenischen Rates der Kirchen und der Ökumenischen Theologischen Ausbildung (ETE), in EMW 2011, 139-147.

Wrogemann, Henning 2016. *Intercultural Hermeneutics.* Downers Grove: InterVarsity Press. (Intercultural Theology Volume One).

Noble Lies, Augustinian Lies and the Post-Modernist Black Hole: Truth, Reconciliation and the Church

Catherine Morris

Abstract

The text of Psalm 85:10-11 provides striking metaphors for the biblical concept of shalom: "Mercy and truth have met each other: justice and peace have kissed." Accordingly, this essay proposes a framework for reconciliation that recognizes truth, justice, forgiveness and peace. The necessity of truth for genuine peace and reconciliation is singled out in light of some North American Christian leaders' engagements with a "post-fact" world. Questions about truth are nothing new. When Jesus told Pilate that he came to testify to truth, Pilate is recorded as retorting: "What is truth?" (Jn 18:37-38). Have church people adopted Pilate's approach by relegating truth into a postmodernist "black hole"? Have church leaders slipped into blind acceptance of Plato's "noble lie" (sometimes known as propaganda)? Are churches endorsing bare-faced lies of the kind Augustine and Aquinas would decry? The essay explores contemporary concerns about truth and lies in light of biblical concepts and statements of Jesus. Drawing on examples from Cambodia, Rwanda, Canada, and the United States, the essay examines historic Christian church complicity with untruths that subvert reconciliation. The essay concludes with suggestions of ways for churches to engage with truths that foster reconciliation, including the tradition of prophetic lament.

1 Introduction

Talk about truth-telling and lying has become increasingly popular and intense in North America as public conflict has become politically polarized, particularly in the United States (US) (United Nations 2017). Christian churches are at the centre of public diatribes that threaten to split congregations and denominations along increasingly thick ideological lines that blur somewhat, as controversies seep across the Canadian border. In the US, hate speech has been dramatically amplified since 2016 and echoes ominous racist ideologies of World War II (WWII) and centuries-old conflicts over slavery and colonization. There are also calls for justice, peace, neighbourly love, and national reconciliation. In August, 2017, the uprooting of civil war memorials in the US and Canada dramatically exposed the depths and darkness of subterranean histories and unhealed wounds of remembered bloodshed and atrocities (Holland 2017, Roache 2018). In this polarized context, there is concern that mendacity is becoming normalized, particularly in the US (Shellnutt 2018). In this essay, written primarily for Christian church audiences, I propose that a deep commitment to truth and truth-telling is the basis of authentic reconciliation. I use a biblical framework for reconciliation found in the vision of *shalom* in Psalm 85, which integrates movements towards truth (Ps 31:5), justice (Is 45:21), lovingkindness (Dt 4:31, Jnh 4:2, 1 Jn 4:8; Ex 34:6, Jn 3:18), and peace (Zch 8:16). Each of these four themes is crucial to a biblical conception of reconciliation, but truth is foundational: God is characterized by truth (Ex 34:6). Jesus describes himself as "the Truth" (Jn 14:16, Jn 1:14). The church is called the "foundation" of truth (1 Tm 3:15). "Speaking the truth in love" is the basis of relational unity of believers in Jesus (1 Tm 3:15, Eph 4:15). Using examples from historic conflicts in Cambodia (Morris 2004; 2016), Rwanda, the US, and Canada, I outline three challenges to truth that are affecting the Church in North America. I conclude with reflections on how to address these challenges in ways that foster genuine reconciliation.

2 A Biblical Framework for Reconciliation

2.1 Why focus on reconciliation?

The recorded purpose of Jesus' ministry is to "reconcile all things" to God, including rescuing humanity from entrapment in all forms of evil and oppression (e.g. 2 Cor 5:18-19). John 17 records the prayer of Jesus for the unity of the future church. "May they be one as we are one," he prays, "so that the world may know that you have sent me and have loved them even as you have loved me" (Jn 17: 11-23). This prayer of Jesus emphasizes that church unity is inextricably connected to the unity of God, with whom Jesus identifies himself as "one." If churches were to join persistently with Jesus in the John 17 prayer, their focus would be directed towards learning to live together in ways that imitate the love of God. People would more frequently witness and experience reconciling love when they are in the midst of church people. The church would become more visible as "the cadre of reconciled individuals" that Schreiter (1998, 116) suggests is essential to social reconciliation.

2.2 Four themes of reconciliation: Truth, Justice, Forgiveness and Peace

What is "reconciliation"? Scholarly literature discloses a confusing array of meanings attached to this term. The fields of dispute resolution, peacebuilding, and international human rights uphold largely liberal democratic frameworks for action towards peace, including independent judiciaries and legal professions (e.g. Morris 2016; Des Forges 1999). Peace and conflict studies also include structuralist (e.g. Galtung 1996) and poststructuralist perspectives, also referred to as "social constructionist" or "postmodernist" perspectives (e.g. Lederach 1996; Pearce and Littlejohn 1997). Within the diverse, interdisciplinary literature, meanings of "reconciliation" range from "thin" ideas of mere coexistence (Ignatieff 2003), or toleration (e.g. Gamberale 2008), which approaches may be accompanied by "social amnesia" (Cohen 2001:132-133, 238-239), to "thicker" (Crocker 2003:54) conceptions of acknowledgment and forgiveness, mercy, shared vision, mutual healing, or harmony (Cohen 2001; Katongole 2005). Meanings of reconciliation vary across religions and cultures (Redekop 2002).

The New Testament definition of "reconciliation" – as translated from the Greek – means "transformation" of relationships, from enmity towards friendship (for discussion see, e.g. Lederach 1999; Schreiter 1998; Tutu 1999; Volf 1996). Mennonite peace and conflict scholar John Paul Lederach locates his conceptual framework for peacebuilding and reconciliation within scripture (Lederach 1997, 1999), particularly the metaphors found in Psalm 85:10-11: "Steadfast love (mercy, lovingkindness)[1] and faithfulness (truth)[2] will meet; righteousness (justice) [3] and peace (shalom)[4] will kiss each other. Faithfulness

---

[1] Hebrew חֶסֶד (kheh'-sed), Also translated as "love" or "loving-kindness".

[2] Hebrew אֱמֶת (eh'-meth), also translated as firmness, reliability, faithfulness.

[3] Hebrew צֶדֶק (tseh'-dek), also translated as righteousness.

[4] Hebrew שָׁלוֹם (shalom, shaw-lome'), also translated as welfare, health, prosperity, friendship. This conception of peace is consistent with the concept of "positive peace" coined by Galtung (1996).

(truth) will spring up from the ground, and righteousness (justice) will look down from the sky."

These verses capture a biblical understanding of reconciliation that recognizes the human needs for truth, justice, mercy, and peace (*shalom*).[5] Such an approach avoids at least three conceptual traps. First, the images of meeting places in the Psalm contradict a notion that processes of "reconciliation" involve placing truth and justice on one end of a balance scale with forgiveness and peace on the other end (resulting in a metaphor that suggests that more justice results in less peace, or vice versa). Second, the metaphor recognizes that the experiences of peacemaking and reconciliation rarely unfold in the tidy, linear sequences often described in Western technocratic approaches to "post-conflict" reconstruction, which emphasize sequential "stages" of peacebuilding. For a critique of a linear, sequential analytic approach to reconciliation, see Lederach and Lederach (2010:41-57). Third, the Psalmist's approach avoids "thin" conceptions of peace that involve acquiescence to power or the mere absence of direct violence, described as "negative peace" by peace scholar Johan Galtung (1996:3).

In real-life experiences, the four themes of truth, justice, compassion, and peace intertwine themselves in people's journeys over time and place – often in tension with one another – through people's needs and yearnings when they are in conflict, including their impulses to "do something" about it. Biblical admonitions concerning the use of power are a key aspect of this model. Followers of Jesus are to exert their full strength in the service of God's purposes, which are constituted in Jesus's ministry of reconciliation (Lk 10:17). Followers of Jesus are to exert this strength not in reliance on political might but on the power of God's Spirit (Zch 3:6, Mt 20:25-28). While each of these themes deserves extensive attention, this essay has its emphasis on truth.

3 Truth: Integral to Justice, Forgiveness and Peace

3.1 Why truth?

Why focus on truth? I have demonstrated Jesus' central concern about the unity of believers. Unifying relationships can develop only when people are able to

---

[5] These needs are congruent with findings of needs theorists, e.g. Redekop (2002). The "capabilities approach" has valuably addressed limitations of needs theory to redress problems of deprivation of human capabilities for functioning towards wellbeing and flourishing (Nussbaum 1999; Sen 1993).

trust one another to be fair and compassionate in their relationships in interpersonal interactions and in governance. The Hebrew word in the Bible often translated as "truth" (אֱמֶת, *eh'-meth*) is more accurately translated as "faithfulness," "reliability," or "trustworthiness." Faithfulness is as important in congregational relationships as it is in marriages, friendships, businesses, and political relationships. If truth – trustworthiness – is crucial to people's wellbeing and relationships, to the social fabric of our congregations and communities, why do people lie?

3.2 Why do we lie?

Literature in the field of negotiation and conflict resolution indicates that outcomes of agreements rooted in reality – and truth-telling about reality – are more stable than those rooted in inaccuracies, falsehoods or deceptions. When misrepresentations – innocent or not – come to light after deals are made or settlements reached, results include mistrust, renewed conflict, or even retaliation and revenge (Lewicki et al. 2001). Despite the risk of unstable outcomes and damage to relationships, negotiators often try to deceive other parties to gain "leverage" for outcomes that favour themselves or their constituents at the expense of others (Lax and Sebenius 1986:363-70). Some writers on negotiation ethics have justified certain kinds of lying as part of the "rules" of the negotiation game (Shell 2004:215-17, but see Menkel-Meadow 1997). Some claim that to "conceal one's true position, to mislead an opponent about one's true settling point, is the essence of negotiation" (White 1980:27-28). In political and other arenas, lying is often defended as sometimes necessary to achieve justice or for the protection of other people, society or the Church (see Chapters 9, 10, 11, 14 in Griffiths 2004; Smith 1911; Verhey 1999;). I will address these justifications below.

When people are accused of wrongdoing, they may go to great lengths to avoid acknowledging responsibility, even when their guilt is obvious (Cohen 1996, 2001). Wrongdoers lie or deny moral responsibility out of fear of reprisals, legal accountability, social ostracization, or loss of political or economic power.

3.2.1 An example from Cambodia: Lies and denials

Rather than turning immediately to the American civil war, I will briefly discuss aspects of a 20th century conflict, the Cambodian "side show" in the major powers' proxy war in Southeast Asia (Shawcross 1979; Kiernan 2004). Churches in North America were far from unified in their stances on the Vietnam War (Wacker 2014; Balmer 2012; Balmer 2016). Christian leaders who encouraged the war feared the communist movements that had emerged as part of nationalist struggles against 19th century European colonization. They supported the containment of communism, which they saw as hostile towards religious and other freedoms (Toulouse 1993). Some Christians opposed the war as being incompatible with traditional just war theory (Toulouse 2007). Christian pacifists opposed the war on the grounds of Jesus' teachings on non-violence (King 1967; and Gordon C. Zahn, see Toulouse 2007).

Starting as early as 1965, the Nixon administration deceitfully escalated the war by means of massive, illegal, and clandestine bombing of Cambodia, killing hundreds of thousands and displacing nearly a third of the population. The bombings are credited with driving "an enraged populace into the arms of an insurgency that had enjoyed relatively little support until the bombing began" (Owen 2006:63). American bombing of Cambodian civilians thus contributed to the rise of Pol Pot's 1975-1979 Khmer Rouge regime, which was responsible for the deaths of at least 1.7 million people; more than a fifth of the population died by summary execution, torture, overwork, or privation (Kiernan 2004:xli).

After the unearthing of mass graves and the scrutiny of thousands of documents, there was plenty of evidence against high-ranking Khmer Rouge officials involved in massive war crimes, crimes against humanity and genocide (Heder and Tittemore 2004; Chandler 1999; Documentation Center of Cambodia). One Khmer Rouge leader, Ieng Sary, who died in 2013 before his international war crimes trial was completed, said he "had no information about ...the killings" (Ehrlich 2001) despite evidence that he publicly encouraged arrests and executions. Nearly all Khmer Rouge regime leaders recited similar litanies of denial (Barber and Munthit 1996; Handley 2017b, 2017a; Thayer 1997). An exception is Kaing Guek Eav (known as "Comrade Duch") who, when the Vietnamese invaded in 1979, made his way to the western border, where "he disappeared into the murky world of secret camps" held by the remnants of the Khmer Rouge (Dunlop 2010:198). In 1996, he was converted to Christianity. When journalists found him living under a false name in 1999, he said "it is God's will you are here... I have done very bad things before in my life. Now it is time for *les represailles* [the consequences] of my actions" (Dunlop 2010:272). He freely admitted overseeing the torture and executions at Tuol Sleng prison, where at least 14,000 people perished (Chandler 1999). Yet Duch, too, reverted to forms of denial during his trial and appeal, saying, he would have been killed if he had not followed orders and that he was "just like a cog in a running machine" with no ability to escape the regime (Carmichael 2015:261, 165-180, 260-266, also see Ledgerwood 2009).

China has become a major donor to Cambodia's current authoritarian government but continues to deny its involvement in assisting the Khmer Rouge regime (Levin 2015). The US points out that it has contributed to the funding of the Documentation Center of Cambodia, which researches Khmer Rouge atrocities, the war crimes and genocide prosecutions of Khmer Rouge officials in the Extraordinary Chambers in the Courts of Cambodia (ECCC), and the clean-up of unexploded ordnance in the region, but the US at the same time continues to demand repayment of US$500 million in loans given to Cambodia's 1970-1975 right-wing coup government that ruled with US support until the Pol Pot regime took Phnom Penh in April 1975 (Wright and Kuch 2017). This demand has nurtured Cambodian bitterness about US atrocities during the 1960s and 1970s.

3.2.2 Ideology and denial of truth

Denials of truth and moral responsibility for wrongdoing are often propped up by ideologies. This is true not only of US officials implicated in the rise of the communist Khmer Rouge regime in Cambodia or Chinese support of the regime from the 1960s throughout the 1980s (Mertha 2014; Wight 2014). For a decade after Vietnam's 1979 expulsion of Pol Pot's Khmer Rouge regime, the anti-communist ideologies of United Kingdom and US governments were used to justify the refusal of official aid to Cambodia's Vietnamese and Soviet backed rulers (Mysliwiec 1988). High ranking officials of the Pol Pot regime have continued to deny their moral responsibility for the atrocities and genocide. The high-ranking Khmer Rouge official, Nuon Chea denied his agency in these crimes until he died in August 2019; before completion of the appeal of his convictions by the ECCC for genocide and other atrocity crimes. He used euphemisms, saying: "I admit that there was a mistake. But I had my ideology. I wanted to free my country. I wanted people to have well-being" (quoted in Leitsinger 2004). At the closing of his trial in 2013, Nuon Chea denied direct knowledge or responsibility for the atrocities of the Khmer Rouge regime, saying, "There is no evidence to prove I did it…" His purpose for participating in the Pol Pot regime was "to liberate Cambodia from colonialism, to protect her from neighboring countries who wanted to swallow Cambodia" (Dernocoeur 2013).

3.3 An old, old story

People deceive to maintain control over information, thus avoiding vulnerability. They may also use lies and denials to manipulate narratives to justify their version of history and maintain legitimacy. At the heart of lying is the purpose of gaining or keeping power or the fear of losing it.

The problem of lying is old. In the biblical account of the rebellion of Adam and Eve against God, the Lord called out to the man, "Where are you?" Adam replied, "I heard…you in the garden, and I was afraid because I was naked; so I hid myself." The man went on to prevaricate by blaming Eve. She, in turn, blamed the serpent for lying to her (Gn 3:1-13). The two of them manoeuvred to try to hide their vulnerability and to control the narrative through denial and deceit. And God expelled them from paradise. Later, after Cain committed the Bible's first recorded murder, God called out to Cain: "Where is your brother Abel?" Cain responded with a lie and a sarcastic retort: "I don't know. Am I my brother's keeper?" God replied, "What have you done? The voice of your brother's blood is crying to me from the ground" (Gn 4:9). God called for truth. In return, God received lies and denials of responsibility. And so it goes.

There are two points to emphasize about these biblical stories. First, the Bible suggests there is no progress towards reconciliation until truth and moral responsibility are acknowledged. Second, from the beginning, God is recorded as having initiated reconciliation and restoration of relationships. God seeks out humankind first, asking for truth and responsibility. The Bible's message about Jesus emphasizes that truthful acknowledgement of responsibility for wrongdoing unlocks people's ability to receive God's grace and forgiveness and results in the invitation to join in Jesus' ministry of reconciliation.

Human experience confirms that truth-telling powerfully releases possibilities for our transformation towards justice as well as possibilities of receiving increased trust and forgiveness from those we have wronged (Govier 2006:58). In contrast, falsehood and denial by a wrongdoer signals a desire to enjoy the power of impunity, not to mention continued danger for victims. Apologies fail to convey moral truth when they are not accompanied by repentance, including reparations and institutional changes to prevent reoccurrence of wrongdoing (Barkan 2006).

4 Three Challenges to Truth: Lies, Noble Lies and the Supposed "Death of Truth"

Churches in North America are currently facing at least three contemporary challenges to truth. First is the need for a return to the virtue of truth-telling. The normalization of lying is harming the personal integrity of church people, the reputation of church and the moral fabric of the broader community. Second is the perpetual temptation for church people to become mired in dominant societal myths that render them vulnerable to propaganda and which are contributing to a sharply polarized political and social climate. Third is concern about cooption by moral relativism – blamed by some on the so-called postmodernist "death of truth."

4.1 The need for renewed church emphasis on truth-telling

Over the centuries, much scholarly ink has been spilled on the topic of honesty and lying. In contemporary North America, church preaching on truthfulness appears to be relatively rare and superficial compared to teaching on other topics.[6] This is despite the emphasis on truthfulness and condemnation of dishonesty and slander throughout the Bible, from the ninth commandment (Ex 20:16), prophets (e.g. Ezk 22:9, Jr 9:4-6), psalms (e.g. Ps 101:5, Ps 120:1-2), and proverbs (Pr 12:22), through to the Gospels (e.g. Mk 7:21-23), letters (Rm 1:29-31; 2 Cor 12:20, Eph 4:31, Col 3:8), and Revelation (Rv 21:8).

Gaps in preaching and teaching about truth-telling may be related in part to historic controversies about the ethics of lying within and outside the church. Augustine in the 4th century, Aquinas in the 13th century, and Calvin in the 16th century taught that lying is sinful, without exception (for discussion, see Griffiths 2004; Tollefsen 2014; Blacketer 2008). Other Christian thinkers, including Chrysostom, Cassian, and Newman, endorsed narrow exceptions to the ban on lying in order to prevent injustice or harm to innocents (see Griffiths 2004; MacIntyre 1994). Often cited in defence of lies is the apparent biblical applause of the lies by the Hebrew midwives to save newborn babies from murder by Pharaoh (Ex 1:15-22) and Rahab's lie to protect Hebrew spies from discovery in Jericho (Jos 2:1-3, 6:17-25, Ja 2:25).

---

[6] A Google search revealed many sermons that discuss the truth of the Bible and the gospels but only a handful on honesty and integrity.

Gaps in Christian literature on truth-telling include a lack of women's scholarship. Among the few ancient or prominent women scholars are Teresa of Avila (1515-1582), who briefly addresses truth-telling. Among Teresa's maxims are: "Never affirm anything unless you are sure it is true," and "Never exaggerate, but utter thy mind in simplicity" (St. Teresa of Avila 1963). In *The Interior Castle*, she writes "never do I wilfully say what is untrue. No; by the mercy of God, I would rather die a thousand times than tell a falsehood: I speak of the matter as I understand it. I believe that in this case the will must in some way be united with that of God" (St. Teresa of Avila, 1577 (1921)). Her understanding of holiness was based on friendship and unity with Jesus, which precluded offending God in any way including by means of lying. A handful of contemporary women scholars have discussed truth-telling briefly (e.g. Sumner 2011).

Paul J. Griffiths adopts Augustine's definition of the lie as "speech that deliberately contradicts what the speaker takes to be true" (Griffiths 2004:25-39, at 31). Christopher O. Tollefson uses the same definition which he refers to as "assertions contrary to belief" (Tollefson 2014:21). I adopt this definition.[7] Thus, lying is always deliberate. A mistake about the truth is not a lie.

In Augustine's view, God is truth, so that lying "ruptures God's image in us" (Griffiths 2004:73; see Gen 1:26-27). Thus, all lying is a wilful denial of our created essence. Lying also misappropriates speech, which God gifts to humankind for God's purposes and for adoration and confession to God (Griffiths 2004:73-84). Speech is not to be appropriated to our own use as we see fit (Griffiths 2004:85-100). Our speech, like everything else, belongs to God, not to us. Speech is to be deployed carefully in the presence of God; as Jesus said, "let your yes mean yes and your no mean no" (Mt 5:37).

According to Griffiths, Aquinas viewed lying not so much as a rupture of the divine image within humankind, but more as a sinful violation against justice. Tollefson argues that Aquinas' proscription of lying is based on more than its likelihood to cause injustice; rather his concern is based in the lie's violation of personal integrity and sociality (Tollefson 2014:102-28, 147). The fundamental purpose of speech acts is to communicate among persons. If one cannot count on truthful communication, social relationships – and society – are injured. Lying is also incompatible with the love of truth, the virtue of truthfulness, and

---

[7] It is beyond the scope of this essay to canvass other definitions. For discussion, see Tollefson (2014:12-30) and Griffiths (2014:73).

friendship with the God of truth. It is important to note that Aquinas, in his articulation of the doctrine of divine simplicity saw God's character of love, justice, and truth as a unified essence (Summa Theologiae, Part 1, Question 3). The corresponding human virtues, e.g. love, justice, and truth (and other virtues) are also interconnected in Aquinas' thinking (Summa Theologiae, Second Part of the Second Part, Question 23 Charity, Question 58 Justice, Question 109 Truth, for discussion see Porter 1993).

While both Augustine and Aquinas banned all lies as sin, both saw some kinds of lies as more serious than others (Griffiths 2004; Tollefsen 2014). Augustine's hierarchy of lies extends from harmless lies that save someone's life or virtue, lies that help someone, and lies that create "smooth discourse," to more serious lies that harm others and help no one. Augustine states that lies told in religious teaching are the most serious of all (Augustine 1952 [395AD]).

An absolute ban on lying was dominant in the church until the 16th century at least, although there has been a less prominent thread that supports lying in narrow circumstances to protect others. Martin Luther is sometimes cited as defending "a good hearty lie for the sake of the good and for the Christian Church, a lie in case of necessity, a useful lie" (Smith 1911; Verhey 1999).[8]

In the context of the current American political ethos, it is important to address some relevant thinking of American theologian Reinhold Niebuhr, given his great influence on American politicians since the mid-20th century (Haas 1999; Niebuhr 1932; Niebuhr 1935/2013; Weitzman 2017). Niebuhr situates Christian ethics in "the tension of historical and the transcendent" (Niebuhr 1935/2013:9). Niebuhr denounces perfectionist approaches to ethics, pointing out that perfectionism is unrealistic in a sinful world in which:

---

[8] While Martin Luther is reported to have defended a hearty, useful lie for the sake of the Church, the context is often ignored. Luther's complete quote is found in the context of correspondence and writings about a controversy in 1540 over whether to confirm information disclosed in confession. Luther is reported as saying "Is it not a good plan to say that the bigamy had been discussed and should not Philip say that he had indeed debated the matter, but had not yet come to a decision? All else must be kept quiet. What is it, if for the good and sake of the Christian Church, one should tell a good, strong lie?" In further correspondence, Luther advised "to give an ambiguous answer by which you could remain." (Smith 1911) In a short article for Christianity Today in 1999, Professor Allan Verhey cites a variation of this quotation without its context, saying, "Luther defended 'a good hearty lie for the sake of the good and for the Christian Church, a lie in case of necessity, a useful lie.' Such lies, he said, 'would not be against God'" (Verhey 1999).

"[S]elf-deception and hypocrisy is an unvarying element in the moral life of all human beings… Naturally, this defect in individuals becomes more apparent in the less moral life of nations. The dishonesty of nations is a necessity of political policy if the nation is to gain the full benefit of its double claim upon the loyalty and devotion of the individual, as his own special and unique community and as a community which embodies universal values and ideals. The two claims, the one touching the individual's emotions and the other appealing to his mind, are incompatible with each other, and can be resolved only through dishonesty. This is particularly evident in wartime… The nation is always endowed with an aura of the sacred, which is one reason why religions, which claim universality, are so easily captured and tamed by national sentiment, religion and patriotism merging in the process… In the life of the simple citizen this hypocrisy exists as a naïve and unstudied self-deception. The politician practices it consciously (though he may become the victim of his own arts), in order to secure the highest devotion from the citizen for his enterprises. The men of culture give themselves to it with less conscious design than the statement because their own inner necessities demand the deceptions, even more than do those of the simple citizens" (Niebuhr 1932:95).

Niebuhr grounds his ethics of "Christian realism" in the belief that "the ideal of love is real in the will and nature of God, even though he knows of no place in history where the ideal has been realized in its pure form" (Niebuhr 1935/2013:8). Pointing to the impossibility of perfection and the universal need for forgiveness, Niebuhrian ethics would mean (in the words of Haas) "fulfilling the law of love to the greatest degree possible, given the world as it is" (Haas 1999:608). According to Niebuhr, the "principles of equal justice are … approximations of the law of love in the kind of imperfect world which we know" (Niebuhr 1935/2013:149). Niebuhr's definition of justice is "the approximation of brotherhood under the conditions of sin" (Haas 1999:626 citing Niebuhr 1949:254). Niebuhrian thinking, according to Haas, would acknowledge that "[t]o use a famous example, a person cannot simultaneously keep his promise to the Jews in his protection and tell the truth to the Nazis" (Haas 1999:623). Thus, exercising responsibility in an immoral world may end up calling for a lie for the sake of justice as the best approximation of love in an imperfect world.

Dietrich Bonhoeffer, who studied with Niebuhr in 1930 (Hauerwas 2013), also seems to contradict Augustine in his assertion that "the essential character of the lie is to be found at a far deeper level than in the discrepancy between thought and speech" (Bonhoeffer 1955:364). Bonhoeffer defines the lie as "primarily the denial of God as He has evidenced Himself to the world." In this, at least, he may be closer to Augustine than is sometimes perceived (Hauerwas 2013). Bonhoeffer also states: "Every word I utter is subject to the requirement that it shall be true" (Bonhoeffer 1955:365). However, he points out that truth-telling, like other ethics, cannot be detached from the larger reality of relationship with God or the particular relationship. Human beings cannot, with reference to themselves alone, decide what is "true" in the context of all relationships and realities. Truthfulness does not "mean the disclosure of everything that exists" or of every opinion or thought (Bonhoeffer 1955:371-72). Speech must be justified and occasioned by the responsibilities of the relationship or office in which it may occur.

Of importance to the topic of reconciliation is Bonhoeffer's overall theme in his *Ethics*, which centres on God's overriding purpose of reconciliation (Bonhoeffer 1955:26). Bonhoeffer shares with Augustine and Aquinas a commitment to truth at all times, based on the central premise that humankind – persons, created in the image of God – originate in God but have misattributed and misappropriated their origin to themselves (Bonhoeffer 1955:18). However, Bonhoeffer's approach to the ethics of truth-telling is not entirely based on an exceptionless "rule" but rather on discernment of the truths to be disclosed within a particular relationship on a particular occasion, centred on relationship with God and God's overriding purpose of reconciliation of "all things." Bonhoeffer is famous for his deceitful involvement in the resistance to the Nazi regime in Germany, so it is important to understand how he characterized his actions. Bonhoeffer was committed to a life of responsibility in a broken world where particular situations might call for action that risks bringing guilt on oneself for the sake of responsible action. Bonhoeffer states:

> "When a man takes guilt upon himself in responsibility, and no responsible man can avoid this, he imputes this guilt to himself and to no one else. He answers for it; he accepts responsibility for it. He does not do this in the insolent presumptuousness of his own power, but he does it in the knowledge that this liberty is forced upon him and that in this liberty he is dependent on grace. Before other men

the man of free responsibility is justified by necessity; before himself is he acquitted by his conscience; but before God he hopes only for mercy" (Bonhoeffer 1955:360).

Thus, in Bonhoeffer's thinking lying always incurs guilt, but some situations in a broken world force responsible action to address evil. In such situations, we rely on God's grace.

It is always an assumption that a wilful lie will, in fact, prevent harm or work for good. Human beings are not omniscient and cannot accurately predict immediate or longer-term consequences of speech acts. It is illogical to imagine that a lie (and only a lie) will successfully stop proverbial murderers at the door from harming their intended victims. It is also important to consider the impact of lying on the liar's integrity, including the possibility that a liar will become inured and practiced in lying to achieve other just ends, resulting in damage to social relationships and to societal trust. Lying also deprives those who believe the lie of the ability to make fully informed choices. Lying is a method of trying to take the future into one's own hands.

There may be other means to achieve good ends or to prevent harms. No Christian commentator suggests that everyone is owed all of the truth all of the time. Some persons are forbidden to pass on information by virtue of their moral or legal duties of confidentiality or privilege. There is no duty to pass along harmful gossip even if one believes it is true – in fact, scripture abundantly forbids gossip and other careless speech (see, e.g. Pr 11:9; Pr 26:20; Mt 12:36; Lk 6:45; Eph 4:29; Ja 1:26; Ja 3:5-11; Tt 3:2). Christian teaching is clear that one is not to associate oneself with wrongdoing or cooperate with evil by means of speech or other actions (e.g. Ex 23:2; Eph 6:10-18). However, resisting evil may not necessitate lying. There is a significant literature on the casuistry of applying the ban on lying in particular situations (Tollefsen 2014:147-97). It is beyond the scope of this essay to fully canvass such approaches, which include creative use of silence and non-verbal misdirection to save someone from the murderer at the door, or camouflaging the truth in self-defence (Griffiths 2004:179), as Abraham did when he said his wife Sarah was his "sister" (which, strictly speaking, was true) (Aquinas, Summa Theologiae, Second Part of the Section Part, Question 110). Finally, it is important to say that untruths that are not formally "lies" (assertions contrary to belief) are not necessarily free of wrongdoing. While I have come to the position of Augustine, Aquinas, Bonhoeffer and others that all lies incur guilt for the liar, it is important to state that other forms of deliberate deception that fall short of outright lies are not necessarily right and must not be undertaken unconscientiously by anyone, particularly to serve one's own individual, social or political interests.

Christian thinkers disagree on the ethics of lying, but they all affirm the virtue of truthfulness and constrict the reasons and range of allowable lies. People differ about where the downward slippery slope begins. Even if one believes falsehoods can be justified "for the sake of the church," there is significant risk of widening the scope too much when our decisions to speak or act fail to discern or seek overall, longer-term purposes of reconciliation.

We do know what can happen to those who slither too far down the slope. Recent decades have seen several well-known North American Christian leaders jailed for fraud after they have misused audience donations (Applebome 1989; Ohlheiser 2015) or lied about their sexual misconduct or crimes even in the face of overwhelming evidence (Friscolanti 2009). Many outside the church mock Christian leaders – and their followers – for justifying or overlooking partisan political lies in aid of a "higher purpose" (Balmer 2018). Non-church people often express contempt for American church people who have supported politicians' obvious lies and other blatant wrongdoing in return for promises to appoint judges (Iszler 2017) and make laws and regulations aimed at furthering particular social, economic, or political goals (Jones 2017).

Christians in North America have become profoundly polarized based on an intertwined combination of political and religious ideology (Miller 2016). Flashpoint controversies surround issues of abortion, rights of LGBTI persons,[9] and immigration. While these three issues have often been conflated in polarized media reporting, it is important to note that Christians hold diverse opinions on each of these issues. Those who support pro-life positions argue that the unborn share with all human beings the image and likeness of God; accordingly, they have inherent dignity and should not be rendered legally expendable.[10] Many Christians hold pro-life positions privately but support pro-choice laws and politics because they oppose the imposition of their values on those

---

[9] LGBTI is an acronym for Lesbian, Gay, Bisexual, Transgender and Intersex persons. LGBTI is the international acronym currently in use by United Nations bodies and experts.

[10] It is important to note that evangelicals in the US opposed restrictions on abortion until the 1970s on the grounds of compassion regarding the devastating consequences on the lives and well-being of some pregnant women. Others considered that the church should not rely on the state to enforce its moral standards (Balmer 2016).

who hold differing religious (or non-religious) views that emphasize women's freedom and equality. Many Christians support pro-life positions on abortion but are in favour of welcoming refugees and immigrants without discrimination. The issue of LGBTI rights is also fraught with contention among Christians who base their views on differing traditions, interpretations, or emphases of the Bible.

Some Christians promote politicians who promise to help Christianize the nation by regulating against abortion, same-sex relationships or immigration from countries where people are predominantly non-Christian, non-Protestant, or non-white (Balmer 2018; Jones 2017). Those who support the creation of a "Christian nation" have been accused of heresy by those who promote allegiance to God alone with clear separations between church doctrines and state regulation (Stevens 2017; Wallis 2018). Some Christians place their emphasis on Jesus' social justice teachings, such as the Sermon on the Mount, advocating government laws and policies to support poor people and promote economic, social and cultural equality. Those promoting social justice themes in the Bible may point out Martin Luther King Jr.'s statement:

> "The church must be reminded that it is not the master or the servant of the state, but rather the conscience of the state…. It must be the guide and the critic of the state, and never its tool. If the church does not recapture its prophetic zeal, it will become an irrelevant social club without moral or spiritual authority" (King 1963/1998).

Church people who support government measures toward economic, gender, or racial equality may be accused of socialism by Christians who believe the Bible supports individualist libertarian and capitalist approaches. Government documents show that during the 1960s Martin Luther King Jr. was branded a communist despite having denounced communism, although he also rejected *laissez faire* economic capitalism (King 1963; Johnson 2018).

Those on all sides of these complex issues may hold sincere views, but public discourse has tended to be marked by discourteous or even hateful accusations that misrepresent their opponents' positions. Compounding this challenge is the fragmentation of media. No longer is mainstream news the only alternative. Numerous alternative news sites, blogs, and social media pages focus attention on issues important to those holding particular religious points of view. There are hundreds of Christian magazines, denominational newspapers and Christian organizations' newsletters.[11] Those writing for most media outlets may express their views truthfully, but some prominent Christians have accused their Christian opponents of lying to accomplish their political goals (Brigham 2018). It is a challenge to discern what information is carefully researched and what is baseless opinion. Media labelled as "Christian," may be no more trustworthy than any other purveyor of information in today's media marketplace. North American church people face the same risks as those outside the church of sliding into lies that distort relationships, subvert social trust, deny God's image, and allow them to fall into the hands of the power-hungry. Isaiah 59:14-15 connects the faltering of public truth-telling with societal injustice:

> So justice is driven back,
> and righteousness stands at a distance;
> truth has stumbled in the streets, honesty cannot enter.
> Truth is nowhere to be found,
> and whoever shuns evil becomes a prey.

People's commitment to truth and the Christian "witness to truth are undermined by lying" (Tollefsen 2014:195). If church people are to be considered trustworthy there is a need for much deeper and wider engagement in concerted discussion and teaching about Christian ethics of truth-telling and the social consequences of tolerating or being associated with public lies and liars.

4.2 Propaganda: religion and culture

It is not enough to avoid being involved in, supporting, or tolerating lies. Church people are warned to avoid being deceived. Jesus warned his disciples: "Be on your guard against the yeast of the Pharisees and Sadducees", by which he meant false teachings (Mt 16:6, Mt 16:12) and hypocrisy (Lk 12:1). Jesus also cautioned his disciples in a paired warning: "… beware the yeast of the Pharisees [meaning religious leaders] and the yeast of Herod [meaning the political establishment]" (Mk 8:15). One American commentator points out that many North American church leaders believe that "the salvation" of the US depends on the ability of religious adherents to "rope a raging bull of political power and get him into our corral," thence getting their "man in office" (Erwin,

---

[11] See, for example, the 206 members listed as publication members of the US-based Evangelical Press Association, https://www.evangelicalpress.com/member-list/. For a list of Protestant Magazines, see World-Newspapers.com, www.world-newspapers.com/protestant-magazines.html. See a list of Catholic magazines published by CatholiCity, www.catholicity.com/links/10/.

n.d.). The attempt of Christian religious groups to harness political power demonstrates a perverse understanding of the kind of power that, according to the biblical record, accomplishes God's purposes.

In a contrasting image, the Bible likens the reign of God to yeast that an ordinary woman kneads through a large quantity of dough until it is all leavened (Mt 13:32-33). Thus, the Bible teaches that people of God are to be thoroughly permeated with the yeast of the Spirit of God. The prophet Jeremiah explains, saying it is "not by power, not by might, but by my Spirit, says the Lord" (Zch 4:6). According to the Bible, the power Christians are to seek is the Holy Spirit enabling them to "knead the dough" toward spreading the leaven of God's reconciling purpose (Lk 13:31-32). Christians are to copy Jesus, not in seeking political power but in resisting cooption by perverse or evil powers. Like Jesus, Christians are to "tell that fox [the ruler, Herod] that I [we] will keep on casting out demons and healing people today and tomorrow; and the third day I will accomplish my purpose" (Lk 13:32).

Historically, church people have frequently become mesmerized by political power and engulfed by propaganda. Jacques Ellul points out the difficulty of resisting social and political propaganda that manipulates powerful metaphors and cultural icons and myths.[12] Each society has deep narratives about the proper social order, who is in charge, who is privileged, and who serves whom. Plato taught that "noble lies" (*gennaion pseudos*) should be instilled in the population through education so as to promote social order and loyalty to the State (Cornford 1945:Chapter X). Plato's famous "myth of the metals" taught that people are created with different metals inherently incorporated into their being: Rulers (which Plato refers to as "Guardians") are gold, auxiliary helpers

---

[12] Jacques Ellul points out that to be effective, propaganda "attach[es] itself to what already exists in the individual, but also … the fundamental currents of the society it seeks to influence. Propaganda must be familiar with the collective sociological presuppositions, spontaneous myths, and broad ideologies." (Ellul 1965:38-39). The full quote is: "Propaganda must not only attach itself to what already exists in the individual, but also express the fundamental currents of the society it seeks to influence. Propaganda must be familiar with the collective sociological presuppositions, spontaneous myths, and broad ideologies. By this we do not mean political currents or temporary opinions that will change in a few months, but the fundamental psycho-sociological bases on which a whole society rests, the presuppositions and myths of not just individuals or of particular groups but those shared by all individuals in a society, including men of opposite political inclinations and class loyalties."

are silver, and farmers and craftspeople are iron or brass. Each class has a function. The myth, which fitted the hierarchical worldview of the ancient Greeks, was intended to train people to acquiesce voluntarily to the State's expectation of them. Historical myths of many societies perpetuate discriminatory social ordering.

Classical liberal theory is supposed to foster equality by restraining executive power with an independent legislature and judiciary. This European idea is one of the guiding myths that ground North American constitutional ideals and frameworks. However, the promises of social equality through the rule of law are often foreclosed by legalized structural power imbalances that favour elites and work against those who have been marginalized or historically colonized. Social inequality has been fostered by the myth of European superiority that infused the colonizing spirit of past centuries, including the "civilizing mission" of states and churches. While this myth has been much assailed since the mid-20th century, the legacy of European supremacy remains alive in North America today. In some quarters in North America, people of European descent who claim Christian identity seem unmoved by the explicit rejection of discrimination and abuse of power by Jesus and the apostles (see, e.g. Gl 3:28, Gl 5:14, Mt 7:12, Rm 2:11, Jn 13:12-20).

Canadian and US governments have not yet acknowledged or grasped the full truth about the history and consequences of centuries of extensive unlawful seizure of Indigenous peoples' lands and forcible relocation of Indigenous peoples. Indigenous peoples' lands and resources have been seen as fair game for European enterprise and settlement (Anaya 2004). Historians are uncovering more and more evidence of genocide of Indigenous peoples in North America (MacDonald and Hudson 2012). In Canada, there has been official recognition that European settlement was accomplished by means of land-grabbing aided by cultural genocide of Indigenous peoples (TRC Canada 2015a). During the 19th and 20th centuries, Canadian governments forcibly removed Indigenous children from their families and cultural communities and placed them in Indian Residential Schools where they were forbidden to speak their own languages and were subjected to neglect and other abuses. Many were subjected to sexual abuse and other forms of torture (MacDonald and Hudson 2012). Thousands of children died, and many disappeared. Some are buried in unmarked graves (TRC Canada 2015a). Several denominations of Christian churches were directly involved in running the schools with government funding (TRC Canada

2015b). The legacy of systemic racism and oppression against Indigenous peoples continues today (TRC Canada 2015a, 2015b)).

Religious traditions and Bible proof-texts have been used to uphold these forms of subjugation (Swartley 1983). American Catholic scholar, Scott Appleby, puts it this way: "Religion is apt to 'hide' in culture, be appropriated by politicians, or blend into society in ways that make it hard to identify as an independent variable" (Appleby 2000:47). Religion and culture are inseparably intertwined. Christians who are not firmly grounded in the ethical teachings of scriptures have little defence against cultural myths or political and social propaganda and may become coopted and aligned with social movements or political leadership that bear no resemblance to the moral character of Jesus.

Europeans were also involved in abduction and slavery of Indigenous peoples from Africa who were forcibly taken to colonies in the Americas. Race-based slavery was not seriously challenged in the Western world until the mid-19th century. Ideas of white superiority were grounded in baseless 19th century notions that harnessed fantasized, Eurocentric interpretations of certain biblical stories (Eltringham 2006).

Western expressions of Christianity played a significant part in the emergence of Cambodia's 20th century conflicts. François Ponchaud, a French priest and historian of Cambodia, argues that from the beginning of the Roman Catholic Church presence in Cambodia in the sixteenth century, the Church was coopted and manipulated over and over again by European rulers seeking economic opportunities and by Cambodian rulers seeking European protection against aggressive neighbours (Ponchaud 1990). The French protectorate in Cambodia (1863 to 1954) was brokered with assistance from Catholic clergy. Church involvements have historically resulted in political entanglements in a succession of Cambodia's political conflicts that led to local resistance to colonization, communist anti-colonial struggles, and the Pol Pot regime. After the fall of the Pol Pot regime, Christian humanitarian organizations who received state funding from their home countries were viewed as directly or indirectly serving their home states' strategic interests (Cormack 1997:437).

In Rwanda, the Church's historical political entanglements, justified by the colonial "civilizing mission", are implicated in the 1994 genocide. In the late 19th century, Christian missionaries took with them Eurocentric and racist theories that included the notion that Tutsi people were superior to Hutu people. The resulting divisions fomented among Tutsi and Hutu eventually led to purges, culminating in the Hutu Power government's highly organized, genocidal killing of between 500,000 and a million Tutsis and moderate Hutus over 100 days. Relentless propaganda over state-owned radio convinced the population that the Tutsi "cockroaches" must be exterminated on the grounds that they were all allied with the invading Rwanda Patriotic Front (Des Forges 1999; Prunier 1997). Land grabbing from Tutsis was among the true motives (Des Forges 1999:12-14). The Hutu Power government purchased huge numbers of machetes, small arms, and grenades and recruited tens of thousands of young people to conduct the massacres (Goose and Smyth 1994; Melvern 2004). The massive atrocities have been called a "Christian" genocide, because 90 percent of Rwandans are church-attending Christians (Longman 2010:3-30). Churches were deeply implicated, often through their silence (Longman 2010; Hatzfeld 2006; Prunier 1997). While many clergy died trying to protect their congregations (Rutayisire 1998, 2007), other clergy became overwhelmed by propaganda and failed to condemn the killings (Longman 2010). Some church-leaders even lured their Tutsi parishioners into massacres, claiming that their choice to sacrifice the lives of Tutsi members of their congregations was justified so as to save the lives of others (Longman 2010:6).

Here is what two of the killers told reporter Jean Hatzfeld. One *génocidaire*, Jean Baptiste, said: "Deep down we knew that Christ was not on our side in this situation, but since He was not saying anything through the priests' mouths, that suited us" (Hatzfeld 2006:145). Another mass murderer, Élie, said:

> All the important people turned their backs on our killings. The blue helmets [UN], the Belgians,… the humanitarian people and the international cameramen, the priests and the bishops, and finally even God. Did He [God] watch what was happening…? Why did He not stab our murderous eyes with His wrath? Or show some small sign of disapproval…? In those horrible moments, who could hear His silence? We were abandoned by all words of rebuke (Hatzfeld 2006:137).

Twenty-five years after the genocide, there remains significant dissension about the truth of what happened before, during, and after the genocide, as the current government constructs and enforces its official narratives of the genocide and suppresses dissenting views about post-genocide atrocities and contemporary human rights abuses. For a recent nuanced examination of efforts at transitional justice and reconciliation processes and human rights during the post-genocidal period, see Longman (2017).

While Rwanda is an extreme example, the church can learn from this history. Extremes do not start out that way; they start out with ideas, sparked by propaganda into brushfires that escalate to consume everything in their paths if they are not stopped. Clergy and lay church leaders, being closely connected to congregations, have the possibility and responsibility of early warning and pastoral rebuke of wrongdoing that has been justified by government lies and propaganda. God is said to speak through believers who have been paying attention. If Christians perceive God calling "where are you?" at times of crisis and overwhelming propaganda, one hopes they will not remain silent for the sake of "political neutrality," or deny responsibility by saying "we are hiding in culture," putting the blame on ideological or political opponents, the education system, the media, or the clergy. When Christians perceive God asking: "where is your neighbour?" one hopes that they will not retort with the denial: "Am I my neighbour's keeper?"

4.3 Postmodernism: The rumoured "death of truth"

A third challenge to the churches is Western postmodernism, which is said to be putting the truth to death. Since the 2016 US election, scholars and commentators have pointed out that "the core concept of truth has become deeply politicized" as President Donald J. Trump's supporters, which include the majority of evangelical Christian voters, have tolerated thousands of easily confirmed untruths promulgated by Mr. Trump during his presidential campaign and his presidency (Edsall 2018; Politifact 2019). Even after facts are publicly corrected, the President has been recorded repeating lies over and over, fanned by political "surrogates" (Goodstein 2018). The President's supporters passionately and persistently believe the lies or deny that they matter (Balmer 2018). This phenomenon has led some to call him the first postmodernist president in that he and his supporters undermine objective reality by manufacturing social truths through the exercise of propagandic power (Heer 2017).

Questions about the meaning of truth are nothing new. During the trial of Jesus, Pontius Pilate questioned Jesus about the charge that he had claimed to be a king. Jesus answered by saying, "My kingdom is not of this world. …You say I am a king. In fact, the reason I was born and came into the world is to testify to the truth. Everyone on the side of truth listens to me" (John 18: 28-40). Pilate's famous retort, "what is truth?", has become a preoccupation of postmodernist thinkers.

Postmodernism defies any simple or convenient definition. The only common thread of postmodernism is the rejection of the modernist "metanarrative" – the elevation of objective, rational epistemology above all other ways of knowing (Olson 2010; Grenz 1996). Postmodernism is often overgeneralized as the idea that all individuals have equal claim to their own truth. "Truth" becomes "truth claims," and all sincere truth claims are said to be equally valid. Thus, postmodernism is often incorrectly assumed to be synonymous with cultural or moral relativism.

Christians have traditionally believed – as an absolute truth – that everyone on the side of truth listens to Jesus who in turn insists that people pay attention to "the law and the prophets" (Mt 5:17). (It is acknowledged that unconvinced rationalists cannot be persuaded by this argument, which is not based on rationalist epistemological foundations, but on faith. Neither can this argument persuade "anti-foundationalists" – those who point out the lack of universal human consensus on truth.) Without a firm grasp on truths revealed by the biblical authors, church people may easily fall into the so-called "post-modernist black hole" (Cohen 1995:12) of post-factual relativism. This is particularly so if there is a lack of focussed moral teaching on truth-telling, a slippage of commitment to honesty, a lack of understanding of how propaganda works, an unwillingness to challenge overt dishonesty of political leaders, and a poor grasp of reconciliation themes of the Bible.

It is important to acknowledge some themes of postmodernism that Christians might welcome while being mindful of darker pitfalls. First, the postmodern "turn," brings welcome relief from the hegemony of Western enlightenment liberal, rationalist, individualistic, humanist, materialist discourse. In today's North American cultural climate, Christian apologists are not compelling when they use rationalist arguments to try to demonstrate that the Christian faith is based on objectively verifiable facts of history (e.g., Francis Schaeffer 1968). Today, there are fewer barriers to recognition of other ways of knowing, including revelation of sacred texts, traditions, symbols, mystical experiences, and spiritual practices. Christians can welcome the demise of the "grand narrative" of Western rationalist enlightenment. The dark side is the lack of agreement on what ideologies and spiritual practices have value, as well as the risk of "anything goes" relativism.

Another welcome postmodernist idea is that minority and marginalised views, including religious views, are no longer to be silenced in favour of perspectives of powerful political, economic, or religious elites.[13] The dark side is that it is difficult to resist voices that oppose oppressed groups and peoples. Ironically, norms of "freedom of speech" are being invoked by claiming an unfettered right to public space to spread discriminatory slander against historically oppressed groups and peoples (Human Rights Council 2013).

It is inaccurate to say that postmodernism denies the existence of verifiable truth. Postmodernists do not suggest, for example, that people should not use road maps or determine facts in courts of law (Dennett 1998). Yet, it is important to acknowledge that even these kinds of every-day truths are socially constructed or discerned through processes of dialogue, debate, and the sifting of evidence. As Christian scholar Stanley Grenz states, "no observer can stand outside the historical process… On the contrary, we are participants in our historical and cultural context, and all our intellectual endeavors are unavoidably conditioned by that participation" (Grenz 1996:166). Where particular conflicts are concerned, Mark Amstutz points out that

> historical truth is not coherent and unitary but contested. It may be possible to develop a high level of agreement about the empirical, objective facts about the past, but developing an authoritative interpretation of past political conflict is likely to be elusive, since perceptions and views will depend on the worldviews of participants (Amstutz 2005).

Postmodernist thinkers acknowledge that people's unique situations make their knowledge subjective. No one knows all or sees from a God's-eye view. The scriptures confirm that we "see through a glass darkly." Despite a common faith in the death and resurrection of Jesus, Christian biblical traditions are not legit-

---

[13] Postmodernist ideas provide a way in which people of faith can insist that their minority moral and spiritual perspectives be respectfully taken into account, including universalist and absolutist perspectives, e.g., those who subscribe to the scriptures common to Judaism, Christianity and Islam.

imately divorced from the talk and actions of communities of believers local-
ized in time and place. Christians in North America are diverse, and their perspectives – including perspectives of women, African Americans, and Indigenous Christians – are now being asserted and must be heard (see e.g. Woodley
2012). Western rational thought dominated by men of European background
can no longer trump. This reality necessitates respectful humility in everything
we assert as "truth."

Christians in the 21st century need to listen more than talk, particularly paying
attention to the voices of those who have rejected Christianity because of oppressive and deceitful behaviour by Christians past and present. Assertions of
Western superiority have no weight except to drag down the reputation of Jesus.

Not all views are morally equivalent. Now in the US and Canada political cen-
trists are being challenged by the so called "alt-right," or "white nationalism,"
insidious euphemisms for a range of anti-socialist, anti-liberal, anti-Semitic,
anti-Islamic, anti-Black, and anti-immigrant groups espousing notions of white
supremacy wrapped in a pastiche of imagery of the 19th century pro-slavery
movement of the American South, various crosses of the Ku Klux Klan, the
20th century Jim Crow era of discrimination, and even the Nazi flag (Politico
2017). While Canada seems less prone to white supremacist extremes, there
have been significant increases in crimes motivated by hatred of particular religions or ethnicities. Anti-Semitic crimes accounted for 18 percent of all hate
crimes, and 17 percent were anti-Islamic hate crimes (Statistics Canada 2019).
Systemic discrimination against Indigenous peoples continues in the US and
Canada.

On the "left" there is a similar diversity – ranging from centrist neo-liberal cap-
italists to moderate social democrats, to smaller groups of Marxian anti-capi-
talists, pacifist anarchists and "antifascists," some of whom are proponents of
nonviolent dissent. Others countenance the use of weapons.

The confusing assortment of actors includes Christian leaders who align themselves in politically partisan ways, stand neutral between "both sides," or remain completely silent. Other church leaders try to remain non-partisan while
condemning discrimination and bigotry and calling for prayer (Green 2017).

Archbishop Desmond Tutu takes a dim view of neutrality, saying "If you are
neutral in situations of injustice, you have chosen the side of the oppressor" (as
quoted in Brown, 1984:19). Ascribing moral equivalence to every truth claim
makes a mockery of justice, truth, and mercy when dominant groups fearfully

claim they are "the real victims" as their previously undisputed power and privilege is questioned by those who have historically enjoyed less clout (Blake 2011). Claims of racist victimization by white people contradict historical truths and thwart possibilities for forgiveness and reconciliation now and in the future.

Pilate's "what is truth?" was a sarcastic rebuttal to Jesus' claim that everyone on the side of truth listens to him. Christians can hardly escape similar criticism for asserting absolute truth, since this claim does not enjoy public consensus anywhere. It would be foolish to deny the fact of multiple truth claims. However, we do need to avoid ascribing positive moral value to just any ideology. It is right to be concerned that a cacophony of truth claims might easily devolve into hyper-individualized, radical forms of factual and moral relativism by which people justify what seems "right in their own eyes" (evoking Judges 17). Those of us who believe the absolute truth of Jesus' claims can ameliorate the seeming arrogance of this truth claim by ensuring that we reject what Jesus rejects – including discrimination, lies, hatred, oppression, and violence. Such attitudes and behaviours are not morally equivalent to the positive ethics Jesus teaches, such as impartiality, justice, careful truth-telling, loving-kindness, and peacefulness.

5 Concluding Thoughts on the Path towards Reconciliation: Confession, Lament and Doxology

How do we as Christians escape entrapment in hyper-individualistic moral relativism and move towards reconciling relationships – both individual and political? What kinds of truth-telling are integral to genuine reconciliation that integrates compassion, justice, and peace?

5.1 Commitment to truth-telling

First, individual Christians need to commit themselves to discerning and telling the truth according to the norms and principles established by scripture. Augustine's views based in the nature of the Holy Trinity, and the nature of speech as a gift of God to be returned to God in confession and adoration are, I suggest, the aspirational benchmarks, keeping in mind warnings that we see our imperfect world "through a glass darkly." Second, Christians can aspire to humble and caring respect of our neighbours as we affirm what we believe to be factual, moral, or religious truth. Third, it is important to develop moral courage to respectfully challenge falsehoods and to curtail any slothful failure to interrogate false claims made by religious or political leaders. Church leaders must be challenged when they demonstrate entrapment in social or state propaganda based on national or cultural myths that have little or no basis in Christian scriptures. These commitments necessitate immersion in the teachings of the Bible, interpreted in ways that are consistent with Jesus' ministry of reconciliation and which emphasize virtues and practices of justice, truthfulness, compassion, and peacefulness.

5.2 What do we do when we hear blood crying out from the ground?

Truthful confession and repentance of wrongdoing are integral to justice, forgiveness, and peace. How can those wishing to deepen engagement in the ministry of reconciliation assist the church in transformation away from denial of societal injustices that are impeding genuine peace?

Blood and bones crying out from the earth are often more than a metaphor (Lederach and Lederach 2010). All over the world there are violently displaced peoples and the unidentified remains of those unlawfully deprived of their lives and identities. Many have been "disappeared." Such atrocities often implicate state officials and elite members of society, including church people.

Europe's, Cambodia's, and Rwanda's mass or unmarked graves, the unmarked graves of slaves in the US (Jones 2018), and Canada's unmarked Indigenous children's graves have not yet yielded the identities of all the victims. Their surviving loved ones and descendants suffer the torment of not knowing the truth about what happened to their loved ones. People in countries where massive atrocities have been perpetrated have a basic need and the right (Naqvi 2006) to know what happened – beyond the rumours, speculations, denials, and lies that circulate and become solidified. Survivors and their descendants struggle to have their stories heard and believed. Future generations need to know the truth if for no other reason than to avoid the resurgence and spread of new lies or justifications for atrocities.

Truth matters – and it is strongly intertwined with demands for justice (Govier 2006). Methods of revealing truth include apologies (Barkan 2006; Govier and Verwoerd 2002; Regan 2007; Tavuchis 1991), reports by journalists, academics, or human rights organizations, trials (Minow 1998:58-59), or truth commissions (Hayner 2001). These methods may produce only partial truths, yet they serve to "narrow the range of permissible lies" that can circulate unchallenged (Ignatieff 1996).

The church can claim additional resources. People of faith are not required to accept the arguments of postmodernist intellectuals or the "cultural alibis" that cover the powerful as "they go on doing what they have always done" abusing their populations and suppressing dissent (Cohen 2001:286, quoting Wole Soyinka). Christians are subject neither to Western enlightenment thinking nor to postmodernist intellectual worries that there are no truths but only truth claims that dissolve into the bottomless void of anti-foundationalism. Christians are entitled to believe and to embrace evidence-based truths and moral values that cohere with historic understandings of scripture, faith, and practice. The core of traditional moral practice of Christians is the teaching that to love God entails loving our neighbour. Jesus defines the neighbour as the one who reaches out to care beyond the comfortably narrow confines of family, friends, and one's own territorial, cultural, or gender-based boundaries.

Christians are not confined to helping that one neighbour. Christians have resources to address broader social issues that overwhelm our efforts to alleviate the suffering of individuals. Christians can align themselves with those advocating social justice and humanitarian concern. Christians can turn to the example of Jesus and the ancient Hebrew prophets who model ways to confront those in power with disagreeable truths of social injustice, including dishonest or oppressive business enterprises, self-seeking elites and rulers, and corrupt justice systems, all of which fail the poor and vulnerable in society.

Such prophets are often associated with harsh, doom-saying criticism. How do we reconcile social critique with Jesus' admonition, "do not judge lest you be judged"? First, it is important to recognize that this admonition against judging refers to condemnation rather than to discernment. Second, as Walter Brueggemann suggests, the task of prophetic ministry is not merely to criticize but to energize people of faith towards an alternative vision for the community. Energization of the community includes piercing our "numbness" about injustice to the point that we can deeply grieve and lament oppression and injustice and embrace the God who exercises sovereign freedom towards love and justice (Brueggeman 1978). Soong-Chan Rah's reflections on the book of Lamentations propose that the church integrate practices of grief and lamentation of injustice and oppression in solidarity with the poor and oppressed within our societies (Rah 2015).

This necessarily entails turning away from celebrating citizens' service to nationalist and civilizational causes, identities, and myths. It entails a dedicated focus on the teaching that followers of Jesus have a new identity based on the victory of Jesus over "the father of lies" who can never prevail over the God of life and truth. This God raised Jesus from the dead and invites people to join him in the ministry of reconciliation. The Christian's true identity is that of daughters and sons of the God of reconciliation. When this truth deeply penetrates our being we receive energy to receive and offer of forgiveness, speak truth, do justice, and move towards the peace of Jesus.

The goal of telling the truth of injustice is not to elicit cheap remorse but rather lamentation that transforms and energizes us to move towards compassion and towards responsibility to participate in dismantling injustices at the root of suffering and societal dysfunction. The Psalmist implies that when the goal of our journeying is *shalom*, we will long for and seek places where compassion and justice embrace. Truth will spring out of the ground to replace denials about the blood, bones, and tears of fallen sisters, brothers, and neighbours. And justice and peace will embrace in God's sovereignty of love.

Finally, we must resist the temptation to imagine that the movement towards reconciliation means merely working harder. Paul Griffiths warns that "[b]ootstrapping ourselves out of sin is impossible" (Griffiths 2004:64). Instead, with Augustine, Griffiths suggests that the remedy for sin is adoration of God through Jesus who "came humbly, although he was most high…[and has] every right to say 'I am the way, and the truth, and the life'" (Griffiths 2004:64). As Walter Brueggemann puts it, doxology (or praise) "sets us before the reality of God," and God's faithfulness "vetoes our faithlessness" (Brueggeman 1978).

Bibliography

Amstutz, M. R. 2005. *The Healing of Nations: The Promise and Limits of Political Forgiveness,* Lanham, Rowman and Littlefield Publishers, Inc.

Anaya, S. J. 2004. The Historical Context. *Indigenous Peoples in International Law.* 2 ed. New York and Oxford: Oxford University Press.

Applebome, P. 1989. Bakker Is Convicted on All Counts; First Felon Among TV Evangelists. *New York Times*, 6 October. Available: http://www.nytimes.com/1989/10/06/us/bakker-is-convicted-on-all-counts-first-felon-among-tv-evangelists.html [Accessed 11 August 2018].

Appleby, R. S. 2000. *The Ambivalence of the Sacred: Religion, Violence and Reconciliation,* Lanham, MD, Rowman & Littlefield.

Aquinas, T. 1920 [1225-1274]. *The "Summa Theologica" of St. Thomas Aquinas. Part I QQ I.-XXVI.* Literally translated by Fathers of the English Dominican Province. Second and revised edition. Available: http://www.newadvent.org/summa/index.html [Accessed 25 July 2019]

Augustine, S. 1952 [395AD]. *Lying*, Catholic University of America Press.

Balmer, R. 2012. Christian Left. *In:* COATES, D. (ed.) *The Oxford Companion to American Politics.* USA: Oxford University Press.

Balmer, R. 2016. *Evangelicalism in America,* Waco, Texas, Baylor University Press.

Balmer, R. 2018 Under Trump, America's religious right is rewriting its code of ethics. *The Guardian*, 18 February Available: https://www.theguardian.com/commentisfree/2018/feb/18/donald-trump-evangelicals-code-of-ethics [Accessed 11 August 2018].

Barber, J. & Munthit, K. 1996. Ieng Sary: *"I never killed anyone"*. *Phnom Penh Post* 20 September. Available: http://www.phnompenhpost.com/national/ieng-sary-i-never-killed-anyone [Accessed 11 August 2018].

Barkan, E. 2006. Group Apology as an Ethical Imperative. *In:* BARKAN, E. & KARN, A. (eds.) *Taking Wrongs Seriously: Apologies and Reconciliation.* Stanford, CA: Stanford University Press.

Blacketer, R. 2008. No Escape by Deception: Calvin's Exegesis of Lies and Liars in the Old Testament. *Reformation & Renaissance Review,* 10, 267-289. Available: https://doi.org/10.1558/rrr.v10i3.267 [Accessed 11 August 2018].

Blake, J. 2011. Are whites racially oppressed? *CNNl*, 4 March. Available: http://www.cnn.com/2010/US/12/21/white.persecution/index.html [Accessed 11 August 2018].

Bonhoeffer, D. 1955. *Ethics,* London and Glascow, Collins.

Brigham, B. 2018. 'Cash before Christ': Bishop William Barber accuses Franklin Graham of being 'bought off' to defend Trump. *Raw Story*, 20 January. Available: https://www.rawstory.com/2018/01/cash-before-christ-bishop-william-barber-accuses-franklin-graham-of-being-bought-off-to-defend-trump/ [Accessed 11 August 2018].

Brown 1984. *Unexpected News: Reading the Bible With Third World Eyes,* Philadelpia, Westminster Press.

Brueggeman, W. 1978. *The Prophetic Imagination,* Philadelphia, Fortress Press.

Carmichael, R. 2015. *When Clouds Fell from the Sky: A Disappearance, A Daughter's Search and Cambodia's First War Criminal,* London, Mason-McDonald Press.

Chandler, D. 1999. *Voices from S-21: Terror and History in Pol Pot's Secret Prison,* Berkeley, Los Angeles, London, University of California Press.

Cohen, S. 1995. State Crimes of Previous Regimes: Knowledge, Accountability, and the Policing of the Past. *Law & Social Inquiry,* 20, 7-50. Available: https://doi.org/10.1111/j.1747-4469.1995.tb00681.x.

Cohen, S. 1996. Government Responses to Human Rights Reports. Claims, Denials, and Counterclaims. *Human Rights Quarterly,* 18, 517-543. Available: http://doi.org/10.1353/hrq.1996.0028.

Cohen, S. 2001. *States of Denial: Knowing about Atrocities and Suffering,* Cambridge, Polity Press.

Cormack, D. 1997. *Killing Fields Living Fields: An Unfinished Portrait of the Cambodian Church - the Church that Would not Die,* Crowborough, UK, Overseas Missionary Fellowship.

Cornford, F. M. (ed.) 1945. *The Republic of Plato,* New York and London: Oxford University Press.

Crocker, D. A. 2003. Reckoning with Past Wrongs. *In:* PRAGER, C. A. L. & GOVIER, T. (eds.) *Dilemmas of Reconciliation: Cases and Concepts.* Waterloo, ON: Wilfred Laurier University Press.

Dennett, D. C. 1998. Postmodernism and Truth. *World Congress of Philosophy,* 13 August Available: https://ase.tufts.edu/cogstud/dennett/papers/postmod.tru.htm [Accessed 11 August 2018].

Dernocoeur, K. B. 2013. *ECCC Grounds Crowded As Defendants Speak On Final Day of Case 002/01* [Online]. Phnom Penh. Available:

http://www.cambodiatribunal.org/2013/10/31/eccc-grounds-crowded-as-defendants-speak-on-final-day/ [Accessed 11 August 2018].

Des Forges, A. 1999. *Leave None to Tell the Story: Genocide in Rwanda* [Online]. New York: Human Rights Watch. Available: https://www1.essex.ac.uk/armed-con/story_id/Leave%20None%20to%20tell%20the%20story-%20Genocide%20in%20Rwanda.pdf [Accessed 11 August 2018].

Documentation Center of Cambodia. *DC-Cam Khmer Rouge History Database* [Online]. Phnom Penh. Available: http://www.d.dccam.org/Documentation_Center_of_Cambodia.htm [Accessed 11 August 2018].

Dunlop, N. 2010. *The Lost Executioner: The Story of Comrade Duch and the Khmer Rouge,* London, Bloomsbury.

Edsall, T. B. 2018. Is President Trump a Stealth Postmodernist or Just a Liar? *New York Times*, 25 January. Available: https://www.nytimes.com/2018/01/25/opinion/trump-postmodernism-lies.html [Accessed 11 August 2018].

Ehrlich, R. S. 2001. Cambodia's Deadly Politics: *"I just did what [Pol Pot] said, because it was my assignment"*. *The Laissez Faire City Times*, 12 March. Available: https://asia-correspondent.tumblr.com/post/35478720660/cambodia-archive-1979-to-2006-copyright-by-richard [Accessed 11 August 2018].

Eltringham, N. 2006. 'Invaders who have stolen the country': The Hamitic Hypothesis, Race and the Rwandan Genocide. *Social Identities,* 12, 425-446. Available: https://doi.org/10.1080/13504630600823619 [Accessed 11 August 2018].

Erwin, G. D. n.d. Leaven of Herod. *Servants Quarters* [Online]. Available: http://www.servant.org/writings/articles/p_loh.php [Accessed 21 August 2017].

Friscolanti, M. 2009. The truth about priests: It is hard to believe, but not every Catholic priest is a pedophile. *Macleans*, 1 December. Available: http://www.macleans.ca/news/world/the-truth-about-priests/ [Accessed 11 August 2018].

Galtung, J. 1996. *Peace by Peaceful Means: Peace and Conflict, Development and Civilization,* London, Sage.

Gamberale, V. 2008. The Role of Economic Development in Reconciliation: One experience from Bosnia and Herzegovina. In: Fleming, C. (ed.) *Pathways to Reconciliation: Between Theory and Practice.* London: Routledge.

Goodstein, L. 2018. Billy Graham Warned Against Embracing a President. His Son Has Gone Another Way. *New York Times*, 26 February. Available: https://www.nytimes.com/2018/02/26/us/billy-graham-franklin-graham-trump.html [Accessed 11 August 2018].

Goose, S. D. & Smyth, F. 1994. Arming Genocide in Rwanda: The High Cost of Small Arms Transfers. *Foreign Affairs*, p.September/October. Available: https://www.foreignaffairs.com/articles/rwanda/1994-09-01/arming-genocide-rwanda-high-cost-small-arms-transfers; full article at http://www.franksmyth.com/foreign-affairs/arming-genocide-in-rwanda/ [Accessed 11 August 2018].

Govier, T. 2006. *Taking Wrongs Seriously,* Amherst, NY, Humanity Books.

Govier, T. & Verwoerd, W. 2002. Taking Wrongs Seriously: A Qualified Defence of Public Apology. *Saskatchewan Law Review,* 65, 139-62.

Graham, D. A. 2017. *'Alternative Facts': The Needless Lies of the Trump Administration* [Online]. Available: https://www.theatlantic.com/politics/archive/2017/01/the-pointless-needless-lies-of-the-trump-administration/514061/ [Accessed 11 August 2018].

Green, E. 2017. How Will the Church Reckon With Charlottesville? . *The Atlantic*, 13 August. Available: https://www.theatlantic.com/politics/archive/2017/08/will-the-church-reckon-with-charlottesville/536718/ [Accessed 11 August 2018].

Grenz, S. J. 1996. *A Primer on Postmodernism,* Grand Rapids, MI, Eerdmans.

Griffiths, P. J. 2004. *Lying: An Augustinian Theology of Duplicity,* Ada, MI, Brazos Press.

Haas, M. L. 1999. Reinhold Niebuhr's *"Christian Pragmatism"*: A Principled Alternative to Consequentialism. *The Review of Politics,* 61, 605-636.

Handley, E. 2017a. Chea challenges forced-marriage claims. *Phnom Penh Post*, 17 May Available: http://www.phnompenhpost.com/national/chea-challenges-forced-marriage-claims [Accessed 11 August 2018].

Handley, E. 2017b. 'We did not exterminate our people': Defiant Khieu Samphan gives final statements at Khmer Rouge tribunal. *Phnom Penh Post* 23 June. Available: https://www.phnompenhpost.com/national/we-did-not-exterminate-our-people-defiant-khieu-samphan-gives-final-statements-khmer-rouge [Accessed 11 August 2018].

Hatzfeld, J. 2006. *Machete Season: The Killers in Rwanda Speak,* New York, Picador.

Hauerwas, S. M. 2013. Bonhoeffer on Truth and Politics *Conference on Lived Theology and Civil Courage.* University of Virginia. Charlottesville, Virginia.

Hayner, P. B. 2001. *Unspeakable Truths: Confronting State Terror and Atrocity,* New York, Routledge.

Heer, J. 2017. America's First Postmodern President. *The New Republic*, 8 July Available: https://newrepublic.com/article/143730/americas-first-postmodern-president [Accessed 11 August 2018].

Holland, J. J. 2017. Cities accelerate Confederate statue removal after Charlottesville rally. *The Associated Press/The Toronto Star*, 15 August. Available: https://www.thestar.com/news/world/2017/08/15/cities-accelerate-confederate-statue-removal-after-charlottesville-rally.html [Accessed 11 August 2018].

UN Human Rights Council. 2013. Annual Report of the United Nations High Commissioner for Human Rights : Addendum, Report of the United Nations High Commissioner for Human Rights on the Expert Workshops on the Prohibition of Incitement to National, Racial or Religious Hatred, 11 January 2013, a/Hrc/22/17/Add.4. Geneva: Human Rights Council, 2013. Available: https://www.ohchr.org/Documents/Issues/Opinion/Seminar-Rabat/Rabat_draft_outcome.pdf [Accessed 20 August 2019]Ignatieff, M. 1996. Articles of Faith. *Index on Censorship,* 25, 110-122.

Ignatieff, M. 2003. Afterword. *In:* Chayes, A. & Minow, M. (eds.) *Imagine Coexistence: Restoring Humanity After Violent Ethnic Conflict.* San Francisco: Jossey-Bass.

Iszler, M. 2017. After Trump's election, NC's Southern Baptists are left to do some soul-searching. *News & Observer*, 9 February 2017. Available:

https://www.newsobserver.com/living/religion/article131794284.html
[Accessed 11 August 2018].

Johnson, B. 2018. The 3 reasons Martin Luther King Jr. rejected Communism. *Transatlantic Blog*. Available: https://acton.org/publications/transatlantic/2018/01/15/3-reasons-martin-luther-king-jr-rejected-communism [Accessed 11 August 2018].

Jones, S. 2017 Evangelicals know Trump is a liar. They just don't care. *The New Republic*, 6 June. Available: https://newrepublic.com/minutes/143213/evangelicals-know-trump-liar-just-dont-care [Accessed 11 August 2018].

Jones, T. L. 2018. Graves of 1,000 enslaved people found near Ascension refinery; Shell, preservationists to honor them. *The Advocate*, 18 March. Available: http://www.theadvocate.com/baton_rouge/news/communities/ascension/article_18c62526-2611-11e8-9aec-d71a6bbc9b0c.html [Accessed 11 August 2018].

Katongole, E. M. 2005. Christianity, Tribalism, and the Rwanda Genocide. *Logos: A Journal of Catholic Thought and Culture,* 8, 67-93. Available: https://doi.org/10.1353/log.2005.0027.

Kiernan, B. 2004. *How Pol Pot Came to Power: Colonialism, Nationalism, and Communism in Cambodia, 1930–1975* USA, Yale University Press.

King, M. L., JR. 1963. Strength to Love. The King Center.

King, M. L., JR. 1963/1998. A Knock at Midnight. *In:* CARSON, C. (ed.) *A Knock at Midnight: Inspiration from the Great Sermons of Martin Luther* New York: IPM/Warner Books.

King, M. L., JR. 1967. Why I Am Opposed to the War in Vietnam, sermon at Riverside Church, New York City. The King Center.

Lax, D. A. & Sebenius, J. K. 1986. Three Ethical Issues in Negotiation. *Negotiation Journal,* 2, 363-370. Available: https://doi.org/10.1111/j.1571-9979.1986.tb00377.x.

Lederach, J. P. 1996. *Preparing for Peace: Conflict Transformation Across Cultures,* Syracuse, NY, Syracuse University Press.

Lederach, J. P. 1997. *Building Peace: Sustainable Reconciliation in Divided Societies,* Washington, DC, United States Institute of Peace Press.

Lederach, J. P. 1999. *The Journey Toward Reconciliation,* Scottdale, PA, and Waterloo, Ontario, Herald Press.

Lederach, J. P. & Lederach, A. J. 2010. *When Blood and Bones Cry Out: Journeys through the Soundscape of Healing and Reconciliation,* New York, Oxford University Press.

Ledgerwood, J. 2009. The Other Day I Saw a Monster *Dara Duong: News about the Khmer Rouge Tribunal*, p.9 August. Available: http://dara-duong.blogspot.ca/2009/08/other-day-i-saw-monster.html [Accessed 11 August 2018].

Leitsinger, M. 2004. 'Khmer Rouge official admits mistake'. *Milwaukee Journal Sentinel (Associated Press)*, 10 January. Available: https://www.freerepublic.com/focus/f-news/1060397/posts [Accessed 11 August 2018].

Levin, D. 2015 China Is Urged to Confront Its Own History. *New York Times*, 30 March. Available: https://sinosphere.blogs.nytimes.com/2015/03/30/cambodian-historians-call-for-china-to-confront-its-own-past/.

Lewicki, R. J., Saunders, D. M., Barry, B. & Minton, J. W. 2001. *Essentials of Negotiation,* Boston, McGraw Hill Irwin.

Longman, T. 2010. *Christianity and Genocide in Rwanda,* Cambridge, Cambridge University Press.

Longman, T. 2017. *Memory and justice in post-genocide Rwanda* Cambridge, UK, and New York, Cambridge University Press.

Macdonald, D. B. & Hudson, G. 2012. The Genocide Question and Indian Residential Schools in Canada. *Canadian Journal of Political Science,* 45, 427-449. Available: doi:10.10170S000842391200039X.

Macintyre, A. 1994. Truthfulness, Lies, and Moral Philosophers: What Can We Learn from Mill and Kant? *The Tanner Lectures on Human Values.* Princeton University.

Melvern, L. 2004. *Conspiracy to Murder: The Rwandan Genocide,* New York, London: , Verso.

Menkel-Meadow, C. 1997. Ethics in Alternative Dispute Resolution: New Issues, No Answers From the Adversary Conception of Lawyers' Responsibilities. *South Texas Law Review,* 38, 407-454.

Mertha, A. 2014. *Brothers in arms : Chinese aid to the Khmer Rouge, 1975-1979* Ithaca, New York, Cornell University Press.

Miller, E. M. 2016. Inauguration speaker Franklin Graham: God allowed Donald Trump to win," *Religion News Service*, 30 December. Available: https://religionnews.com/2016/12/30/inauguration-speaker-franklin-graham-god-allowed-donald-trump-to-win/ [Accessed 11 August 2018].

Minow, M. 1998. *Between Vengeance and Forgiveness: Facing History after Genocide and Mass Violence,* Boston, Beacon Press.

Moon, R. 2016. Religion and Hate Speech in Canada: The Difficulty in Separating Attacks on Beliefs from Attacks on Believers. *SSRN* [Online]. Available: https://ssrn.com/abstract=2911528 [Accessed 11 August 2018].

Morris, C. 2004. Cases in Religion and Peacebuilding: Cambodia. *In:* Coward, H. & Smith, G. (eds.) *Religion and Peacebuilding.* New York: SUNY.

Morris, C. 2016. Justice Inverted: Law and human rights in Cambodia. *In:* Brickell, K. & Springer, S. (eds.) *Handbook of Contemporary Cambodia.* New York: Routledge.

Mysliwiec, E. 1988. *Punishing the Poor: The international isolation of Kampuchea,* London, Oxfam.

Naqvi, Y. 2006. The Right to the Truth in International Law: Fact or Fiction. *International Review of the Red Cross,* 88, 245-362. Available: https://www.icrc.org/en/international-review/article/right-truth-international-law-fact-or-fiction.

Negash, G. 2006. *Apologia Politica: States and Their Apologies by Proxy,* Lanham, MD, Lexington Books.

Niebuhr, R. 1932. *Moral Man and Immoral Society,* New York, Charles Scribner's Sons.

Niebuhr, R. 1935/2013. *Interpretation of Christian Ethics,* Louisville, Kentucky, John Knox Press.

Niebuhr, R. 1949. *The Nature and Destiny of Man,* New York, Charles Scribner's Sons.

Olson, R. E. 2010 Evangelicalism and postmodernism. *Patheos*, 27 August. Available: http://www.patheos.com/blogs/rogereolson/2010/08/evangelicalism-and-postmodernism/.

Owen, T. 2006. Bombs Over Cambodia: New information reveals that Cambodia was bombed far more heavily than previously believed. *The Walrus*, 12 October. Available: https://thewalrus.ca/2006-10-history/ [Accessed 11 August 2018].

Pearce, W. B. & Littlejohn, S. W. 1997. *Moral Conflict: When Social Worlds Collide,* Thousand Oaks, CA, Sage Publications.

Politico. 2017. Chaos and violence: Scenes from Charlottesville's white nationalist rally. *Politico*, 12 August 2017. Available: https://www.politico.com/gallery/2017/08/12/photos-charlottesville-white-nationalist-rally-002467?slide=3 [Accessed 13 August 2018].

Politifact. 2019. *Donald J. Trump's file* [Online]. Available: https://www.politifact.com/personalities/donald-trump/ [Accessed 25 July 2019].

Ponchaud, F. 1990. *The Cathedral of the Rice Paddy: 450 Years of History of the Church in Cambodia,* Paris, Le Sarment, Fayard.

Porter, J. 1993. The unity of the virtues and the ambiguity of goodness. *Journal Of Religious Ethics,* 21, 137-163.

Prunier, G. 1997. *The Rwanda Crisis: History of a Genocide,* London, Hurst & Company.

Rah, S.-C. 2015. *Prophetic Lament: A Call for Justice in Troubled Times,* Downers Grover, IL, IVP Books.

Redekop, V. N. 2002. *From Violence to Blessing: How an Understanding of Deep-Rooted Conflict Can Open Paths to Reconciliation,* Ottawa, Novalis.

Regan, P. 2007. An Apology Feast in Hazelton: Indian Residential Schools, Reconciliation, and Making Space for Indigenous Legal Traditions. *In:* Canada, L. C. O. (ed.) *Indigenous Legal Traditions.* Vancouver: UBC Press.

Roache, T. 2018. History Decolonized: A closer look at Edward Cornwallis and why his statue toppled. *APTN*, 6 February. Available: http://aptnnews.ca/2018/02/16/history-decolonized-a-closer-look-at-edward-cornwallis-and-why-his-statue-toppled/ [Accessed 11 August 2018].

Rutayisire, A. 1998, 2007. *Faith Under Fire: Testimonies of Christian Bravery,* Buckhurst Hill, Essex, UK, African Enterprise.

Schaeffer, F. A. 1968. *The God Who Is There,* London, Stodder and Houghton.

Schreiter, R. J. 1998. *The Ministry of Reconciliation: Spirituality and Strategies,* Maryknoll, NY, Orbis Books.

Shawcross, W. 1979. *Sideshow: Kissinger, Nixon and the Destruction of Cambodia,* New York, Simon and Schuster.

Shell, R. G. 2004. Bargaining with the Devil Without Losing Your Soul: Ethics in Negotiation. In: Menkel-Meadow, C. & Wheeler, M. (eds.) *What's Fair: Ethics for Negotiation.* San Francisco: Jossey-Bass.

Shellnutt, K. 2018. No Lie: Americans Still Ascribe to the Ten Commandments. *Christianity Today*, 28 March. Available: https://www.christianitytoday.com/news/2018/march/ten-commandments-survey-lying-murder-deseret-news-yougov.html [Accessed 11 August 2018].

Smith, P. 1911. *The Life and Letters of Martin Luther,* Boston and New York, Houghton Mifflin Company.

St. Teresa of Avila 1577 (1921). *The Interior Castle or The Mansions,* Grand Rapids, MI: , Christian Classics Ethereal Library.

St. Teresa of Avila 1963. Maxims for Her Nuns. *In:* PEERS, E. A. (ed.) *Complete Works St. Teresa of Avila.*

Statistics Canada. 2019. Police-reported hate crimes, 2017. Available: https://www150.statcan.gc.ca/n1/pub/85-002-x/2019001/article/00008-eng.htm [Accessed 11 August 2018].

Stevens, S. 2017. Stop repeating the heresy of declaring the United States a 'Christian nation'. *Washington Post* 9 February. Available: https://www.washingtonpost.com/news/acts-of-faith/wp/2017/02/09/stop-repeating-the-heresy-of-declaring-the-united-states-a-christian-nation/?noredirect=on&utm_term=.a9dd3624bfc6 [Accessed 11 August 2018].

Sumner, S. 2011. The Seven Levels of Lying. *Christianity Today*, 20 May p.5. Available: https://www.christianitytoday.com/ct/2011/may/7-levelslying.html [Accessed 11 August 2018].

Swartley, W. M. 1983. *Slavery, Sabbath, War & Women: Case Issues in Biblical Interpretation,* Harrisonburg, VA Herald Press.

Tavuchis, N. 1991. *Mea Culpa: A Sociology of Apology and Reconciliation,* Stanford, CA, Stanford University Press.

Thayer, N. 1997. Pol Pot: Unrepentant. *Far Eastern Economic Review*, 30 October 1997. Available: http://natethayer.typepad.com/blog/2011/11/pol-pot-unrepentant-an-exclusive-interview-by-nate-thayer.html [Accessed 11 August 2018].

Tollefsen, C. O. 2014. *Lying and Christian Ethics,* New York, Cambridge University Press.

Toulouse, M. G. 1993. "Christianity Today" and American Public Life: A Case Study. *Journal of Church and State,* 35, 241-284.

Toulouse, M. G. 2007. Christian Response to Vietnam: The Organization of Dissent. *Religion and Culture Web Forum* [Online]. Available: https://divinity.uchicago.edu/sites/default/files/imce/pdfs/webforum/062007/vietnam.pdf [Accessed 11 August 2018].

Truth and Reconciliation Commission of Canada (TRC Canada 2015. *Missing Children and Unmarked Burials: Research Recommendations, Working Group on Missing Children and Unmarked Burials*. Winnipeg: Truth and Reconciliation Commission of Canada.

Truth and Reconciliation Commission of Canada (TRC Canada) 2015a. *Honouring the Truth, Reconciling for the Future: Summary of the Final Report of the Truth and Reconciliation Commission of Canada*. Winnipeg, Truth and Reconciliation Commission of Canada. Available: http://www.trc.ca/websites/trcinstitution/File/2015/Findings/Exec_Summary_2015_05_31_web_o.pdf.

Truth and Reconciliation Commission of Canada (TRC Canada) 2015b. *What We Have Learned: Principles of Truth and Reconciliation,* Winnipeg, Truth and Reconciliation Commission of Canada. Available: http://www.trc.ca/websites/trcinstitution/File/2015/Findings/Principles%20of%20Truth%20and%20Reconciliation.pdf.

Tutu, D. 1999. *No Future Without Forgiveness,* New York, Doubleday.

United Nations. 2017. UN rights experts criticize US failure to unequivocally reject racist violent events. 23 August. Available: http://www.un.org/apps/news/story.asp?NewsID=57399 [Accessed 10 August 2018].

Verhey, A. 1999. Directions: Is Lying Always Wrong? *Christianity Today*, 24 May, p.6. Available: http://www.christianityto-day.com/ct/1999/may24/9t6068.html [Accessed 11 August 2018].

Volf, M. 1996. *Exclusion and Embrace: A Theological Exploration of Identity, Otherness, and Reconciliation,* Nashville, TN, Abingdon Press.

Wacker, G. 2014. *America's Pastor,* Cambridge, MA, Harvard University Press.

Wallis, J. 2018. Reclaiming Jesus: Speaking Up for the Integrity of Our Faith *Sojourners*, 30 March. Available: https://sojo.net/media/reclaiming-jesus-speaking-integrity-our-faith [Accessed 11 August 2018].

Weitzman, S. 2017. *The Theology Beneath the Trump-Comey Conflict* [Online]. Available: https://www.christianitytoday.com/ct/2017/may-web-only/theology-of-james-comey-fbi-niebuhr-trump.html [Accessed 11 August 2018].

White, J. J. 1980. Machievelli and the Bar: Ethical Limitations on Lying in Negotiation. *American Bar Foundation Research Journal* 926-938. Available: http://onlinelibrary.wiley.com/doi/10.1111/j.1747-4469.1980.tb01041.x.

Wight, E. 2014 The China connection: new book reveals Khmer Rouge relationship. *Phnom Penh Post* 14 February. Available: https://www.phnompenhpost.com/7days/china-connection-new-book-reveals-khmer-rouge-relationship [Accessed 11 August 2018].

Woodley, R. S. 2012. *Shalom and the Community of Creation: An Indigenous Vision,* Grand Rapids, MI, Eerdmans.

Wright, G. & Kuch, N. 2017. With War-Era Debt Demands, US on Shaky Moral Ground. *Cambodia Daily* 17 February. Available: https://www.cambodiadaily.com/news/with-war-era-debt-demands-us-on-shaky-moral-ground-124912/ [Accessed 11 August 2018].

Violence, Trauma, and Reconciliation – the Role of the Church after Community Trauma in Guatemala

Marcus Weiand

Abstract

This chapter discusses reconciliation efforts after events that caused community trauma. The chapter focuses in particular on a case study conducted in Guatemala in 2012. The paper shows that traumatised communities are often caught in a circle of violence that could last for centuries. The paper begins with a definition of individual trauma and community trauma. After that, it tries to define reconciliation and discusses its specific challenges in an environment of community trauma. The question will be raised whether reconciliation is a realistic option or if mere co-existence might be an intermediary aim that is more adequate to the inflicted injuries. The case study that was conducted in Guatemala will then show how diverse the opinions on the best way towards reconciliation are. People who are actively involved in churches emphasise forgiveness as a key to reconciliation. Non-church actors prefer talking about (transitional) justice. The study shows that both groups have significant insights into understanding the prerequisites of reconciled community. In the end the paper shows that in order to leave the circle of violence it is necessary to talk about safety and non-recurrence, truth, justice, grace and forgiveness. It will be necessary to acknowledge the victims' feelings of revenge and their need to get rid of the "demons" of the past. Simultaneously, the offenders' needs also require attention, to also get rid of their "demons" of the past that lead to self-justification, shame and fear.

1 Introduction

My chapter is about community trauma and reconciliation with a specific emphasis on the role of the church. It is based on a case study on the situation in the Central American country Guatemala.

In the year 2012, I had the pleasure to visit Guatemala to conduct interviews with pastors, church leaders, specialists in the psychosocial area, activists and members of public institutions. I asked them about forgiveness, reconciliation and community trauma. In contrast to the beauty of the landscape and the friendliness of the people I met, Guatemala has a history full of violence. Guatemala has one of the highest rates of homicides in the world. During large parts of the past century, Guatemala experienced a gruesome civil war.

2 The Situation in Guatemala

This is a country, in which almost 90%[1] of the citizens are somehow affiliated to a church. 45% belong to the Roman Catholic Church, 43% to one of the protestant congregations – of which most belong to one of the numerous Pentecostal Churches. It is a country, where most of the people would call themselves Christians.

How is it possible that a country suffers from violence and at the same time, so many people are dedicated Christians? What went wrong? Unfortunately, the teachings of the church leaders were not always very helpful. That is not only the case in Guatemala. A young Guatemalan pastor told me:

> "(...) for too long they have preached to us about a violent God. A God who is love and a consuming fire, whom no one should anger because if he is angry he kills whoever comes in his way, he is a violent God." (C10, 2012)

This pastor lives in Guatemala City and is working with young people in a part of the city that is one of the "red zones", a neighbourhood with high rates of criminality. On a daily basis, he witnesses the violence that affects almost every aspect of life in Guatemala. Being robbed is a common experience in the everyday life. Domestic violence is a huge problem. Corruption is endemic.

In addition, this young pastor witnesses congregations who teach that violence is part of a godly character. When God kills everybody who provokes his anger, why should we not emulate this behaviour? Why should we not just do the same? Why should Christians not take part in this kind of eradication of evil?

Killing bad people has been one of the driving forces of the counterinsurgency efforts during the civil war that lasted 36 years until 1996. It was led by the

---

[1] This and the following numbers are from Prensa Libre, 31 May 2015 (http://www.prensalibre.com/guatemala/comunitario/catolicos-evangelicos-cifras-en-cuesta, retrieved, 2017.08.30).

Guatemalan state and its allies – namely the United States until the mid 1980s. 200.000 people were killed – men, women and children. What was left, was a country scarred by violence and corruption.

But what has happened?

Guatemalans, in particular indigenous people, go back in their analysis as far as the 16th century. They insist that everything began with the invasion of their country by the Spanish in the 16th century. Even though the preceding time of Mayan rule wasn't just a time of peace and prosperity, the invasion by the Spanish has become a "chosen trauma", as Vamik Volkan (1997) called it.

Over centuries, a ruling class oppressed large parts of the population. Big landowners mostly dictated the fate of the villages and cities, ensuring that their workers stayed poor and dependent. However, this system came under threat by the new agrarian reform law from 1944. A law that also affected large US companies.

This led to serious tensions between Guatemala and the United States. Guatemala was stigmatised as a country ruled by communists. The United States finally supported a *coup d'état* in 1954 (Jonas 1991). This was the end of some sort of "Guatemalan spring".

As a consequence, parts of the army rebelled against this overthrow of the government and started to form the first guerrilla group (Bornschein 2009). The following decades were shaped by a political, economic and social system that rested on overt terror (Kantowitz and Çelik 2009). The separation between government and military became nonexistent.

Still, social movements emerged all over the country despite the fact that everything that sounded like being in favour of the poor was synonymous of being communist and therefore inimical to the state. Of substantial importance was the role of the Catholic Church. Catechists were trained and sent all over the country to provide spiritual assistance, to help reduce poverty and oppression and to denounce military violence against the population (CEH 1999, chap. I, sect. 199-207). The Catholic Church, who had been a loyal partner of the ruling class over centuries, now became a target of the military.

In the early 1980s, a particular violent time began under the rule of General Efraín Rios Montt. He began to systematically brutalize the population by forming civilian self-defence patrols (PAC). The Guatemalan armed forces ordered that all males had to join the patrols and forced many to commit atrocities against alleged insurgent groups or collaborators who frequently happened to be neighbours, friends or even relatives. This system of total control destroyed the traditional system of indigenous authority and solidarity (ibid., chap. II, vol. 1, sect. 497).

Rios Montt was a member of a Pentecostal church, preaching regularly on Sundays. No wonder, that during his presidency, parts of the newly founded Protestant churches backed the counterinsurgent policy and permitted the military to recruit young church members during youth group sessions.

Some pastors of Pentecostal and some other Protestant groups were active PAC members or PAC leaders, in some cases giving names of suspects to the military even from within their own congregations (CEH 1999 chapt I, sect. 404). In some instances, local authorities issued identification cards naming the respective church membership. Members of evangelical churches could move more freely whereas members of the Catholic Church were much more in danger (ibid., chapt I, sect. 406).

During Montt's reign of terror, it was particularly difficult for Protestant churches not to follow the logic of violence. It was so easy to fall into categories of black and white, good and evil.

An evangelical pastor described her experiences during her youth (C5, 2012):

> "The church didn't take up their role as an institution for healing. They didn't make us conscious about this historical moment in which we were living. Their fundamentalism led to a discourse that was primarily concerned with salvation. ... I remember vividly that some songs came into fashion and other historical hymns were taken out of the hymn books. They wanted us to sing only happy praise songs, very entertaining and relaxing. They didn't encourage us to become aware of this historical moment."

In 1996 a peace treaty was signed. It became clear that neither the army nor the insurgent groups were able to win the war – in particular because the USA had changed their policy and had ceased to back the Guatemalan government and its violent approach towards the indigenous population. An official historical commission was installed to investigate the atrocities of the previous decades (Commission para el Esclarecimiento Histórico, CEH). The Catholic Church under Bishop Gerardi also set up a commission to remember what has happened

(Recuperación de la Memoria Histórica, REMHI). This quest for truth, however, was strongly opposed by politicians, army officials and the former leaders of the guerrilla groups, who also committed atrocities. Just two days after presenting the REMHI-report, Bishop Juan Gerardi was murdered.

3 The Consequences: Community Trauma

A violent history like this has consequences far beyond the directly affected people. The Guatemalan society has become a traumatised community, even though the general population in the big cities had not been affected much during the war.

Traumatic events in communities shape the collective memory of a group. These events become deeply ingrained into a community's view of history and influence its identity and future expectations (Robben and Suárez-Orozco 2000).

Community trauma has certain characteristics:

1. It distorts community values: values like the respect for life and property, for not being harmed, honesty and to make contracts in good faith – all these values seem not to be relevant anymore.
2. Communities function in a survival mode: decisions are made on a short-term basis – just for the sake of survival for the next day, week or month. Or just for themselves. There is no sense of a healthy community needed in order to prosper. People have lost the ability to think about long term investments. People with a short-term orientation do not save money, they do not invest in education and they are not concerned with the well-being of the wider society. Their motto is: My family and I, we have to survive, no matter what.
3. Communities are shaped by feelings of guilt and humiliation leading to an increased group identity that sees the group as victim: Each side of the Guatemalan civil war perceives themselves as a victim. People who have committed atrocities stick together in defending their actions. They feel victimised by

the international community, the reports on historical clarification or by the judicial institutions.

Victims of military violence on the other hand, are ashamed of what happened, that they were not able to protect their loved ones. This can lead to a new group identity that says, "We are always victims". Especially indigenous people feel that way.

4. This can then lead to the next characteristic of community trauma: a unidimensional and good versus evil narrative, which dehumanises the enemy and may ultimately lead to new violence as an attempt to achieve justice (Schirch 2008; Gilligan 1997).

4 How the Church Is Dealing with the Consequences

What can the church do to help overcome community trauma? What can be done in a country, where most people's single tool for dealing with conflicts is violence?

One of the participants of the case study, an expert not affiliated with a particular church, remarked:

> "[T]he church in general has an important role to play in the process of individual and communal recovery, even at a national level, by providing leaders with sound ethical convictions. Churches have an influence on their members when urging them to be just in their actions" (NC11 2012).

A church leader adds:

> "It is, however, unfortunate that a number of churches are solely interested in their own wellbeing in terms of increasing membership and economic prosperity and are not willing to be involved in any project for the wider community" (C14 2012).

This marks one of the key problems. Churches usually think of themselves as bringing good news for the world. Even from an outside perception, people expect churches to be lighthouses in dark times. However, the content of the Good News is disputed.

On the one hand, there are congregations who combine spiritual, psychological and physical care. They offer spaces for grief and help people to deal with their daily challenges. Yet not all churches are perceived as looking for the good of the community. Participants in the case study criticise in particular a gospel of prosperity that focuses on individualism rather than the restoration of relationships and communities. Also some other evangelical churches are being criticised for preaching eternal salvation but not supporting their brothers and sisters who suffer from an unjust, violent and corrupt system. These churches tend to turn a blind eye on questions of justice and truth.

No wonder that there is considerable dispute in Guatemala on what it means to forgive and to reconcile. In 2010 numerous churches in Guatemala launched the campaign "40 days of forgiveness". "Forgive and everything will get well" was the main slogan. Forgiving and forgetting was promoted as being the best way of dealing with the past. The need for justice did not gain much attention. While forgetting might be important at some stage, as Miroslav Volf (1996) argues, looking into the past and condemning what went wrong is crucial for restored relationships and changed behaviours. A Guatemalan pastor depicts the consequences, when forgiveness is not dealing with the past. He remarks:

> This is the traditional preaching in our church. When a wife is beaten by her husband we tell [her]... : 'forgive your husband, love him, give him love. Don't report him, don't go to the police, don't go to the authorities. That won't help anything. Love him, forgive him and one day God is going to do a miracle and is going to transform your husband's life.' – Well, if he doesn't kill her first; but this is what we say in the churches, you have to forgive. Forgiving is understood as leaving all abuses unpunished. Not seeking justice. Not fighting for the rights of each person, each individual. (...) It is more like keeping it secret, not even talking about the things that we suffer from, simply forgive and forget."

Forgiveness is central to all churches. Every single congregation readily affirms: Jesus teaches us to forgive. The differences mostly consist in how to align forgiveness and reconciliation with justice and truth. A Guatemalan Christian leader argues (C16 2012):

> "I believe that forgiving doesn't mean that there won't be a process of justice. I can forgive a person, but this person has to abide by the

> law. I can forgive that person for my own peace of mind and for the
> wellbeing of the other. But this doesn't mean that on a social level
> this person cannot be tried by the law of the countries."

Many Guatemalan Christians, however, oppose this view. For some it is a matter of survival and not motivated by theological exegeses. Bringing up the truth, involving the authorities, can be very dangerous in Guatemala. Some of the victims are just scared of revealing the truth. Would people believe them? What would be the consequences of revealing the truth? Does the perpetrator have good connections to the police? Rather than risking one's life, forgiving is a safer option. This is even more difficult, when the offender is part of the government or the security forces. President Rios Montt was tried and convicted for genocide in 2013 with the support of the United Nations.

An evangelical pastor commented this: "Why did they arrest them? Let them die peacefully in their beds; after all, they will have to pay one day for all they did to the Guatemalan people." (C6 2012) When taking into account that to this day the former government and military officials do not reveal the truth about many murders and atrocities and that at the same time the relatives of victims who have disappeared still are longing for knowing the truth about the whereabouts of their dead, this pastor's comment is utterly distressing for the surviving victims.

The court decision on Rios Montt was overturned in the same year by the constitutional court.

Still, the government of Guatemala wanted to go on, to leave the bad days behind. They wanted to have a reconciled country. President Álvaro Arzú chose therefore to ask his country for forgiveness for the atrocities committed by politicians and security forces. Some saw this as a sign of reaching out to the victims, of acknowledging the suffering of so many people, and of bringing justice to those who suffered injustice. However, the disillusion followed quickly. The government promised reparations yet failed to deliver. There were no acts that would prove a change of mind towards the victims. One of the participants in the case study comments:

> "Real forgiveness leads to a new situation in which the harm doesn't
> continue. And this is a very difficult step, especially if there is a sim-
> plistic theology saying: 'You have to forgive ...'. Because it seems

to me that forgiveness cannot leave the situation as it was, but instead it has to lead towards a new reality" (C9 2012).

The power of forgiveness is to bring healing into broken relationships, to make way for reconciliation. Another Christian leader therefore emphasises (C2 2012):

> "Perhaps what is most important for the victim is to understand that he who offended him really wants to take steps to show his repentance for what he has done, that's where I believe the truth becomes important, where restitution and reparation are important as part of a process of forgiveness".

In the case study it became clear that for most participants reconciliation is about restored relations that are built on truth and mercy, on forgiveness and love. Moreover, those who are on the way towards reconciliation know about its inherent imperfection yet will not let themselves be discouraged by this. One Christian leader is convinced that

> "[w]e can neither repair nor compose this society by destroying those who harm, destroying those people who offend, those who commit crimes; we cannot compose society that way. The only way to heal this society is to follow ... the way of the gospel, which is a way that invites us to heal and to forgive" (C2 2012).

On this difficult path, Jesus calls victims, perpetrators and bystanders to follow him on the way to overcome enmity and restore communion with God and with others. Consequently, the church in Guatemala should assess its own role in the conflict. Many congregations had been passive bystanders during the war. They had turned a blind eye towards their brothers and sisters who suffered under the cruel oppression. Churches preferred good connections with those in power instead of raising their prophetic voice in a time of distress.

It seems to me that the churches need to repent for failing to protect the weak, for being passive bystanders or for having sided with the oppressors. When the Church becomes aware of its own sinfulness and limits, victims might invite the Church to take an active part in promoting reconciliation. The Church will then have to assume responsibility by raising its prophetic voice even in the face of threats and violence. This prophetic voice of the Church consists of the many voices of the followers of Jesus who take up their cross by speaking out against injustice, by insisting on revealing the truth, and by putting love at the centre of their actions. The Eucharist and baptism become places of encounter where participants deal with the needs of each other and commit themselves to end separation.

5 Love as a Way Towards Reconciliation

I propose that when the Church speaks of reconciliation between enemies, love should be the central concept even after traumatic events. This has to do with the identity-giving characteristic of love.

Traumatic events can destroy identity. People no longer know who they are, everything has changed, and relationships have been damaged beyond recognition. This is a characteristic of hell, as philosopher and theologian Clemens Sedmak puts it, a place of "impersonal beings without identity" (2007). It is a place without love. "Crises of identity take away the power to love", concludes Sedmak. (ibid.)

Identity means finding a place "from which I speak and in which I want to be spoken to" (ibid.). Identity develops through an exchange with others within a communion of the "self among selves" (ibid.). That is, what we can call love: those who love know who they are because they have built relationships which determine, what is meaningful to them (Sedmak, 20).

Love is the centre of the gospel (Sedmak 2007) embodied in Jesus Christ. Christ invites his followers to emulate him in his love for the world. John Howard Yoder argues that Jesus' main intention was to lead to a new communion of love. This however, leads towards opposing a system of social oppression and enmity. Love ultimately enables victims to risk new relationships with former oppressors.

The Mennonite sociologist John Paul Lederach points out that reconciliation necessarily entails encounters at specific places. Referring to the encounter of Esau and Jacob (Gen 33), he remarks that the journey towards reconciliation entails encounters "with self, with the enemy, and with God" (1999). Encounter means to realise that in the presence of true evil (ibid.) the voice of evil is not the only one. There is another voice, "the voice of God's search for reconciliation as a call to love those who do us harm" (ibid.).

Lederach, however, adds that there is no "easy peace accomplished through promises of humanistic love. There is nothing human about loving one's enemy. Living faithfully in the face of enemies is only possible with deep spiritual connection to God's love and a willingness to live as vulnerably as Jesus did" (ibid.). As can be seen in numerous Psalms, that a "theology of the enemy" (ibid.) honours "the cry for deliverance and also acknowledge[s] and give[s] legitimate place for anger" (ibid.).

Victims, perpetrators, and bystanders long for safety, good living conditions, intact relationships, and acknowledgment of their respective situations: their pain, their efforts in fighting for peace, their fear and their concern for their own well-being. It is this "common humanity" that is most important and that is a common denominator in the needs of all three groups. Yet, it is extremely challenging to grant these human rights to the enemy and to see the other as a fellow human being. On this path towards healing and reconciliation each group and each individual has his or her specific way to go.

In particular, the situation of passive bystanders has often been neglected. The psychological effects of being a passive bystander are similar to the effects of perpetration. Bystanders are likely to accept justifications offered by the perpetrators, distancing themselves from the victims (Staub et al. 2008). Sometimes they believe that if the victims had not done anything wrong they would not suffer (ibid.). Passivity of bystanders is the norm even though some risk their lives to help others (ibid.).

Love as a driving force of reconciliation has consequences for victim, perpetrator and bystander. As mentioned before, in Guatemala, many of the victims, perpetrators, and bystanders are somehow affiliated to a church. The churches have therefore the possibility of enabling victims, perpetrators and passive bystanders to meet in an attitude of identity-affirming love. This is one of the churches' most difficult tasks, yet core to their mission of becoming reconciled communities (2 Co 5:19-20).

At this meeting place, each party contributes in a specific way to overcoming trauma and enmity:

- the perpetrators with acts of repentance;
- (passive) bystanders by taking responsibility for past failures and for the future development of their society;
- the victims contribute with their willingness to walk on the path towards reconciliation by forgiving and inviting the perpetrators to perform acts of repentance;

180

- the churches help victims, perpetrators, and bystanders assuming their responsibility by reflecting on their own past, engaging in acts of repentance, and caring for the victims through offering practical and spiritual support;

The meeting place, where victims, offenders and bystanders meet, is then becoming a place where the "art of loving" (cf. Sedmak 2007) is being practiced and identities are being complexified and strengthened (Sen 2006; cf. Nussbaum 2003)[2]. All parties have to take difficult steps towards each other and to acknowledge that there can be no reconciled community without the other person. In the midst of these challenges, participants can trust in God who promises his presence and his peace (Jn 14:27) to those who meet in his name in order to work for the restoration of the communion (cf. Mt 5:9; 18:20).

Then the churches all over the world are able to help shape their communities after community trauma:

1. The unidimensional narrative of good versus evil widens into a common humanity. The enemy is a human being after all.
2. Congregations offer spaces for repentance, forgiveness and healing, while the churches themselves repent for times when they had been mainly preoccupied with their own wellbeing. Congregations then become a place, where guilt, humiliation and shame can be worked through.
3. The community's survival mode turns into hope for the future.
4. Congregations become an example of healthy community values: People can trust each other. They care for each other. They do not seek first their own kingdom but God's.

---

[2] Sen (Sen, A. 2006. *Identity and violence : the illusion of destiny,* London, Allen Lane) lists, how complex identities can be: Identity can be defined by a person's citizenship, residence, geographic origin, gender, class, politics, profession, employment, food habits, sport interests, taste, music, and social commitments (ibid.). Nussbaum (Nussbaum, M. C. 2003. The complexity of groups. *Philosophy & Social Criticism,* 29, 57-69). notes: "for many people, their most fundamental identifications may be with groups that I shall henceforth call 'dispersed groups' – groups that are communities of interest and aspiration across regional and even national boundaries" (ibid.).

That is, where the kingdom of God starts to grow. "It is like a grain of mustard seed that a man took and sowed in his garden, and it grew and became a tree, and the birds of the air made nests in its branches." (Lk 13:19)

Bibliography

Bornschein, D. 2009. Vergangenheitspolitik im Prozess der Demokratisierung Guatemalas (1990-2007). PhD, University of Hamburg.

C2 2012. Interview. Guatemala.

C5 2012. Interview. Guatemala.

C6 2012. Interview. Guatemala.

C9 2012. Interview. Guatemala.

C10 2012. Interview. Guatemala.

C14 2012. Interview. Guatemala.

C16 2012. Interview. Guatemala.

Ceh 1999. Guatemala, memoria del silencio : informe, Guatemala, Comisión para el Esclarecimiento Histórico (Guatemala).

Gilligan, J. 1997. Violence: reflections on a national epidemic, New York, Vintage Books New York.

Jonas, S. 1991. The battle for Guatemala: rebels, death squads, and U.S. power, Boulder, Westview Press.

Kantowitz, R. & Çelik, A. B. 2009. Trauma and forgiveness: comparing experiences from Turkey and Guatemala. In: Block-Schulman, S. & White, D. (eds.) Forgiveness: Probing the Boundaries. Oxford: Inter-Disciplinary Press.

Lederach, J. P. 1999. The journey toward reconciliation, Scottdale, Pa., Herald Press.

NC11 2012. Interview. Guatemala.

Nussbaum, M. C. 2003. The complexity of groups. Philosophy & Social Criticism, 29, 57-69.

Robben, A. C. G. M. & Suárez-Orozco, M. M. (eds.) 2000. Cultures under siege: collective violence and trauma, Cambridge [u.a.]: Cambridge Univ. Press.

Schirch, L. 2008. Trauma, identity and security: How the U.S. can recover from 9/11 using media arts and a 3D approach to human security. In: Hart, B. (ed.) Peacebuilding in traumatized societies. Lanham, Md.: University Press of America.

Sedmak, C. 2007. Die politische Kraft der Liebe: Christsein und die europäische Situation, Innsbruck, Tyrolia.

Sen, A. 2006. Identity and violence: the illusion of destiny, London, Allen Lane.

Staub, E., Pearlman, L. A. & Bilali, R. 2008. Psychological recovery, reconciliation and the prevention of new violence : an approach and its uses in Rwanda. In: Hart, B. (ed.) Peacebuilding in traumatized societies. Lanham, Md.: University Press of America.

Volf, M. 1996. Exclusion and embrace: a theological exploration of identity, otherness, and reconciliation, Nashville, Abingdon Press.

Volkan, V. D. 1997. Bloodlines: from ethnic pride to ethnic terrorism, New York, Farrar, Straus and Giroux.

The Peace Witness of the Church - Swords into Plowshares - and "Building Leaders For Peace" (BL4P)

Randy Friesen

Abstract

This paper will draw from both Isaiah's vision (Isaiah 2:1-5) and Paul's vision of "one new man" (Eph 2:15) in describing the reconciling dimensions of the gospel. Case studies from the Building Leaders for Peace program will offer rich illustrations of Christ's reconciling presence in conflict zones today. The Church is called to be good news, not just to verbalize good news. The world's conflict zones have never needed that good news more than now!

1 Introduction

In August of 2016, several kilometers from the Syrian border, 25 North Americans, 35 Syrians and 15 Turks (ages 18-30) met for a week to share their life stories and aspirations for peace. Both, Muslims and Christians, were drawn by the living presence of Jesus and His peace. Many of these "BL4P" participants were from Aleppo, some 90 km away. Their neighborhoods had become war zones controlled by many different militias and factions, all with different agendas and alliances.

Between July 2012 and December 2016 the siege of Aleppo left some 31,000 people dead, and resulted in some 700,000 people fleeing a city that formerly was home to 2.5 million people. Most of these refugees are either living in Turkey waiting to return home or beginning new lives in the West. Their story is that of countless other refugees fleeing conflict zones around the world. With the global media giving us real-time news from many of these conflicts and from the growing number of terrorist attacks in western cities, the aspiration for peace and reconciliation amongst those most affected by violence is growing.

It was during a generation of similar conflict and extended city sieges that Isaiah was given a vision (Isaiah 2:1-5) of the nations streaming to the mountain of the Lord's temple in the last days and leaving with new capacities to live in peace. There are few biblical texts which have inspired peacemaking initiatives more than this picture of "beating swords into plowshares." Does this text just ask us to wait for a future golden era of peace at the return of Christ or are their applications to guide the Church in our witness in the world today?

This vision of transforming "swords into plowshares" inspired the writing of Isaiah 2:4 on the granite "Isaiah Wall" of the Peace Park across from the United Nations headquarters in NYC, as well as a bronze statue in front of the UN building. While the world acknowledges this vision of peacemaking and aspires toward it, the global structures appear powerless to transform conflict zones, and especially human hearts, from violence to peace.

What are the key elements of peacemaking found in Isaiah's vision and how are they fulfilled in Christ's first coming as our "Prince of Peace?" How is the Church called to live into this vision today?

There are a number of prominent symbols in Isaiah's peacemaking vision which must be understood before an application of the text can be made. These include: "the mountain of the Lord's temple", God's interaction with the "nations", God's way of peace, and the call to walk in the light of the Lord.

2 The Mountain of the Lord's Temple

Isaiah saw a vision of the mountain of the Lord's temple in Jerusalem being raised up in global prominence, such that all nations will stream to it. The temple was the physical location of God's dwelling on earth in the form of his glory. The Holy of Holies, the inner sanctum of the temple, was marked by a gold-covered ark containing the ten commandments and above the ark was the Shekinah glory of God, his very presence.

Jesus said he would destroy the temple and rebuild it in three days. His followers later realized he meant his body. This temple is now called the body of Christ, more commonly known as the Church.

Paul points to the resurrected Christ: "far above all rule and authority, power and dominion" and "head over everything for the church, which is his body..." (Ephesians 1:21-22). The body of Christ, his Church, is "raised up with Christ and seated with him in the heavenly realms in Christ Jesus..." (Ephesian 2:6). This is the mountain of the Lord's temple, raised above all other mountains and hills with all nations streaming to it.

Jesus said he would build his church "and the gates of Hades will not overcome it" (Matthew 16:18). The word "church" is the Greek word "ekklesia" here, which refers to an assembly of people set apart to govern the affairs of the state or nation. In the case of Rome, the ekklesia were to alter the culture of a region until it looked like that of Rome. (Sheets, 2010, p. 61)

Jesus promised to build his Church, a body of people that would represent his throne room and express the culture of the kingdom of heaven on earth. The gates of Hades also represent authority. The Bible often illustrates that the affairs of the city were governed by the gathered leaders at the gates (2 Samuel 19:8; Ruth 4:10-11). The governmental plans of hell will not be able to withstand the advance of the ekklesia. The Church is not a passive, hidden worship service, but a body of people who are expressing the culture of the Kingdom of heaven on Earth, bringing transformation to every nation and sphere of society.

Jesus promised his disciples that where "two or three come together in my name, there am I with them" (Matthew 18:20). The Church gathered in any place at any time expresses the presence of Christ in the world. "A city on a hill cannot be hidden" (Matthew 5:14).

BL4P

Several weeks after the attempted coup in Turkey in August 2016, a group of Christ-followers traveled to southeastern Turkey to host a peace-camp for 75 young people from Turkey, Syria, Iraq, Armenia, Canada, USA, and Mexico. Half of the participants were Muslims; the other half were Christians. They called their gathering "Building Leaders for Peace" (BL4P). Participants from various cultures shared rooms and ate together. Late night conversations opened up personal stories and trust was built. Participants spent the week learning and practicing five peace values: celebrating diversity, collaboration, conflict resolution, catalytic leadership through reconciliation and forgiveness, and changing the world.

After being immersed in these topics, learning from each other, and growing as a community, participants spent the last two days serving Syrian refugee children. At the peace-camp, cultural tensions were broken down, language barriers were overcome, and lasting friendships were built. (BL4P, 2017)

Fear fueled by terrorism and war has caused some in the West to retreat and close their doors. This is not an option for Christ's Church. We embody the peace of Christ and his very presence. Our collective witness to Christ's reconciling presence in the midst of conflict is why Jesus called his disciples the "salt of the earth" (Matthew 5:13) and the "light of the world" (Matthew 5:14). Jesus is building his Church in the midst of the "gates of hell."

What is ironic to some is that at the very point in history when Muslims are crying out for peace and looking for a better way to live, many Christians in the West are retreating in fear. Now is the time of God's favor, now is the day of salvation" (2 Cor 6:2). Could God be using this time of conflict to "save" the Church from her self-protection and reach our Muslim neighbors?

In the "now and not yet" dimensions of prophetic fulfillment, Isaiah's vision is of the Church, positioned in the center of the nations, visibly demonstrating God's peaceful ways, and expressing Christ's Kingdom culture. Isaiah's vision points to the collective witness of the Church in the midst of conflict beyond our individual gospel witness.

3 God's Love for the Nations

The nations matter to God. He placed Israel in the center of the nations as a visible witness of his covenant and ethical ways. Isaiah's vision is of all nations streaming to the mountain of the Lord's temple (Isaiah 2:2).

Jerusalem's strategic location in the center of Israel and at the confluence of several strategic trade routes linking Egypt with Babylon, Assyria and the Hittites meant the nations were aware of Israel's temple in Jerusalem. The fame of Solomon's temple project and his wisdom had been far reaching. However, when the nations came to Jerusalem, what did they see? This was an aniconic religion without any statues of God. In the temple was a box with the laws of God. Essentially, this was a religion of ethics. Ethics that were to be lived out in community, a community that was strategically placed at the center of the nations. Why? So that the nations could see a demonstration of God's higher and better ways in a community living in covenant with him. Ken Esau, Professor of Old Testament at Columbia Bible College, has developed this concept in greater detail in his Old Testament survey course.

This is not a vision of God pleading with the nations to learn from him, but rather, the vision is of a magnetic pull of influence in which the nations desire to learn from God. "Come, let us go up to the mountain of the Lord...He will teach us his ways, so that we can walk in his paths" (Isaiah 2:3).

Isaiah's vision also includes an outward movement of God's authority, as "the law will go out from Zion, the word of the Lord from Jerusalem" (Isaiah

2:3). Christ's call to the Church to "make disciples of all nations" (Matthew 28:18-20) is consistent with the mission impulse of Isaiah's vision.

Paul's letter to the Ephesians reminds us that Christ "himself is our peace." (Ephesians 2:14). In Christ, God is creating or recreating "one new humanity out of two, thus making peace" (Ephesians 2:15). Through Christ, all nations "have access to the Father by one Spirit" (Ephesians 2:18). Jews and Gentiles are now being "built together to become a dwelling in which God lives by his Spirit" (Ephesians 2:22). In Christ, "the whole building is joined together and rises to become a holy temple in the Lord" (Ephesians 2:21).

The Church is to be the place where the nations are reconciled to God and to each other. Jesus is God's peace plan, and the Church is his peace vehicle. Are we living this mission vision?

Jesus points to God's love for the nations as he announces his fulfillment of Isaiah's gospel of the Kingdom (Isaiah 61:1-2) in his home synagogue in Nazareth (Luke 4:16-30). Everyone enjoyed this reading of Isaiah until Jesus applied it to the Lebanese widow in Elijah's day and the Syrian general in Elisha's day – then they wanted to kill him! Extending the "Missio Dei" to "unclean" nations was not popular in Christ's day, and it is still not popular when the Church becomes insular.

The story of Pentecost in Acts 2 records people from all over the known world attracted to Jerusalem by the feast of Shavuot when the Spirit was poured out and the Church was birthed. At its inception, this was a multinational Church. God's mission has always been about the nations.

Will God's covenant community live the "Missio Dei" amongst the nations or will we live for ourselves? Will we welcome the nations who are streaming to the mountain of the Lord's temple? Will we engage in reconciliation and peace-making as an expression of our gospel witness, even amongst nations known as our enemies?

The Church's collective witness as a reconciled covenant community living as ambassadors of reconciliation in the world (2 Cor 5:18-20) is to be so astounding that "the manifold wisdom of God should be made known to the rulers and authorities in the heavenly realms" (Eph 3:10).

BL4P

Something beautiful happens when cultures come together in the presence of the Lord. The testimony of Christ's followers who had experienced the gospel of peace from Mexico, North America, and Armenia was very attractive to the participants from Iraq, Syria and Turkey and they had many questions.

A woman from Syria shared with her Canadian roommate a dream of Jesus she had several years ago. Jesus, or Isa as she knew him, walked up to her in a meadow of flowers. What struck her about Jesus though was the circle of thorns on his head. When he looked at her, it seemed as if he knew her. This dream made her curious to learn more about Jesus. The roommates spent the night reading what Jesus said in the Bible about how we can know him personally.

Today, this Syrian refugee has led her sister, brother and now best friend to Jesus. Many Muslims are experiencing dreams of Jesus. Where will they go with their questions if the Church is not present?

4 God's Way of Peace

The way of God most prominently illustrated in Isaiah's vision is peace. The nations stream to the mountain of the Lord's temple to learn how to resolve their conflicts and live by God's peaceful ways. They beat their "swords into plowshares, and their spears into pruning hooks" (Isaiah 2:4). It is God's peace plan to refocus the resources of nations from destructive to constructive purposes, from instruments of death to food production!

God's peace is "shalom," a Hebrew word that is much richer in meaning than our word peace. Shalom represents wellbeing in all areas of life, wholeness and contentment. Isaiah's prophecy of the coming Messiah included the title, "Prince of Peace" (Isaiah 7:6). "Of the greatness of his government and peace there will be no end" (Isaiah 7:7). This expression of peaceful authority will happen because "the zeal of the Lord Almighty will accomplish this" (Isaiah 7:7). Shalom is the experience of those who live in covenant relationship with the Prince of Peace.

Isaiah's day saw the Assyrian army advancing through Judah sieging city after city into submission. Their attack against Jerusalem is recorded in Isaiah 36-37, and it is the opposite of Isaiah's vision! The Assyrians came to mock and destroy Jerusalem, not learn of God's ways. However, they did learn that God cannot be mocked, as 185,000 of them were killed in one night by the angel of the Lord. What can we learn of God's peaceful ways from that story?

God's shalom is not at odds with his holiness. This is not peace at all costs or the peace of appeasement. God's peace is not the absence of conflict or a nego-tiated settlement to the lowest common denominator. God's peace is found in his presence, expressed in the Prince of Peace, Jeshua the Christ. Jesus would later say to his disciples, "Peace I leave with you; my peace I give you. I do not give to you as the world gives. Do not let your hearts be troubled and do not be afraid" (John 14:27).

What is this peace that Jesus offered his disciples? He spoke these words as he was about to go to painful death on a cross to atone for the sins of the world. God's wrath against sin has not changed. The atonement of Christ for our sin is the only way peace with God is possible, so that the peace of God can be experienced in our relationship with him and others.

As Isaiah later testifies, "Lord, you establish peace for us; all that we have ac-complished you have done for us" (Isaiah 26:12). God's peace is a gift of grace we receive and then share with others. Isaiah goes on to lament that rather than share this gift, "we have not brought salvation (literally "Jeshua") to the Earth, and the people of the world have not come to life" (Isaiah 26:18).

Christ came as the sinless Lamb of God who was killed for the sin of the world, that we might know peace with God. He promised to return again, as the Lion of the tribe of Judah. The Lion and the Lamb are both expressing dimensions of God's peace. It is Jesus who is our peace (Ephesians 2:14).

However, this peace Christ offered is not just with God. Jesus took the Mosaic law and relational ethics to a new level with his call to love our enemies and pray for those who persecute us "that you may be sons of your Father in heaven" (Matthew 5:44-45). Our identity as children of God is evidenced by whether we love our enemies as our heavenly Father does. This is one of heaven's pa-ternity tests!

For several centuries the Church lived this ethic and willingly died as martyrs rather than lead insurrections and revolutionary movements under the yoke of Roman persecution and Emperor worship. The Church was collectively known as peacemakers and scorned for it. With the conversion of Constantine and the inauguration of "Christendom", the ethics of Jesus related to peacemaking were largely replaced with the just war theory in the fourth century. Later interpretations of Jesus' teachings relegated peacemaking to the private sphere.

The early Anabaptists in the sixteenth century revived the literal interpretation of Jesus' call to love our enemies. They paid the ultimate price for their rejection of the marriage of Church and State and many died at martyrs at the hands of Catholics, Lutherans, and Calvinists. Over the past five hundred years since the Reformation, the Church has struggled to consistently live with shalom and it has limited our prophetic witness of a covenant community living Christ's call to costly love.

The current legitimizing of terrorism as a God sanctioned "jihad", which appears to be Islam's version of the just war theory, frequently preys upon the fears of Middle Eastern immigrant delinquents in Europe who know their sins disqualify them from heaven. The promise to jihadi martyrs that they will avoid the scales of justice and go straight to heaven is an effective recruiting tool. However, it is not much different than the promises made to Christian knights as they rode off to their crusades in the Middle Ages.

Our influence as the Church in this world is not found in legitimizing conflict and promising eternal reward for it, rather, we are citizens of the kingdom of heaven first. We are to collectively express the values and culture of the kingdom of heaven here on earth as salt and light. The culture and ethics of the kingdom of heaven most succinctly expressed by Jesus in Matthew 5-7 is the way we are to live out our collective witness. Jesus' call to make disciples of all nations (Matthew 28:18-20) is not disconnected from these ethics and this collective witness.

When the gospel is reduced to a sin exchange and witness is only personal, the transformation of the cultures of this world by the culture of the kingdom of heaven is diminished. Shalom is our collective witness that we are at peace with God and each other. This is a better way to live!

BL4P

Participants of the BL4P program learn reconciliation skills and how to practice forgiveness. The concept of forgiveness, which many Christians take for granted, is not well understood in cultures that highly value honor and revenge.

Many participants in the 2016 BL4P program were from Aleppo, a city which was separated into at least 12 zones, all ruled by different warring factions and militias. Snipers guarded the boundaries of each zone and revenge killing was a daily experience.

A young man from Aleppo fled with his family to Turkey, living as refugees in one of the larger cities. His Kurdish background and Syrian refugee status exposed him to many insults from his Turkish schoolmates. At BL4P, he learned the importance of forgiveness and he heard the stories of Turks publicly repenting for the atrocities of the Armenian massacre one hundred years ago. As he listened to that story of reconciliation he was convicted of his own animosity toward the Turks. When given an opportunity, he publicly forgave the Turks present at the BL4P program and asked them to forgive him for his anger toward them. Several young Turkish men left their seats and embraced him as they responded to his words and tears.

5 Walking in the Light of the Lord

Isaiah's vision concludes with an invitation to the house of Jacob, "let us walk in the light of the Lord" (Isaiah 2:5). The implication being that if God's covenant people do not walk in the light of the Lord, the nations won't see a collective witness of God's ways and be drawn to live them as well.

The vision of Isaiah in 2:1-5 is either a judgment oracle, a salvation oracle, or an indictment oracle. The surrounding texts in Isaiah speak of God's judgment of Israel and Jerusalem for her idolatry and apostasy – that is clearly not the focus of this vision. The book of Isaiah is also full of salvation oracles which prepare God's people for the Messiah. This text anticipates the coming Messiah but is also an indictment that Israel has not walked in the light of God's covenant ways so that the nations are drawn to know him.

Isaiah prophesied that in the future God would honor "Galilee of the nations" (Isaiah 9:1). In the future, "The people walking in darkness have seen a great light, on those living in the land of deep darkness a light has dawned" (Isaiah 9:2). Jesus' life and ministry in Galilee as a fulfillment of Isaiah's prophesy is noted by Matthew, the gospel writer, as he describes the beginning of Christ's public ministry (Matthew 4:15-16).

What does this light practically look like in this world according to Jesus the Messiah? Jesus' description of the culture of the kingdom of heaven here on Earth begins with the beatitudes (Matthew 5:3-12). "Blessed are the peacemakers, for they will be called sons of God" (Matthew 5:9). This peacemaking is often done from a position of weakness, not strength. "Blessed are those who are persecuted because of righteousness…Blessed are you when people insult you, persecute you and falsely say all kinds of evil against you because of me…" (Matthew 5:10-11).

Jesus describes these kinds of disciples as the "light of the world" (Matthew 5:14-16). Jesus came as the light of the world to indwell those who give their lives to him, so we too can live as the light of the world, often because of the cost.

The cost of being light is our pride, anger, and sin being consumed by the fire of God's presence in our lives. "Therefore, if you are offering your gift at the altar and there remember that your brother or sister has something against you, leave your gift there in front of the altar. First go and be reconciled to them; then come and offer your gift" (Matthew 5:23-24). Initiating reconciliation in relationships is walking in the light.

"You have heard that it was said, 'Eye for eye, and tooth for tooth.' But I tell you, do not resist an evil person. If anyone slaps you on the right cheek, turn to them the other cheek also" (Matthew 5:38-39). Not taking revenge against those who have wronged us is walking in the light.

"You have heard that it was said, 'Love your neighbor and hate your enemy.' But I tell you, love your enemies and pray for those who persecute you, that you may be children of your Father in heaven. He causes his sun to rise on the evil and the good and sends rain on the righteous and the unrighteous" (Matthew 5:43-45). Actively loving our enemies is walking in the light of the Lord and evidences we are part of God's family.

This light-filled behavior is our collective witness as the Church in the world that we are citizens of Christ's Kingdom and His light fills us.

We anticipate the fullness of this vision of the "New Jerusalem" when the light of God's glory is the only light. "The city does not need the sun or the moon to shine on it, for the glory of God gives it light, and the Lamb is its lamp. The nations will walk by its light, and the kings of the earth will bring their splendor into it" (Revelation 21:23-24).

John's revelation echoes that of Isaiah's vision of the nations streaming to the temple of the Lord. Isaiah's vision is written with definitive language, "Many peoples will come…", "the law will go out from Zion…", "He will judge between the nations…" (Isaiah 2:3-4). This same vision of the nations being drawn to the light of God's glory was given to God's servants over the generations to encourage us that God's Kingdom mission will be accomplished.

The last days were inaugurated by Christ's first coming and commence with his second coming. We live in the age of grace where the opportunity to join God's kingdom and join him in his mission is available to all. Living in the light of God's ways as his Kingdom citizens transformed by his gospel includes reconciliation and peacemaking. Our potential as the Church to transform culture is connected to our collective expression of Jesus' Kingdom culture in peacemaking and reconciliation, not just in our individual gospel witness.

Isaiah prophesied about the coming Messiah when he wrote: "How beautiful on the mountains are the feet of those who bring good news, who proclaim peace, who bring good tidings, who proclaim salvation who say to Zion, 'Your God reigns!'" (Isaiah 52:7). Peace with God through Christ brings the peace of God and the invitation to join Christ's mission as ambassadors of reconciliation. Will we walk in the light of the Lord?

BL4P

The BL4P story continues as young leaders walk in the light they have received. Syrian and Iraqi participants returned to their communities and started local BL4P chapters, teaching the peacemaking principles they had learned to their families and in local schools. Western participants returned to their communities and schools to actively befriend their refugee neighbors and those from different faith backgrounds.

New BL4P programs are starting in Colombia with the demobilized FARC guerillas and in Eastern Ukraine between Russians and Ukrainians.The Church is awakening to her calling to walk in the light, rather than sleep in the light. www.BL4P.com is connecting interested peacemakers around the world with local initiatives in their area. It is a movement and it is time.

Bibliography

BL4P. 2017. *Peace Camps.* Available at: http://www.bl4p.com/category/peace-camps/ (Accessed: March 1, 2017).

Esau, K. 2017. Conversation with Prof. Ken Esau, April 7, 2017

194

Sheets, D. 2010. *Authority in Prayer*. Minneapolis, MN: Bethany House Publishers.

Sustainability - Reconciliation with Creation, Global Neighbours and Future Generations

Thomas Kroeck

Abstract

Reconciliation, a key term in Christian theology, is not restricted to the relationship of individuals to God, but also includes the relationships to other humans and to non-human creation. In the context of today's economic and ecological challenges wholistic reconciliation is a Christian perspective on sustainable development with the aim of global, intergenerational and ecological justice. This contribution introduces the concept of sustainability, provides a summary of theological views related to it and encourages the Christian church to work for reconciliation with our global neighbours, future generations and the whole of creation.

1 Introduction

The heading of this paper combines concepts from different disciplines. Sustainability comes from the natural sciences and development studies, while reconciliation plays an important role in theology. This paper attempts to bring these perspectives together as a wholistic approach to a major challenge for mankind in this century.

The German equivalent to sustainability, "Nachhaltigkeit", can be traced back to Hans Carl von Carlowitz, who in 1713 advocated sustainable forest management in order to secure the future supply of timber for the growing mining industry. Although it is a quite old concept, the term, sustainability has gained much more prominence during the past 50 years. The study commissioned by the Club of Rome on the "limits of growth" (Meadows et al. 1972) was an important milestone. During the following years and decades, the dangers of air pollution, nuclear waste, the loss of biodiversity, deforestation and global climate change became major concerns. Efforts have been made to save energy, to reduce air pollution and to recycle waste. However, in spite of these efforts, at least in Germany, the amount of waste and the air pollution from motor vehicles continues to increase (Asendorpf 2017; Renn s.a.). This indicates that sustainability is not only a matter of technology, but also of mindsets and values.

2 Sustainability: A Global Challenge

What are the reasons that made sustainability such an important concept? Over centuries mankind has been fighting for survival. They modified their natural environments, but these changes have generally been on a local or regional scale. This has dramatically changed due to the industrial revolution and economic development in Europe and North America since the end of the 18th century. By using new technologies, the industrialized countries were able to dramatically expand their economic output and the consumption of their population. As the British economist Angus Maddison estimated around the year 1000 A.D., the average GDP per capita in Western Europe was lower than that of Latin America, Asia and Africa. By the year 1700, GDP per capita in Western Europa was less than double compared to these regions, but by the end of the 20th century the per capita production of Western Europe, North America and Japan was six times that of the rest of the world. (Maddison 2010:46).

This dramatic economic growth was possible because of technologies that used fossil energy in form of coal and crude oil and raw materials from the colonies. The burning of coal and oil has increased emission of carbon-dioxide and other gases. A major effect is global warming due to the greenhouse effect. Since the start of the industrial revolution the global temperature increased by 0.8 °C (Messner & Rahmstorf 2010:262), which is almost as much as the warming during the 1000 years after the ice age. There is now general agreement among scientists that these changes are a result of human activity. They result in the change of climate patterns, increase of extreme weather conditions (storms, flooding and drought), the melting of glaciers and the acidification of the oceans, which endanger marine ecosystems and are affecting people all around the globe. Other effects of our present economic system are the destruction of tropical forests, desertification and the extinction of species.

The technologies which have been used during the past 200 years have cumulative effects that threaten the existence of mankind. Therefore, the Jewish philosopher Hans Jonas demands of us to take responsibility for the long-term effects of our collective behaviour and to consider the moral entitlement of nature (Jonas 1986:26-29, 80). 30 years ago, the former Norwegian Prime minister Gro Harlem Brundtland wrote in the UN-report "Our Common Future":

"Many of the development paths of the industrialized nations are clearly unsustainable. And the development decisions of these countries, because of their great economic and political power, will have a profound effect upon the ability of all peoples to sustain human progress for generations to come." (Brundtland-Commission 1987)

Recently, the goal of sustainability has gained more public recognition through the Sustainable Development Goals (SDGs), adopted by the UN in 2015 (UN-DESA 2015), and the Paris Agreement of 2016 for fighting climate change. However, as we all know, this is not unchallenged and the implementation is rather slow.

As the way we live, produce and consume effects the livelihood of people around the globe, future generations and the whole ecosystem, we have an issue of justice (Kröck 2016), globally, intergenerational and ecologically.

2.1 Global justice

Our lifestyle and its effects on nature are issues of global justice. While in previous centuries environmental devastation only affected people living in the same location, now pollution and overconsumption in the global North is affecting people on the whole globe, and the whole earth shares the same fate (Vogt 2009:68). However, the advantages of industrialization and the hazards of climate change are unevenly distributed. People in the industrialised countries have benefited from economic growth during the past two centuries. Our consumption patterns are the reason why natural forests are converted into soybean fields and palm oil plantations.

Meanwhile, millions of people in the global South are struggling to survive. There are local causes that threaten their livelihoods and well-being, like population growth, non-sustainable agricultural practices and failure of political and economic systems; but today the poorer sections of humanity suffer increasingly from the effects of global climate change. Since the 1980s, the frequency of natural disasters related to climate has doubled (CRED 2015:7). Tropical storms, extreme rainfalls as well as increased periods of drought can be directly linked to climate change. Those affected are in particular the poor who cannot afford solid houses, who live on sites that are exposed to flooding and landslides and who have to live and survive in fragile environments, e.g. areas with poor soils and unreliable rainfall. It has been estimated that more than 90 % of fatalities due to natural disasters occur in developing countries (Dikau & Voss 2000). The poor are not only more often affected, they also lack the resources needed to recover from disasters. In order to survive, many people migrate to areas where their livelihood is less at risk. A recent study states that between 2008 and 2015 about 203 million people were displaced by natural disasters (Bedarff & Jakobeit 2017:12). Although the majority of these are internally displaced persons, an increasing number may try to migrate to countries of the global North.

Thus, climate change and the unsustainable patterns of our economies and lifestyles threaten particularly the livelihood and survival of the poor. Moreover, it will eventually increase national and global conflicts and therefore affect all of us.

2.2 Intergenerational justice

The goal of preserving resources for future generations is the central aspect of the concept of sustainability. The Brundtland Report speaks of sustainable development that "meets the needs of the present without compromising the ability of future generations to meet their own needs" (Brundtland-Commission 1987).

While most people may agree that future generations have the right to meet their needs, the practical implementation is rather difficult. On the one hand, we are used to our lifestyle and do not like to give up the amenities and pleasures we enjoy just for future effects that we are not yet tangible and that we are not sure of. On the other hand, there is an academic debate on how different resources should be valued and whether they can be substituted. The concept of "weak sustainability" advocates that the overall capital stock must not decline. This includes natural resources, as well as infrastructure, buildings, technologies, etc. According to this view natural resources can be substituted by man-made capital. The concept of "strong sustainability" does not agree with this option to substitute natural resources, such as the genetic diversity of plant and animal species and natural ecosystems with other forms of capital. (Perdan 2011:21) This is not only an academic question but has very practical implications for economic activities and the development of infrastructure.

In order to handle the effects of climate change and loss of biodiversity, a fundamental change of our mode of production and consumption will be necessary. Scientists use the term "great transformation" to indicate that the change will have to be as radical as the transition of our ancestors from the economy of hunters and gatherers to sedimentary farming 10.000-5.000 years ago (WBGU 2011:66).

2.3 Ecological justice

Dealing with climate change and environmental destruction is not just a political and technical issue but "entails changing how we understand and how we relate to the lives and functioning of others— from individual animals to large-scale ecosystems" (Schlosberg 2012:165). The campaign for a Universal Declaration of Rights of Mother Earth aims at creating a legal basis similar to the human rights (Culinan 2010). There is a wide range of positions regarding the relationship and rights of humans and nonhuman species. This ranges from extreme anthropocentrism (see Lüke 2001:243) to biocentric egalitarianism (Keller 2008:207).

The renowned philosopher Hans Jonas held what we may call a mild anthropocentric position. In his major work "The imperative of responsibility" he focused his ethics on the obligation of humankind for its existence (Jonas 1986:29). However, he did not restrict the purpose of nature on the survival of mankind but gave nature a value of its own and an entitlement for care (:245).

In development studies most academics seem to hold more or less anthropocentric positions. The philosopher Martha Nussbaum, however, includes in her capabilities approach animal entitlements and sees "the living individual, not the species" as the focus of a concern for justice (Nussbaum 2011:159). Schlosberg also uses the capabilities approach to discuss climate justice but focuses on the integrity of habitats and ecosystems (Schlosberg 2012:176).

An extreme anti-anthropocentric position is "deep ecology", whose adherents "recognize the equal intrinsic worth of all biota" (Keller 2008:206) independently of its usefulness or value to humans. Human beings are considered one of the many species of animals with the same rights as all other species.

3 Ecology and Faith

How are these scientific and political issues related to religion in general or more specific to the Christian faith?

Throughout church history theologians have dealt with the relationship between nature and faith. A prominent example was Francis of Assis in the 12th century (Hofer 2008). At the end of the 17th century the „physicotheologists", such as the British theologian William Derham (1657-1735), the German Johann Albert Fabricius (1668-1726) and the Swedish biologist Charles of Linné (1707-1778), combined natural sciences with a Christian worldview (Krolzik

1989:21ff). The integrity and value of other creatures was also valued by
Philipp Jacob Spener (1635-1705) and German pietism (Jung 1999).

However, there have also been voices which made the Christian teaching on
creation responsible for the ecological crisis. Two proponents of this view were
the American historian Lynn White jr. (1967) and the German author Carl
Amery (1972). Their publications triggered a theological discourse on ecological responsibility (see Schaeffer 1970; Auer 1984; Moltmann 1985). In 1991
the South African Missiological Society devoted its conference to the topic
"Mission and ecology" (Bosch 1991).

Since then a vast number of articles and books on theological views on ecology
and creation, as well statements of churches and ecumenical bodies, have been
published[1]. The encyclical letter "Laudato Si" of Pope Francis I in 2015 received worldwide attention. The Evangelical Church in Germany (the umbrella
of the mainline Lutheran and reformed churches) published several papers on
these topics[2]. The Lausanne Movement published a call to action during its
"Global Consultation on Creation Care and the Gospel" in 2012 (Lausanne
Movement 2012). A number of religious organisations and networks have been
formed to strengthen the Christian involvement for creation care, such as the

- Alliance of Religions and Conservation (www.arcworld.org),
- European Christian Environmental Network (www.ecen.org),
- Evangelical Environmental Network (www.creationcare.org),
- A Rocha International (www.arocha.org),
- Groene Kerken (www.groenekerken.nl),
- Christian Ecology Link (www.greenchristian.org.uk).

It has to be noted that the care for creation is not a specifically Christian concern. More sustainable lifestyles are also advocated by members of other religions, e.g. Islam (www.ifees.org.uk).

In spite of this discourse, the Catholic theologian Dirk Ansorge stated in 2012
that (in the German speaking context) the ecotheological enthusiasm of the
1980s and 90s seems to have faded and that in spite of the global challenge of
climate change an elaborate ecological theology is missing (Ansorge 2012:4f).

---

[1] For an overview see: Vogt (2010) & Conradie (2012).

[2] e.g. EKD (2009) & EKD (2015).

3.1 Reconciliation – restoring relationships

As others have elaborated on this term and enlightened our understanding of reconciliation, I will only briefly summarise some aspects related to my specific topic.

As mentioned in the introduction, the Apostle Paul used the term reconciliation to characterise his mission. This term is not only rooted in the New Testament but is a basic concept of the whole biblical story. Reconciliation is about relationships, and the triune God is a God in relationship within the trinity as well as his creation (see Moltmann 1991:119; Reimer 2013:150ff). According to Welker, creation can be understood as the formation and maintenance of a network of interdependent relationships (Welker 1995:24, quoted in Volf 2012:77). As these relationships have been affected by the fall, they need to be reconciled. According to Langmead (2008:7), reconciliation can be understood as "a governing metaphor, a model that shapes our whole approach to mission". Bryant Myers elaborates on a concept of Jayakumar Christian, who sees broken and unjust relationships as the fundamental cause of poverty and understands development as the restoration of the relationships to God, to self, to community, to others and to the environment (Myers 2011:143ff). The orthodox patriarch Bartholomew I sees these relationships closely linked to each other when he states: „[…] the way we relate to nature and the biodiversity of creation directly reflects the way we relate to God and to our fellow human beings" (Bartholomew I 2015:o.S.). We will now take a brief look at these relationships.

3.2 The relationship between God and Nature

Traditionally humans have been considered as the crown of creation and the exclusive objects of the redemptive work of Christ (van Houtan 2006:132). Therefore, nature has been understood as the backdrop which provides an environment and the necessary resources for mankind and is of little relevance in God's salvation.

However, when we read the biblical texts, we find that nature is God's creation (Gen 1+2) and his property (Ps 24:1) and continues to be related to Him. God sustains nature (Ps 104), blesses it (Gen 1:22) and includes it in his covenant (Gen 9:8-17; Ex 12:12-14). By their existence the creatures are glorifying God (Ps 69:34; Ps 103:22; Ps 145:21; Ps 148; etc.) (Link 1991:136; Bookless 2008:41; Ansorge 2012:8).

The relationship between God and his creatures is expressed in the Sabbath. With the Sabbath the purpose of creation is realised: God, humans and animals resting in harmony (Moltmann 1985:20, Hieke 2013:17). Animals and the land are explicitly included in the law of the Sabbath, so that life and fruitfulness can be sustained (DeWitt 1995:6; Bookless 2008:43).

Like humans, nature is also affected by the fall (Gen 3:14-19) and longs for redemption (Rom 8:19-23). According to Douglas J. Moo and Christopher Wright, the redemption and renewal of creation is included in biblical eschatology (Moo 2006:482f; Wright 2010:59ff; see also Link 1991:143; Bookless 2008:43). The value of the natural world is demonstrated by the incarnation and resurrection of Christ (Moo 2006:482f; Schaeffer 1970:45f). Moltmann (1985:19) understands the „messianic time" as focused on "the liberation of mankind, the pacification of nature and the redemption of the community of man and nature from negative powers and death"[3]. The hope for the redemption of the whole creation also characterizes the WCC Affirmation on Mission and Evangelism "Together Towards Life" (WCC 2012).

As shown, nature should not only be regarded as a resource for the use of humans but as God's creation with its own intrinsic value (Ansorge 2012:8; Vogt 2009:269). Therefore, many authors advocate to consider the common position of humans and nature as God's creatures and to show more respect for nature as our fellow creatures (Bartholomew I 2015; Francis I 2015:81; Schaeffer 1970:35f,40f; Moo 2006:486). Some philosophers and theologians however go a step further towards biocentrism and attribute spiritual qualities to nature. In this regard, Kritzinger cautions that "God could (again) be identified with nature to such an extent that any transcendent dimension gets lost. The cosmos itself could become an eternal, sacred entity." (Kritzinger 1991:14) He insists that "not humankind, not the wonders of nature, but God the Creator is the centre of the universe" (:17)

How we understand the relationship between God and Nature will also influence, how we relate to nature.

3.3 Our relationship to nature

The role of humans in nature is a central and at the same time a rather controversial point in this debate. As shown above the opposing positions can be identified as anthropocentrism respectively biocentrism. As Gen 1:26-28 speaks of

---

[3] Original: „auf die Befreiung der Menschen, auf die Befriedung der Natur und auf die Erlösung der Gemeinschaft von Mensch und Natur von den Mächten des Negativen und des Todes ausgerichtet".

humans being created in the image of God, they can be regarded as central in creation (Van Houtan 2006:132). This is strongly opposed by White (1967), Amery (1972) and others, who criticise that this passage of scripture has been used as a justification for the right of humans to exploit nature. Schaeffer (1970:35), Kritzinger (1991:8) and Münk (1987) argue that such an understanding is not truly Christian. According to Münk (1987:169ff), it was not Christian theology but philosophers like Francis Bacon (1561-1626) and Rene Descartes (1596-1650) who paved the way to the exploitation of nature. It seems that today most theologians attribute a unique status to humans in creation but hold different positions in-between extreme forms of anthropocentrism and biocentrism (e.g. Kritzinger 1991:13f; Bookless 2008: 41; Wright 2010:50ff)

A commonly used paradigm for the relationship between humans and nature is stewardship (EKD 2015:47, CSJE & ARC 2014; DeWitt 2012). The idea is also implied in the subtitle of the encyclical letter Laudato Si (Francis I 2015): "on the care for our common home". The American biologist Calvin DeWitt defines the concept of stewardship as follows:

> "Stewardship is environmentally responsible behavior that involves an interactive relationship of human beings with their dynamic environment. Stewardship integrates science, ethics, and praxis; [...] Overall, stewardship shapes and reshapes human behavior in the direction of maintaining individual, community, and biospheric sustainability. It is practiced in behalf of future generations, in behalf of the biosphere and its component systems, in behalf of the processes and persons that sustain the biosphere, and in behalf of their Creator." (DeWitt 2012:2).

However, the concept of stewardship has been criticised for being too anthropocentric and being too demanding in practice (Moo 2006:486f). Warners et al (2014:225) propose to replace it with the paradigm of ecological reconciliation. Unlike stewardship, reconciliation emphasises that humans are not opposed to nature, but are part of it (:227f).

3.4 Our relationship to other humans

The concern for nature is sometimes understood as being opposed to the care for people. However, if we see these concerns in the framework of justice, they do not need to be opposites. The affluence of large parts of the population in the industrialised countries is directly connected to global climate change and environmental degradation, which affects the poor in countries of the global South in particular, as well as future generations on the whole earth. Therefore, attempts to reduce climate change and to protect natural resources and biological diversity are a matter of justice for nature as well as for humans (Kröck 2016:133f; Miegel 2012:3f).

As Reder (2013:111) shows, climate change affects basic human rights. Environmental degradation also violates important Christian values such as the „golden rule" of Mat 7:12 (Lienkamp 2013:123), love for one's neighbour (Moo 2006:485), human solidarity (Vogt 2009:67, Bartholomew I 2015), justice (EKD 2009:110) and peace (Vogt 2009:73). Justice and solidarity are major aspects of denominational statements on climate change (Bartholomew I 2015, Deutsche Bischöfe 2007, EKD 2009:109, Francis I 2015:85).

Therefore, our relationship to nature is of great significance for the human community and touches central concerns of the Christian faith. As Vogt (2009:73) says:

> "Peace is a central topic of the Christian faith [...]. The secret of peace is the protection of human dignity. Today this has to be spelled out regarding its ecological dimensions and includes dealing with creation in a responsible manner."[4]

In other words, reconciliation with less advantaged people in the global South and with coming generations involves reconciliation with nature.

3.5 Our relationship to God

Finally, we come to the question, what sustainability has to do with reconciliation with God. Several scholars and official statements point out that the ecological crisis is not only a scientific or technological problem but also a spiritual crisis (Nasr 1968; Stückelberger 2011; EKD 2015:50; Francis I 2015: 89; etc. see also Nasr 1976, Boff 1994, Conradie et al. 2016). This spiritual crisis is rooted in a distorted relationship to God and a misconception of ourselves. It leads to the question of our own position in relation to other humans and to nature (Vogt 2010:2; Francis I 2015:68) and the question of prerequisites for

---

[4] Original: „Frieden ist ein Zentralthema des christlichen Glaubens [...]. Das Geheimnis des Friedens ist die Wahrung der Menschenwürde. Diese muss heute auch hinsichtlich der ökologischen Dimension ausbuchstabiert werden und den verantwortlichen Umgang mit der Schöpfung einbeziehen."

human well-being. As our relationship to other humans and to nature has been touched above, I would like to make a few remarks on the last question.

While the poor in the global South suffer from a lack of basic requirements, such as food, safe water, education, medical services, etc., for many people in the North consumption not only serves as the fulfilment of material needs but often as a surrogate for immaterial needs, such as status, harmony and joy (Renn o.J.:18f). As these needs cannot be permanently satisfied this way, they demand an ever-increasing consumption of new goods. This increased consumption offsets the progress made with the development of environmentally friendly technologies (Renn s.a.:22). An example is the trend to large and heavy SUV cars, which increases fuel consumption in spite of more efficient engines. These trends influence not only society in general but also members of Christian churches. Our behaviour is frequently shaped by the messages of advertising and the example of our neighbours rather than by Christian teaching. The need for "a basic change of values and goals at individual, national, and world levels" was already mentioned in the report "The limits to growth" in 1972 (Meadows et al. 1992:195) and the German Evangelical Church (EKD 2015:25) calls for a revolution of sufficiency by remembering the Christian value of modesty (Mt 6:31f; 1.Tim 6:8; Heb 13:5).

It is in the relationship to God our creator that the needs for belonging, harmony and joy can be met and values are transformed. Therefore, reconciliation with the creator is an important step towards reconciliation with his creatures, other human beings and nature. On the other hand, our behaviour towards them is an indicator of our relationship to God. The two following quotes bring these aspects together:

> "Today the commitment for global justice and the protection of creation as the habitat of all creatures is the hallmark of our belief in creation. Responsible action for the future of creation is a witness for the presence of God in this world. Protecting our environment is practiced belief in creation." (Vogt 2009:270)[5]

---

[5] Original: „Der Einsatz für weltweite Gerechtigkeit und die Bewahrung der Schöpfung als Lebensraum für alle Kreaturen ist heute Bewährungsfeld für den Schöpfungsglauben. Denn das verantwortliche Handeln für die Zukunft der Schöpfung ist ein Zeugnis für die Gegenwart Gottes in der Welt. Umweltschutz ist praktizierter Schöpfungsglaube."

"If I don't love what the Lover has made- ... and really love it because He made it - do I really love the Lover at all?" (Schaeffer
1970:67)

3.6 The mission of the Church

In spite of the vast biblical and theological evidence on the importance of nature
in God's dealing with his creation and the links between our relationships to
God and to his creation, the non-human creation has not been considered an
important concern for the mission of church.

However, there is a growing awareness that the mission of God includes all of
creation. An example is the Lausanne Global Consultation on Creation Care
and the Gospel, which states:

> "[...] we reaffirm that creation care is an issue that must be included
> in our response to the gospel, proclaiming and acting upon the good
> news of what God has done and will complete for the salvation of
> the world. This is not only biblically justified, but an integral part of
> our mission and an expression of our worship to God for his won-
> derful plan of redemption through Jesus Christ." (Lausanne 2012)

And the British theologian Christopher Wright writes:

> "[...] our mission as created human beings is to care for the earth
> God created. And that mission is intensified for us as redeemed hu-
> man beings because we look forward to the redemption of creation
> as well. Our ecological activity as Christians has both a creational
> and a redemptive dimension. It is a missional response to what our
> biblical theology teaches us about God's purpose for creation, from
> the very beginning and the very ending of the Bible." (Wright
> 2010:61)

Besides this biblical mandate, the church should care for creation because climate change and loss of natural resources are among the most pressing issues
today, and the church has to deal with it if it wants to be relevant in society.

Churches have many opportunities and resources to do so. Haluza–Delay
(2014:4) sees religions as playing an important role in the societal response to
climate change, because

- of "their influence on believers' worldviews or cosmologies and the moral duties that they promote."
- they "are able to engage a broad audience, many of whom accept and respect their moral authority and leadership",
- they "have significant institutional and economic resources at their disposal" and
- they "have the potential to provide connectivity (e.g., in the form of social capital) that fosters achievement of collective goals".

One way for churches to take action is to manage and use their property, buildings, vehicles etc. in a manner that is more sustainable and supports biological diversity (see Melander, Diefenbacher & Bismark 2010; FEST 2016; www.groenekerken.nl; www.kirchliches-umweltmanagement.de).

An important task as well as great opportunity for churches is to encourage their members to review and correct their theologies, prophetically challenge the predominant worldview and values and take individual and collective action towards a more sustainable lifestyle. This can lead to a process of reconciliation with nature.

In this process, Warners et al. consider similar steps necessary as in the process of reconciliation between people or groups of people – regret for our personal complicity and dedication to correcting harms.

> "Once this new commitment is made, and efforts are extended toward healing past wrongs, creation will respond. [...] New life will return to the stream, butterflies and birds will find the native plants, and the preserved forest will be able to supply environmental and aesthetic services that will benefit all kinds of creatures once again." (2014:226f)

With global climate change, the enormous loss of animal and plant species and the depletion of natural resources, we are today facing challenges that endanger the survival of mankind. I have tried to show, that these issues touch central aspects of the Christian faith and theology. As they concern our relationships to nature, other human beings and to God, reconciliation is a concept that helps us to deal with these issues theologically and that guides us to take practical steps toward a more sustainable way of life. This is not just an interesting topic for academic discussion, but a matter of life or death for millions of people.

Bibliography

Amery, Carl 1972. Das Ende der Vorsehung: Die gnadenlosen Folgen des Christentums. Reinbek bei Hamburg: Rowohlt.

Ansorge, Dirk 2012. Ökotheologie heute: Vortrag in Budapest am 16. August 2012. URL: http://www.kas.de/wf/doc/kas_31886-544-1-30.pdf?1 [accessed 2.9.16].

Asendorpf, Dirk 2017. Recycling: Voll daneben. Zeit-Online 10.5.17. URL: http://www.zeit.de/2017/20/recycling-muell-barbara-hendricks-verpackungsgesetz/komplettansicht [accessed 27.5.17].

Auer, Alfons 1984. Umweltethik: Ein theologischer Beitrag zur ökologischen Diskussion. Düsseldorf: Patmos Verl.

Bartholomew I 2015. Creation Care and Ecological Justice: Reflections by Ecumenical Patriarch Bartholomew. Oxford. URL: https://www.patriarchate.org/-/creation-care-and-ecological-justice-reflections-by-ecumenical-patriarch-bartholomew [accessed 9.8.16].

Bedarff, Hildegart & Jakobeit, Cord 2017. Klimawandel, Migration und Vertreibung: Die unterschätzte Katastrophe. Eine Studie im Auftrag von Greenpeace Deutschland. Hamburg. URL: http://gpurl.de/ttZMd [accessed 27.5.17].

Boff, Leonardo 1994. Von der Würde der Erde: Ökologie, Politik, Mystik. Düsseldorf: Patmos Verl.

Bookless, Dave 2008. Christian Mission and Environmental Issues: An Evangelical Reflection. Mission Studies 25, S. 37–52.

Bosch, David 1991. Mission and Ecology. Missionalia 19 (1), S. 1–3.

Brundtland-Commission 1987. Report of the World Commission on Environment and Development: Our Common Future. New York. URL: http://www.un-documents.net/wced-ocf.htm [accessed 2.9.16].

Carlowitz, Hans C. 2013. Sylvicultura oeconomica: Oder Haußwirthliche Nachricht und Naturmäßige Anweisung zur Wilden Baum-Zucht. München: oekom-verl. Ges. für ökologische Kommunikation.

Conradie, Ernst M. 2012. The journey of doing Christian ecotheology: A collective mapping of the terrain. Theology 116 (1), S. 4–17.

Conradie, Ernst M.; Tsalampouni, Ekaterini; Werner, Dietrich 2016. Manifesto for an Ecological Reformation of Christianity. The Volos Call. URL: https://www.oikoumene.org/en/resources/documents/other-ecumenical-bodies/manifesto-on-an-ecological-reformation-of-all-christian-traditions [accessed 19.7.17]

CRED 2015. The Human Cost of Natural Disasters: A Global Perspective. Brussels: Centre for Research on the Epidemology of Disasters.URL: http://cred.be/sites/default/files/The_Human_Cost_of_Natural_Disasters_CRED.pdf [accessed 17.8.15].

CSJE; ARC 2014. Stewardship of God' Creation. A Catholic Environmental Toolkit for Catechists and Seminarians. Nairobi: CUEA Press. URL: http://www.arcworld.org/downloads/Catholic-Stewardship-CUEA.pdf [accessed 10.6.15].

Cullinan, Cormac 2010. The legal case for the universal declaration of the rights of mother earth. URL: http://therightsofnature.org/wp-content/uploads/pdfs/Legal-Case-for-Universal-Declaration-Cormac-Cullinan.pdf [accessed 9.8.17].

DeWitt, Calvin B. 1995. Ecology and Ethics: Relation of religious belief to ecological practice in the biblical tradition. Biodiversity and Conservation (4), 838–848.

DeWitt, Calvin B. 2012. Environmental Stewardship: For the Green Salon Jan 7, 2012 in Madison, Wisconsin. URL: http://faculty.nelson.wisc.edu/dewitt/docs/environmental_stewardship.pdf [accessed 2.9.16].

Dikau, Richard & Voss, Holger 2000. Naturkatastrophen: Lexikon der Geowissenschaften. Heidelberg: Spektrum Akademischer Verlag. URL: http://www.spektrum.de/lexikon/geowissenschaften/naturkatastrophe/10985 [accessed 24.7.15].

Deutsche Bischöfe 2007. Der Klimawandel: Brennpunkt globaler, intergenerationeller und ökologischer Gerechtigkeit: Ein Expertentext zur Herausforderung des globalen Klimawandels. 2., aktualisierte. Bonn. URL: https://www.misereor.de/fileadmin/publikationen/expertentext-klimawandel-deutsche-bischoefe-2006.pdf [accessed 17.7.17].

EKD 2009. Umkehr zum Leben: Nachhaltige Entwicklung im Zeichen des Klimawandels. Eine Denkschrift des Rates der EKD. Gütersloh: Gütersloher Verl.-Haus.

EKD 2015. »... damit sie das Leben und volle Genüge haben sollen«: Ein Beitrag zur Debatte über neue Leitbilder für eine zukunftsfähige Entwicklung; eine Studie der Kammer der EKD für nachhaltige Entwicklung. EKD Texte 122. Hannover: Evang. Kirche in Deutschland (EKD).

FEST 2016. Erstellung von Klimaschutzkonzepten und Umweltkonzepten. Heidelberg. URL: http://www.fest-heidelberg.de/index.php/arbeitsbereiche-und-querschnittsprojekte/frieden-und-nachhaltige-entwicklung/klimaschutzkonzepte?lang=de [accessed 3.8.16].

Francis I 2015. Encylical Letter 'LAUDATO SI' of the Holy Father Francis on Care for our Common Home. Rome. URL: http://w2.vatican.va/content/dam/francesco/pdf/encyclicals/documents/papa-francesco_20150524_enciclica-laudato-si_en.pdf [accessed 17.7.17].

Haluza-DeLay, Randolph 2014. Religion and Climate Change: Varieties in Viewpoints and Practices. WIRES Climate Change 5(2), 261–279.

Hieke, Thomas 2013. Alles nur Mythos? Impulse für heutiges Handeln aus biblischer Schöpfungsrede, in Geiger, Gunter & van Saan-Klein, Beatrice (ed.): Menschenrechte weltweit - Schöpfung bewahren!: Grundlagen einer ethischen Umweltpolitik. Opladen: Budrich, 13–31.

Hofer, Markus 2008. Franz von Assisi. Seine Spiritualität der Schöpfung. Feldkirch. URL: http://www.kath-kirche-vorarlberg.at/organisation/ethikcenter-alt/artikel/franz-von-assisi.-seine-spiritualitaet-der-schoepfung [accessed 4.4.16].

Jonas, Hans 1986. Das Prinzip Verantwortung: Versuch einer Ethik für die technologische Zivilisation. Frankfurt a.M.: Insel Verl.

Jung, Martin H. 1999. Der Gerechte erbarmt sich seines Viehs: Der Tierschutzgedanke im Pietismus, in Janowski, Bernd (ed.): Die Zukunft der Tiere: Theologische, ethische und naturwissenschaftliche Perspektiven. Stuttgart: Calwer, 128–154.

Keller, David R. 2008. Deep Ecology, in Callicott, J. B. & Frodeman, Robert (ed.): Encyclopedia of environmental ethics and philosophy. Detroit: Macmillan, 206–211.

Kritzinger; J.J. 1991. Mission, Development, and Ecology. Missionalia 19 (1), S. 4–19.

Kröck, Thomas 2016. Klimawandel - Eine Frage der (Un-)Gerechtigkeit, in Faix, Tobias, Kröck, Thomas & Roller, Dietmar (ed.): Ein Schrei nach Gerechtigkeit: Ein Buch über Glauben, Menschenreche und den Auftrag der Christen. Marburg: Francke-Buchhandlung, 129–138.

Krolzik, Udo 1989. Vorläufer ökologischer Theologie, in Altner, Günter (ed.): Ökologische Theologie: Perspektiven zur Orientierung. Stuttgart: Kreuz-Verl., 14–29.

Lausanne Movement 2012. Lausanne Global Consultation on Creation Care and the Gospel: Call to Action. URL: https://www.lausanne.org/content/statement/creation-care-call-to-action [accessed 20.4.16].

Lienkamp, Andreas 2013. Der Klimawandel als ethisches Problem, in Geiger, Gunter & van Saan-Klein, Beatrice (ed.): Menschenrechte weltweit - Schöpfung bewahren!: Grundlagen einer ethischen Umweltpolitik. Opladen: Budrich, 121–154.

Link, Christian 1991. Schöpfung: Schöpfungstheologie angesichts der Herausforderungen des 20. Jahrhunderts. Gütersloh: Gütersloher Verl.-Haus Mohn.

Lüke, Ulrich 2001. Bio-Theologie: Zeit - Evolution - Hominisation. Zugl.: Münster (Westfalen), Univ., Habil.-Schr. 2., korr. Aufl. Paderborn: Schöningh.

Maddison, Angus 2010. The world economy: A millennial perspective. Reprinted. Paris: OECD.

Meadows, Dennis L.; Meadows, Donella H.; Zahn, Erich; Milling, Peter 1972. The limits to growth: A report for the Club of Rome's Project on the Predicament of Mankind. 2. ed. New York: Universe Books.

Melander, Dan; Diefenbacher, Hans; Bismark, Antoinette 2010. Klimaschutz in Kirchen. Vom christlichen Auftrag zur Praxis. Berlin: Erich Schmidt.

Messner, Dirk & Stefan Rahmstorf 2010. Kipp-Punkte im Erdsystem und ihre Auswirkungen auf Weltpolitik und Wirtschaft. In: Debiel, T.(ed.): Globale Trends 2010: Frieden Entwicklung Umwelt. Stiftung Entwicklung und Frieden, Hrsg. Bonn. (Bundeszentrale für Politische Bildung, 1025), 261–278.

Miegel, Meinhard 2012. Welches Wachstum und welchen Wohlstand wollen wir? APuZ 62(27-28), 3–8.

Moltmann, Jürgen 1985. Gott in der Schöpfung: Ökologische Schöpfungslehre. München: Chr. Kaiser.

Moltmann, Jürgen 1991. Reconciliation with Nature. In: Word & World 11 (2), 117–123.

Moo, Douglas J. 2006. Nature in the New Creation. New Testament Eschatology and the Environment. JETS 49 (3), S. 449–488.

Münk, Hans J. 1987. Umweltkrise - Folge und Erbe des Christentums? Historisch-systematische Überlegungen zu einer umstrittenen These im Vorfeld ökologischer Ethik. JCSW 28, S. 133–206.

Myers, Bryant L. 2011. Walking with the poor: Principles and practices of transformational development. Rev. and updated ed. Maryknoll N.Y.: Orbis Books.

Nasr, Seyyed H. 1968. The encounter of man and nature: The spiritual crisis of modern man. London: Allen & Unwin.

Nussbaum, Martha C. 2011. Creating capabilities: The human development approach. Cambridge, Mass.

Perdan, Slobodan 2011. The Concept of Sustainable Development and its Practical Implications, in Azapagic, Adisa & Perdan, Slobodan (ed.): Sustainable development in practice: Case studies for engineers and scientists. Chichester: Wiley-Blackwell, 3–25.

Reder, Michael 2013. Ethik der Menschenrechte und Klimawandel, in Geiger, Gunter & van Saan-Klein, Beatrice (ed.): Menschenrechte weltweit - Schöpfung bewahren!: Grundlagen einer ethischen Umweltpolitik. Opladen: Budrich, 107–120.

Reimer, Johannes 2013. Die Welt umarmen: Theologie des gesellschaftsrelevanten Gemeindebaus. 2. Auflage. Marburg an der Lahn: Francke

Renn, Ortwin s.a. Ökologische Orientierung: Anmerkungen zu den Aufgaben der Kirchen. URL: www.akademie-rs.de/fileadmin/user_upload/.../Renn__KircheNach.pdf [accessed 30.7.16].

Schaeffer, Francis A. 1970. Pollution and the death of man: The Christian view of ecology. London: Hodder & Stoughton.

Schlosberg, David 2012. Justice, Ecological Integrity, and Climate Change, in Thompson, Allen & Bendik-Keymer, Jeremy (Hg.): Ethical adaptation to climate change: Human virtues of the future. Cambridge, Mass.: MIT Press, 165–183.

UN-DESA 2015. Sustainable Development Goals. URL: https://sustainabledevelopment.un.org/sdgs [accessed 8.7.17].

van Houtan, Kyle S.; Pimm, Stuart L. 2006. The Various Christian Ethics of Species Conservation. in David M. Lodge und Christopher Hamlin (ed.): Religion and the new ecology. Environmental responsibility in a world in flux. Notre Dame: Univ. of Notre Dame Press, 116–147.

Vogt, Markus 2009. Prinzip Nachhaltigkeit: Ein Entwurf aus theologisch-ethischer Perspektive. Univ., Habil.-Schr.-Luzern. München: oekom Verl.

Vogt, Markus 2010. Worin besteht die theologische Kompetenz im Umweltdiskurs? Überlegungen aus katholischer Sicht. 14. Internationaler Renovabis-Kongress „In Verantwortung für die Schöpfung". Freising, 02.09.2010. URL: http://www.kaththeol.uni-muenchen.de/lehrstuehle/christl_sozialethik/personen/1vogt/texte_vogt/theol-kompetenz_umweltdiskurs.pdf. [accessed 13.7.17].

Volf, Miroslav 2012. Von der Ausgrenzung zur Umarmung: Versöhnendes Handeln als Ausdruck christlicher Identität. Marburg an der Lahn: Francke.

Warners, David, Ryskamp, Michael & van Dragt, Randall 2014. Reconciliation Ecology: A New Paradigm for Advancing Creation Care. Perspectives on science and Christian faith 66(4), 221–235.

WBGU 2011. Welt im Wandel: Gesellschaftsvertrag für eine Große Transformation. 2., veränd. Aufl. Berlin: Wiss. Beirat der Bundesregierung Globale Umweltveränderungen (WBGU). URL: http://www.wbgu.de/hauptgutachten/hg-2011-transformation/ [accessed 19.7.17]

WCC 2012. Together Towards Life: Mission and Evangelism in Changing Landscapes. Commission on World Mission and Evangelism. URL: https://www.oikoumene.org/en/resources/documents/commissions/mission-and-evangelism/together-towards-life-mission-and-evangelism-in-changing-landscapes?set_language=en, (accessed 13.7.17).

White, Lynn, JR. 1967. The Historical Roots of Our Ecologic Crisis. Science 155(3767), 1203–1207.

Wright, Christopher J. H. 2010. The mission of God's people. A biblical theology of the church's mission. Grand Rapids Mich.: Zondervan.

Reconciliation Meetings in Egypt

Jonathan Andrews and Christof Sauer

Abstract

So-called *reconciliation meetings* are often held in the aftermath of sectarian violence involving Christians and Muslims in parts of Egypt. Upon critical investigation, it is found that such meetings involving representatives of religious communities have no standing in law and therefore neither fulfil nor remove the State's obligation to file cases against perpetrators of assaults, vandalism or threats where there is clear evidence that a criminal act has been committed. In practice, such meetings bring reconciliation and peace only in the sense of the unconditional surrender of the weaker party.

1 Introduction

This paper examines the practice of 'reconciliation meetings' in Egypt. Typically, these occur following sectarian violence involving Muslims and Christians. Community leaders gather, often with the key participants, to agree a way of restoring communal harmony. In the vast majority of cases the agreed remedies include exemption from prosecution for those who perpetrated acts of violence. In some cases, Christians are obliged to move away from the area.

Are these practices effective? What happens to the role of the State in maintaining law and order including holding those to account before the law who commit criminal acts?

Reconciliation meetings are a specific type of procedure used in some locations to address local conflicts. Yet, they illustrate much that is dysfunctional in local communities, the nation state and the wider Middle East region, in which Egypt is a significant country. These problems include discrimination on religious lines, the subversion or circumvention of criminal justice and the exacerbation of violence, oppression and forcible displacement.

2 What Are 'Reconciliation Meetings'?

In this opening section we present a set of case studies that describe how *reconciliation meetings* operate, the situations they normally address and the typical actions that result.

2.1 A case study from 2011

On 20 March 2011 Ayman Anwar Mitri was attacked in Qena over an alleged affair. His ear was cut off. Ayman is a Christian and his attackers Muslims. On 23 March a *reconciliation meeting* was held at which one assailant acknowledged that the accusation was false and apologised for the unwarranted assault. The police proceeded with a case against the attackers. On 22 April 2012 a judge exonerated and released the attackers following intense pressure on Ayman to pardon them. This was a clear case of witness intimidation leading to a miscarriage of justice.

2.2 Seven case studies from 2012

During 2012 there were seven reported occurrences of *reconciliation meetings*. They are all listed here to show the prevalence of such events.

On 28 January 2012 a large mob of Muslims attacked Christian owned homes and businesses in Kobry-el-Sharbat (el-Ameriyah), Alexandria Province. Two Christians and one Muslim were injured. A rumour had circulated that a Christian man had an intimate photo of a Muslim woman on his mobile phone. Violence erupted, following which a number of *reconciliation meetings* between Muslim and Christian leaders were held. Initially, Muslim leaders were insistent that all Christian families must leave the village. Eight families were forced to leave, with the sale of their homes and businesses overseen by a Muslim leader. On 16 February a parliamentary fact-finding commission issued a proclamation cancelling all evictions and confiscations of property and asserting that the law gave all Christian families the right to reside in the village. The commission included two Christians, two moderate Muslims and a Salafist[1] MP who had been involved in the *reconciliation meetings*. In this case, the parliamentary commission overturned at least some of the injustice that the *reconciliation meetings* had imposed. No action was taken against the perpetrators of criminal acts of vandalism.

On 4 March 2012 a mob of Muslims brandishing swords and knives surrounded a guesthouse in Abu Al-Reesh, Aswan province, terrorising two nuns trapped inside. The next day a school on the same site was threatened. The nuns were

---

[1] Salafism is a puritanical form of Sunni Islam with 'quiet', 'active' and 'jihadist' forms of spreading the Islamic faith. The quiet form spreads the faith by example, proclamation and debate; the active form adds pressing the authorities to enact Islamic law; the jihadist form adds the concept of holy war, spreading Islam by conquest.

not physically hurt but were traumatised. Attendance at the school dropped by a third following the incident. At a *reconciliation meeting* held in April, Muslims demanded that ownership of the guesthouse be transferred. This claim was resisted. However, the victims felt obliged to drop complaints against the assailants.

In early August 2012 there were sectarian clashes in Sohag province. There was some damage and looting of Christian properties on a relatively small scale. The Christian community decided that it was in their best interest to participate in a *reconciliation meeting* – rather than to pursue legal action against the perpetrators – in order to diffuse the tension.

On 19 September 2012 there was a sectarian incident in Samalout, Minya province. The incident started over a traffic accident in which a 13-year-old Muslim boy hit a Christian man with his tuk-tuk. An argument ensued and became heated when family members intervened, some of whom were injured. A mob of Muslims then surrounded the Christian's home, creating a threatening situation. Police intervened and calmed the situation. At a *reconciliation meeting* held on 23 September it was agreed that the Christian parties involved would pay the Muslim parties EGP30,000[2] and if either side resumed hostilities then it must pay EGP150,000[3] to the other party. So, despite being the victim of the original incident, the Christian community paid financial compensation to others to resolve the situation.

In September 2012 there was an altercation between a Muslim teacher and a Christian pupil, both female, and their respective families in a town in Assiut province. An argument led to the teacher filing an adverse report about the pupil with the police. The two families held a *reconciliation meeting*, which appeared to resolve the situation. However, one week later three members of the teacher's family attacked the pupil's uncle's home, looting it and setting it on fire. The uncle and his family left the village. There were no reports of action being taken against the perpetrators of the criminal violence.

In late September 2012, in Ezbat Marko, Beni Sweif province, two boys aged 9 and 10 were observed by a passing Imam allegedly defacing a Qur'an. Dissatisfied with the reprimand administered by a priest, Muslims submitted a

[2] Approximately US$4,000 at that time.

[3] Approximately US$21,500 at that time.

complaint, together with evidence, to the police. Police acted to diffuse clashes and a *reconciliation meeting* was held. However, on 2 October the two boys were taken into protective custody and questioned further. They were released on 4 October, but investigations continued, with a hearing scheduled for 7 October. On 10 October the case against them was dropped following a meeting involving Christians, Muslims and local security officials.

On 28 October 2012 at least five Christians were injured when a mob of Salafi Muslims surrounded a church in Tala-el Fashn, Beni Sweif province, and assaulted worshippers as they left mass. The church serves a number of neighbouring villages that do not have a church building. The priest was unable to leave the building for several hours. He called the police, but they failed to respond until the head of the Egyptian Union of Human Rights Organization complained to the Ministry of the Interior. A *reconciliation meeting* was held, at which it was agreed that anyone could attend worship services, but only local residents could attend assembly meetings. It was further agreed that the state would pay damages. Both Muslim and Christian leaders agreed that EGP500,000[4] would be paid by any party that broke the agreement reached.

2.3 Occurrences from 2013 onwards

Reconciliation meetings continue to occur as shown by surveys by the Egyptian Institute for Personal Rights which notes 45 occurrences of such practices in the period 2011 to early 2015 (EIPR 2015:17). The report categories the incidents under a number of causes including the opening of church buildings, alleged romantic relationships, disputes over land and property, political engagement and religious expression, notably 'liking' pages on social media websites (EIPR 2015:20-7).

There is no reason that suggest the practice has been discontinued since then.

3 Analysis

In this section of the paper we analyse the practice and underlying causes of *reconciliation meetings* and accompanying unjust practices in Egypt. This necessitates looking at the socio-political-economic context of Egypt within the Middle East and wider Arab world.

---

[4] Approximately US$71,500 at that time.

Reconciliation meetings involve key participants in the incident and local community leaders. Such meetings have no official standing in law and therefore neither fulfil nor remove the State's legal obligation to file cases against perpetrators of assaults, vandalism and threats where there is clear evidence that a criminal act has been committed. In many cases *reconciliation meetings* result in members of minorities being forced to accept a degree of injustice and allow perpetrators to escape legal sanction for their crimes. At times they do not constitute a closure of a case: further hostilities ensue against Christians. They are an expression of Christians being treated as second class citizens, a practice known as *dhimmitude*.

3.1 Why do 'reconciliation meetings' occur only in some parts of Egypt?

An analysis of examples of *reconciliation meetings* reveals that the practice is confined to a few governorates. The primary ones are Minya, Beni Sweif, Assiut and Sohag, although there are examples from elsewhere, including one cited above from Alexandria.

A wider observation is that this practice is confined to Egypt: it is not seen in other countries in the Middle East.

We need to consider why these *reconciliation meetings* occur only in Egypt and within that country, why they are more prevalent in some parts than others. To address these questions, we need to explore the sociological conditions present.

3.1.1 Why only in Egypt?

Some Muslims ask, "Why, if Islam is superior, is God not blessing us? Why are they – that group that is clearly different – doing better than we are in terms of wealth or political power. It cannot be that God is not strong enough, since he is almighty. Therefore, it must be that God is not pleased with us; clearly, we are not good enough Muslims. What do we need to change in us and our environment?"

Two things emerge from this. First, the concept of purity in individual behaviour and the need for purity in society. The presence of a non-Muslim group is seen by some as polluting. One response is to encourage either conversion or expulsion of the other. Of note is that such practices are not applied only to Christians: other religious groups are also affected and frequently the group most affected are 'Muslims of the wrong type'. One example is the severe suppression of Egypt's small Shi'a community (al-Monitor 2016b).

Second, a sense of shame at the failure to be good enough Muslims. One expression of such shame can be rage, expressed in violent behaviour. Therefore, sectarian clashes can be viewed as an act of rage rooted in shame. The cultural and social context in Egypt allows this expression of rage whereas in other Middle Eastern countries it does not.

We must note that many Muslims emphasise that their faith takes justice very seriously. Underlying justice is what legal framework applies which determines what is regarded as just and unjust. In practice, this varies from one location to another including amongst Muslim communities.

In Iraq since 2003 there have been several occurrences of sectarian violence, often leading to Christians and others being forced to move elsewhere. By 2006 much of Baghdad had become segregated on religious lines, affecting Sunnis and Shi'a perhaps more than the Christians. In such circumstances there was no attempt at reconciliation or seeking to restore communal harmony: everyone was obliged to adapt to a new situation where each community defends itself against any that attacks it, as the law enforcement services could not be trusted to act impartially. Some Christians were obliged to pay the jizya tax in order to remain. Technically, this is a tax paid in lieu of not being allowed to participate in the defence forces. This is enforcing dhimmitude: there is no attempt at reconciliation.

One common element in these explanations is the lack of respect for diversity.

The former Deputy Prime Minister and Foreign Minister of Jordan Marwan Muasher describes the events from 2011 onwards as a battle for pluralism in the Middle East (Muasher 2014). He uses the title Arab Awakening for what was first termed the Arab Spring, reflecting his view that the root aspirations expressed were a cry for greater dignity and more and better jobs. To achieve this, societies would need greater respect for diversity which is a creative force that improves the economic conditions and hence the wealth of the society as a whole. This requires greater respect for religious diversity and freedom of religion and belief for all (Muasher 2014:168-70).

3.1.2 Why only in parts of Egypt?

It is clear from above that the practice of *reconciliation meetings* is restricted to some parts of the country. It seems that the attitude of local law enforcement officials is significant, as is the attitude of community leaders. Lack of respect for diversity would end if local community and religious leaders demanded that it do so. One aspect of this is the attitude and behaviour of governors.

The practice appears restricted to smaller towns. In Egypt, many of these have religiously mixed populations. Elsewhere in the Middle East, the vast majority of Christians live in the major cities or in villages and other settings which are overwhelmingly Christian. It is in those places with a more balanced number of Muslims and Christians that appear prone to the practice of *reconciliation meetings*.

We noted above the effects of extremist violence when considering Iraq. The northern Sinai area of Egypt has also been affected by the emergence of ex-tremist armed groups. Some Christians have felt obliged to leave. Local tribes armed themselves and started cooperating closely with the army to restore order (al-Monitor 2017). In contrast to Iraq, the security forces in this part of Egypt are trusted to act decisively against the extremists. This illustrates that extremist excesses can be dealt with if there is the collective will to do so.

3.2 Accompanying injustices in Egypt

There are a number of other areas in which the enforcement of law and order and the criminal justice system treat Muslims and Christians differently. We list a few here to illustrate that the unjust practices seen in *reconciliation meet-ings* are not an isolated occurrence.

3.2.1 Poor policing

One factor in much injustice is poor police procedures, or poor application of such procedures, in handling complaints and initial investigations. An extreme example of this occurred in al-Kosheh in 1998 concerning the murder of two Christians. In summary, numerous Christian residents of the area were detained and brutally interrogated whilst the police chose not to investigate suspects who were regarded as Muslim. The injustice in this first criminal act and an inter-twined web of social, economic, political and religious factors created tensions that erupted in sectarian violence on 31 December 1999 (Sennott 2013:167-173,191). The de facto granting of impunity earlier emboldened some to act violently, confident that they would not be held to due account for their behav-iour.

In her address to the European Parliament in June 2017 Eva Saenz-Diez cited several examples of the police failing to respond promptly and effectively to reports by Christians that a sectarian incident had been initiated (Saenz-Diez

2017). Clearly, discrimination in police practices continues to affect parts of Egypt. The same applies for the fire service in cases of arson.

3.2.2 Blasphemy laws

Another area in which Christians and Muslims are treated differently has emerged since 2011. Egypt's blasphemy laws date from the President Mubarak era (1981-2011) but were applied very rarely. This changed in 2012 when at least three Christians were imprisoned after being convicted on blasphemy charges. All denied any wrongdoing and noted that due attention was not paid to the evidence during their trials. A higher profile case started on 9 May 2013 when Demiana, a 24-year old Christian teacher, was arrested following complaints by a number of parents and pupils concerning the content of a class she taught on 8 April. Two independent investigations were conducted, one by the school council representing parents and teachers and the other by the local office of the Ministry of Education. Both found no basis for the allegations. Ten of the 13 pupils interviewed during these investigations stated that the accusations were false. Despite this, lawyers representing the parents of one pupil went to the prosecutor's office and filed a complaint. This prompted the arrest of the teacher and a court case. Demiana was released on bail before the end of May. On 11 June she was convicted. The judge did not give her a custodial sentence but imposed a fine of EGP 100,000.[5] An appeal was submitted. The judge agreed that the report from one of the initial investigations could be read in court during the appeal hearing. The report exonerated the teacher. She was cleared on appeal but denied permission to return to her job. The teacher consistently denied any wrongdoing. Her life was irreversibly changed by the false accusations, the failure to apply the law justly and the denial of full restoration.

In Egypt's honour-shame dominated culture, right and wrong, legal and illegal is of less significance than what is perceived to be honourable and shameful. We need to ask what in Demiana's situation is *honourable* about the conduct of those who falsely accused her and sat in judgement of her. Is it truly honourable to ignore evidence and the outcomes of independent investigations? Is it truly honourable to effectively end the career of a young teacher to satisfy the whims of a few? Why can the actions of a few override the majority consensus that no wrong had been committed?

---

[5] Equivalent to approximately US$14,000 at that time.

3.2.3 Human rights violations

We can summarise the human rights violations seen in *reconciliation meetings* and other situations as being rooted in discrimination based on religious grounds. This is expressed within the police system by poor investigations and slow responses to emergency calls from Christians. Within the justice system, we have seen examples of evidence being disregarded and impunity granted when it is clear that victims have been pressured to withdraw complaints. The system grants impunity to some of those who perpetrate criminal acts. A number of the victims of human rights abuses did not receive due recompense even when they were exonerated; the teacher, for example, was not reinstated in her job.

3.3 The underlying system – religious segregation in the Middle East

What underlies these situations in which some Muslims exploit, marginalise and minoritize Christians? Why is justice being circumvented? These questions lead us to explore the underlying system operative throughout society that segregates everyone on religious lines.

The religious registration system assigns every person to a religious belief at birth. This allocation might be generic, such as Christian or Muslim, or very specific, such as Roman Catholic, Syrian Orthodox or Anglican. The registration determines which religiously based legal system applies to each individual for personal status matters, such as marriage, divorce, custody of children, religious education in schools, burial and inheritance. There is no civil marriage, everyone is obliged to use a religiously based system. This leads to restrictions on who can marry whom, notably that a woman registered as a Muslim can only marry a man with the same registration.

The same system is applied in all Middle Eastern countries. There are variations across the region in the list of what registrations are permissible. The assignment generally follows that of the father, except in Israel where it follows the mother, including for Israeli Arabs. The registration is recorded on birth certificates, on identity cards in many countries and within government computer systems.

Changing the registration is problematic everywhere. In most places it is a one-way street, i.e. to Islam. The exceptions are Lebanon, Turkey and for Israeli Arabs, where to change the registration from Muslim to Christian is legal, although social and cultural restrictions affect many. This creates problems for those who convert from Islam to Christianity: they live and worship as Christians but are treated as Muslims by their country's legal system. This provides a clear demonstration that the system, despite its name, does not describe people's religious beliefs or practices.

The system creates a variety of other challenges. For example, how should one determine who is a Muslim? Religious registration can make this clear although it ignores factors such as how an individual lives or how a community conducts its affairs. What is the role of ethics, behaviour and attitudes, to say nothing of religious belief and practice? So, does religious registration really identify who is a Muslim? Surely the answer is: only if one excludes belief, practice and lifestyle. Religious registration reduces the terms Christian and Muslim to social labels.

One group subtly challenging the system are those describing themselves as "Muslim atheists". These people are describing themselves as Muslim in a social sense but not as adherents of a religion. The prevalence of this phenomenon has been presented in a survey of websites across the Arab world (Ibrahim 2017).

3.4 What is meant by peace, reconciliation and justice?

Finally, in our analysis, we need to be clear how the terms peace and reconciliation are being used since these words can mean different things to different audiences.

Peace can mean the absence of overt conflict. For example, some wars end when one party surrenders to the other. The vanquished are then at the mercy of the victors; the latter able to do anything they wish to the other party: might they act magnanimously seeking to establish a sense of shared community and hopes for the future or will they choose to be oppressive and exploitative?

The Biblical use of the term peace is much deeper. Primarily, it is about peace with God, marked by a relationship of trust and love. God's love for us has been demonstrated in his creation and, primarily, his redemption through the life, death, resurrection and ascension of Jesus Christ. In practical expression, many Christians seek to be agents of God's peace in the sense of seeking the best for society as a whole.

What is understood by reconciliation in *reconciliation meetings*? In practice it means that there will be harmony if the minority community agrees to live with whatever conditions the majority stipulates. Right and wrong, in the sense of what is lawful and criminal, is a secondary consideration. It is establishing peace in the sense of an end to overt conflict, effectively by the unconditional surrender of the weaker party. It is not peace and harmony in the sense of a mutual respect that recognises and affirms distinctions and differences and seeks to allow everyone to flourish.

We need to keep in mind that it is the religious registration system that underpins the treatment of Christians as a powerless minority obliged to be *reconciled* in the sense of accepting whatever the majority imposes.

This prompts consideration of what is meant by justice? Clearly, acting justly, but underlying this is a shared understanding of what just behaviour is, of what legal framework is operative. In *reconciliation meetings* the criminal code is being overridden by an interpretation of justice imposed by some upon others.

The Egyptian practice of *reconciliation meetings* has been shown to be far from just, peaceful and true reconciliation: all-too-often the practice is the imposition and justification of exploitation.

4 Proposed Remedies

Having described the practice of *reconciliation meetings* and analysed the causes and effects thereof, we move now to propose some possible remedies.

4.1 Overcoming religious segregation and dhimmitude

Tackling religious registration as a system is problematic from the perspective of supporting the indigenous Christians across the region. Many Church leaders across the Middle East assert that they appreciate religious registration since it identifies who they have authority before the state and society to work with. In contrast, almost all converts from Islam to Christianity state that this system is the root of many the challenges they face. Finding a way through this pronounced difference of perspective is a challenge (Andrews 2016:12).

One approach is to show how religious registration affects society as a whole since it is symptomatic of and a key contributor to a pluralism deficit, a deficit that reduces the economic dynamism within society.

4.1.1 Historical precedents

Historically, what we see today is a continuation – with some subtle tweaks – of the Ottoman Empire's Millet System. The Millet System was not static during the Ottoman era: it was adapted on several occasions as more groups sought to be recognised as distinct. Such recognition enabled them to celebrate marriage, births and deaths according to their beliefs, applying their own rituals to mark these key events in people's lives. However, the Millet System predates the Ottoman Empire and indeed the founding of Islam. Its history can be traced to the fourth century. The earliest recorded use is in the fourth century when it was applied to the communities of the Church of the East under the Sassanid Persian Empire. This empire's state religion was Zoroastrianism. The Christians formed the Church of the East, whose leader was responsible to the Persian king for the Christians within the Empire. The intention then was to facilitate use of Christian rites of passage such as marriage whilst affirming the loyalty of the Christian communities to the political rulers. These honourable and laudable aspirations are far from the practices seen today: all too often, we see the current versions of the system used as control mechanisms.

So, there is precedent for the adaptation of the system. In recent years there have been a few positive developments. In 2014 the Palestinian Authority removed religion from identity cards although the system remains operative, including restricting who can marry whom. In 2011 Egypt's Supreme Administrative Court issued a decisive ruling allowing people registered as Christian at birth to re-convert to Christian if their registration had been changed to Muslim for any reason.

4.1.2 Majority and minority

We need to redefine the concept of majority and minority, of stronger and weaker communities as assessed numerically. There are numerous examples across the Middle East where those who think of themselves as the majority supress and oppress the minority, e.g. Sunnis supressing Shi'a in Egypt and Saudi Arabia. There are also examples where a minority is the dominating group, for example Bahrain where Sunnis hold all the political power and much of the economic wealth despite being numerically smaller than the Shi'a.

In recent years Syrian Christian leaders have asked an international association of Christians not to refer to their communities as a 'minority'. They point out that no group forms a majority under an ethnic-religious-tribal view of society. Labelling Christians as a minority differentiates them from society as a whole, making them more vulnerable. Instead they request that Syria's Christian communities be described as an integral part of a multi-ethnic and multi-religious society. Segregating society on religious lines is not helpful in their context.

Similarly, some members of Turkey's Christian communities have suggested that it is not helping them to think of themselves as minorities, since it tends to imply that they should be quiet for fear of attracting attention. A more positive and outward looking view is being promoted by some; a view that says Christians are an historic and integral part of society, whose presence enriches the whole (Andrews 2016:73).

So how might we determine who is a majority? An alternative approach was suggested by Dr Martin Accad, who is Lebanese (Accad 2014). He suggested that if one looks for those who desire the best for all fellow citizens, who seek to use their religious belief and practice as a motivation for seeking and serving the common good, then such people would be a clear majority in all countries across the Middle East.

This approach is an appeal to the majority of Muslims to act as agents of change within their own communities so that what is often termed 'the silent majority' is heard. It also amounts to a call for the broadening of interfaith dialogue to include transforming the cultural context for the benefit of all.

Finally, this approach is a direct challenge to the practice of *reconciliation meetings* since it addresses the underlying assumption about one party exploiting and minoritizing the other.

4.2 Applying and enforcing justice equitably

The latest Egyptian constitution was adopted in 2014, the third revision in three years. This is evidence of the political system seeking to be seen to respond to the calls for greater dignity and more and better jobs.

We do need to be clear that how constitutions are understood and operate varies by regional context. The typical Western view is that they are the highest form of law. In contrast, in the Middle East they are seen as statements of aspiration and intent. Consequently, internal tensions are to be avoided at all costs in the West but accepted as normal in the Middle East. (Cf. Andrews 2016:307)

Egypt's 2014 constitution articulates that society should be based on equal citizenship. This is a profound change from the current situation rooted in tribalism and the concept of patronage.

4.2.1 Citizenship-based societies

The need for consistently high policing standards is one aspect of the transition to a society based on citizenship since the clear rule of law applied equally to all is a foundational component. We have seen that *reconciliation meetings* are situations in which the rule of law is overtly suppressed. Article 94 of the 2014 constitution states, "The rule of law is the basis of governance in the state." (Constitute 2017:29) We have seen that *reconciliation meetings* violate this article.

Achieving citizenship-based societies would become more manageable if both top-down and bottom-up approaches were adopted. Top-down requires the president, senior politicians and parliament to assert that this is what is expected. They would need to ensure that governors of all governorates are clear about what is expected. This would need to lead to clear instructions to the heads of law enforcement and the criminal justice system together with a mechanism to hold them accountable. Likewise, the senior figures would need to be clear to their subordinates: those that failed to implement the transition towards citizenship would need to be removed from office.

The bottom-up element is the clear and consistent call of community leaders and the people in general that this is what they expect. The establishment of a mechanism for reporting violations would need to be initiated. In Western contexts such mechanisms can be referred to as whistleblowing.

A report summarising human rights violations of Egyptian Christians in the period 2011 to 2015 notes that, "The starting point to resolve sectarian conflicts should be ... the immediate application of the provisions of the Constitution and the laws related to these conflicts, without discrimination or bias." (EIPR 2015:4)

4.2.2 Honour-shame

In the story of Demiana we asked how the concept of honour and shame was to be applied.

Some differentiate between two types of shame; positive and negative. The former is an awareness of what would be considered shameful and hence needs to be avoided. One example is the concept of modesty in dress, which gives us a sense of what is appropriate attire and what is not.

If the desire for the clear rule of law was present, then it would be seen to be shameful to act in violent ways towards others in the community, including those of different religious persuasions. Then the positive sense of shame would act as a deterrent of resorting to violence.

4.2.3 Egyptian debate on removing religion from identity cards

During 2016 the Egyptian parliament considered legislation to remove religious registration from the state's identity cards. The motive appears to be to reduce discrimination and a step towards implementing the constitution's aspiration for citizenship (al-Monitor 2016a).

It appears that one group in society opposed to the move were church leaders in towns with mixed Christian and Muslim populations. In these locations people wishing to attend church services are required to show their identity cards in order to gain admittance. This self-imposed practice is to ensure that no Muslims – meaning people registered as Muslim – attend, since these church leaders feared that such legislation would be used as an excuse for mob violence against the church building and the Christian community. The ideal response to these concerns would be greater respect for freedom of religion and belief by all and, until that is achieved, effective policing and the maintenance of law and order that effectively addresses mob violence.

4.2.4 Debating divorce law

In 2017 President Sisi remarked that the divorce laws should be changed to give greater equality to women seeking divorce. The religious authority of al-Azhar responded that the current laws were based on the requirements of Shari'a and must be maintained. We might more accurately note that they are based on one interpretation of Shari'a; different interpretations are cited by others. This exchange happened in public, which is to be welcomed. It illustrates the issue as to the balance of power between political and religious bodies in Egypt. Changing the structure of society, the context within which *reconciliation meetings* occur, seems likely to take many years.

4.3 Creating more pluralistic societies

Earlier we remarked on the lack of respect for diversity (see 2.2.1). The Arab Awakening can be regarded as a battle for pluralism (Muasher 2014). The segregation of society on religious lines, enshrined by the religious registration system, effects society as a whole since it underpins discrimination, undermines the clear rule of law applied equally to all and fuels violence. Note the careful language here; it rarely causes violence but, where violence occurs, it exacerbates and intensifies it. Consequently, the religious registration system hinders meeting the aspirations expressed in the Arab Awakening from 2011 onwards. To use a religious and harsher metaphor, it is more of a curse than a blessing (Andrews 2016:327).

Addressing the lack of respect for diversity will require change at several levels. What is the role of the education system? One specific issue for Egypt is its long history. The history curriculum includes ancient Egypt, the Before Common Era period, and then skips across the Christian era very quickly, before picking up from the arrival of Islam in the seventh century. Such a biased approach needs correction. The long-standing presence of Christians in Egypt needs to be acknowledged and affirmed. This would need to be reinforced within the religious education curriculum, which should make clear that religious diversity is a feature of an Egyptian society based on citizenship.

5 Concluding Comments

Reconciliation meetings are a symptom of deeper issues within Egyptian society which affect everyone profoundly. They are an example of the exploitation of some by others, an expression of the absence of a clear rule of law applied equally to all and symptomatic of a pluralism deficit.

Why is Egypt, and the wider Middle East, the way it is? One reason is the profound and widely felt effect of segregation on religious lines, which is enshrined in the religious registration system. For Egypt and the Middle East to flourish, authentic local solutions need to be implemented. Embracing diversity, including religious diversity, as crucial to creative and vibrant social, economic and political activity is essential. The majority, however understood, needs to stop exploiting others. Freedom of religion and belief for all needs to become accepted as fundamentally beneficial to everyone and as an integral aspect of a society based on citizenship.

The practice of *reconciliation meetings* is symptomatic of many of the challenges confronting Egypt: it needs to be brought to an end. Criminal behaviour needs to be treated as such. Community leaders at all levels need to insist that law-and-order and criminal justice systems are effective and applied to all as an essential component of a truly harmonious society.

Bibliography

Accad, M. 2014. *Christians at the Heart of the Middle East's Future*; IMES Blog entry, 2 October 2014; https://imeslebanon.word-press.com/2014/10/02/christians-at-the-heart-of-the-middle-easts-future/ (accessed 15 August 2017)

Andrews, J. 2016. *Identity Crisis – Religious Registration in the Middle East*; Gilead Books Publishing (www.GileadBooksPublishing.com/identity-crisis)

Constitute. 2017. *Egypt's Constitution of 2014*; June 2017; www.constituteproject.org/constitution/Egypt_2014.pdf (accessed 21 August 2017)

Egyptian Initiative for Personal Rights. 2015. *According to Which Customs*; June 2015; https://eipr.org/sites/default/files/reports/pdf/imposing_biased_outcomes.pdf (accessed 16 August 2017)

Ibrahim, H. 2017. *Atheism: a Phenomenon in the Islamic Arab World*; Muslim World Forum operated by Global Connections, London, June 2017

al-Monitor. 2016a. *Will Egypt stop listing religion on official IDs*; 14 June 2016; www.al-monitor.com/pulse/originals/2016/06/egypt-citizenship-draft-religion-discrimination.html (accessed 21 August 2017)

al-Monitor. 2016b. *How do Egypt's official religious authorities view Shiites?*; 12 August 2016; www.al-monitor.com/pulse/originals/2016/08/egypt-divide-sunni-shiites-accusations-abuse-azhar.html (accessed 21 August 2017)

al-Monitor. 2017. *Why did tribes take up arms in Egypt's Sinai?*; 20 August 2017; www.al-monitor.com/pulse/originals/2017/08/egypt-sinai-tribes-arms-army-extremism.html (accessed 21 August 2017)

Muasher, Ma. 2014. *The Second Arab Awakening and the Battle for Pluralism*; Yale University Press

Saenz-Diez, E. 2017. *Freedom of Religion and Belief in Egypt: Official discourse vs. reality on the field*; 28 June 2017; www.blog.sami-aldeeb.com/2017/06/30/freedom-of-religion-and-belief-in-egypt-official-discourse-vs-reality-on-the-field/ (accessed 16 August 2017)

Sennott, C. 2003. *The Body and the Blood* (paperback edition); Public Affairs

Inter- und (verdeckt) transsexuellen Menschen versöhnt begegnen

Martina Kessler

Abstract

This article focuses on the pastoral treatment of intersex and transsexual people. Both intersexuality and transsexuality are reflected. A short questionnaire shows that church-people lack sufficient information about these terms. A model with five facets is introduced: 1. biological identity, 2. sexual identity, 3. sexual orientation, 4. legal gender and 5. cultural expectations.

From the following, the current theological discussion shows that many questions are still open. Since transsexuality is more difficult to grasp and more complex than intersex, theological approaches to it are also difficult. Following the concept of "Toleranz aus Glauben" (Eckstein 2010), a separate theological positioning is derived in order to facilitate reconciliation.

1 Einleitung

Wie können christliche Kirchen und Gemeinschaften inter- und (verdeckt) transsexuellen Menschen versöhnt begegnen? Alle bisherigen Gespräche mit Leiter/-innen aus christlichen Gemeinden und Werken zeigen, dass der Umgang mit der steigenden Anzahl von Intersexuellen, Transsexuellen oder „Trans*Menschen" irritiert.[1] Dieser Artikel bietet, ausgehend von einem Model nach Balswick & Balswick (1999), ein Analysetool, verhilft zur Orientierung, fördert Sprachfähigkeit und bietet eine seelsorgerliche Positionierung, aus denen angemessene Entscheidungen folgen können, damit sich Betroffene in christlichen Gemeinden und Werken angenommen und geborgen erleben. Der alternative theologische Ansatz hilft, in konkreten Situationen ethisch, seelsorgerlich und pragmatisch entscheiden zu können.

Im ersten Abschnitt wird anhand einer begrenzten empirischen Forschung bei christlichen Leiter/-innen die Informationsnotwendigkeit aufgedeckt. In Ab-

---

[1] Unter „christliche Leiter/-innen" sind hier sowohl Geistliche, als auch Leiter/-innen von christlichen Organisationen, wie auch engagierte Laien zusammengefasst.

schnitt zwei werden die wesentlichen Begriffe erläutert. Des Weiteren ist herausgearbeitet, wie inter- und transsexuelle Menschen biologisch, in ihrer sexuellen Identität, der sexuelle Orientierung, bezüglich des rechtsgültigen Geschlechts und im Rahmen kulturspezifischer Erwartungen differenzierter verstanden werden können.

Nachfolgend ist die aktuelle theologische Diskussion aufgegriffen. Daraus geht hervor, dass theologisch noch viele Fragen offen sind. Im Kontext der unterschiedlichen Kirchen wird verschieden angesetzt und liegen unterschiedliche Antworten vor. Da Transsexualität schwieriger zu erfassen und komplexer als Intersexualität ist, ist es auch theologisch schwieriger, hilfreiche Ansätze dazu zu finden. Nach dem Konzept der „Toleranz aus Glauben" wird anschließend eine eigene theologische Positionierung abgeleitet, um Versöhnung zu ermöglichen (in Eckstein 2010). Aber auch danach werden Fragen offen bleiben.

2 Motivation

Theologisch sollten auch Trans- und Intersexualität ausgehend von Genesis 1,27 beleuchtet werden. Dort wird die Erschaffung der Menschen in schöpfungsmäßiger Gottebenbildlichkeit und als zweigeschlechtlich beschrieben.[2] Gottebenbildlichkeit drückt sich also auch gleichzeitig im Mannsein und Frausein aus.

Viele Stellen im Alten Testament zeigen Gott männlich als Vater (5Mo 32,6; Ps 89,27; Ps 68,6; Ps 103,13 u.v.a.m.), aber in einigen Texten ist auch von Gottes weiblichen Attributen die Rede (Gott tröstet wie eine Mutter: Jesaja 66,10-14; Gott hat seine Kinder geboren: Jesaja 42,11; er stillt sie: 4. Mose 11,12; u.a.). Diese Wahrnehmung führte wohl dazu, dass schon der flämische Maler Rembrand (1606-1669) in seinem berühmten Werk „Der verlorene Sohn" Gottvater mit einer männlichen und einer weiblichen Hand darstellte. Gleichzeitig „ist es erstaunlich, dass die Geschlechtsproblematik in vielen theologischen Anthropologien ausgeblendet wird" (Iff 2013:21).

---

[2] „Gott schuf den Menschen zu seinem Bilde, zum Bilde Gottes schuf er ihn und er schuf ihn als Mann und Frau".
Die Gottebenbildlichkeit des Menschen wird in diesem Artikel nicht weiter beleuchtet und als Ausgangsbasis vorangestellt, da die Menschen auch heute als Gottes Ebenbilder auf der Erde leben (vgl. Kessler 2009). Vergleiche zu Zweigeschlechtlichkeit auch Westermann (1974:221 und 2000:33), Wolf (1994:243), Bräumer (2000:28-37) und Oorschot (2000:7-31).

2.1 Fallstudien

Folgende Praxisbeispiele waren der Ausgangspunkt für die Beschäftigung mit diesem Thema:

In einer Gemeinde wurde bekannt, dass eine Frau, die schon länger in der Kinderarbeit mitarbeitet, eine „Geschlechtsumwandlung" vollzogen hatte. Sie wurde umgehend aus der Kinderarbeit entlassen. Daraufhin verließ sie die Gemeinde.

Eine Person will sich als Erwachsene in einer Gemeinde taufen lassen. Dass eine „Geschlechtsumwandlung" stattgefunden hatte, ist bekannt. Nun entsteht aber in der Gemeinde eine große Unsicherheit: Wo soll sich die Person nach dem Taufakt umziehen? Sowohl bei den Männern, als auch bei den Frauen erscheint es unpassend. Die Person verlässt die Gemeinde und suizidiert sich später.

Ein Missionar teilt seiner Familie und der sendenden Missionsgesellschaft mit, dass er fortan als Frau leben will. Alle, Familie und Missionsgesellschaft, sind irritiert und wissen nicht damit umzugehen.

Diese Einzelschicksale zeigen die Unsicherheit und seelsorgerliche Unkenntnis der jeweiligen Leiter/-innen auf. Daher sehe ich es, aus der Arbeit bei der *Akademie für christliche Führungskräfte* und bei der *Stiftung Therapeutische Seelsorge* heraus, als eine Aufgabe, sich mit diesem Thema auseinanderzusetzen.

2.1.1 Empirische Erkenntnisse zum Kenntnisstand von christlichen Leiter/-innen

Um herauszuarbeiten, wie gut Leiter/-innen von Kirchen und Gemeinden tatsächlich über Intersexualität, Transsexualität oder andere genderspezifische Begriffe informiert sind, habe ich 2016 in einer ersten begrenzten Umfrage Pastoren und Absolvent/-innen einer Theologischen Hochschule aus derselben freikirchlichen Denomination nach ihren Kenntnissen zu einzelnen Worten aus der gendertypischen Sprache befragt. Ziel war es, erstens, herauszufinden, wie der aktuelle Kenntnisstand ist, ob es, zweitens, einen Unterschied zwischen Pastoren im Dienst und Hochschulabsolvent/-innen kurz vor Dienstantritt gibt und ob, drittens, die einzelnen Begriffe ihrer Bedeutung gemäß gefüllt werden können.[3]

Von 17 angefragten Pastoren (28-40 und 47 Jahre alt) beteiligten sich 6 an der Befragung. Von 16 Hochschulabsolventen nahmen 7 (5 Männer, 2 Frauen; 25-27 und 37 Jahre alt) an der Befragung teil. Die Beteiligten kamen aus Dörfern und mittelgroßen Städten. Keiner war in einer Großstadt zu Hause.[4] Am Ende der Befragung war vor allem ein Unterschied zwischen den befragten Gruppen zu erkennen: Die Hochschulabsolvent/-innen antworteten insgesamt häufiger, auch wenn die Antwort falsch war. Die Pastoren im Dienst waren zurückhaltender. Alle weiteren Angaben deckten sich in beiden Gruppen so sehr, dass sie im Folgenden gemeinsam dargestellt werden können.

Intersexualität: Da zu diesem Thema verschiedene Begrifflichkeiten im Umlauf sind, wollte ich herausfinden, welcher der folgenden Begriffe verstanden wird.

Intersexualität	4 Leute definieren richtig 9 falsch oder ohne Interpretation
Intergeschlecht-lichkeit	5 Leute definieren richtig 8 falsch oder ohne Angabe
Hermaphroditen	2 definieren richtig. einer falsch, alle anderen äußern sich nicht
Zwitter	12 definieren richtig eine Person äußert sich nicht

Transsexualität: Hierbei haben ähnliche Begriffe unterschiedliche Bedeutungsschwerpunkte. Es ging darum Erkenntnisse dazu zu bekommen, ob die Begriffe im Sinne ihrer Bedeutung verstanden werden.

---

[3] Es handelt sich hierbei nicht um eine umfassende empirische Studie, sondern lediglich um eine Begründung dafür, wie wichtig es ist, christliche Leiter/-innen über das hier behandelte Thema zu informieren.

[4] Da es z. B. in der nordreinwestfälischen Stadt Siegen (ca. 100.000 Bürger/-innen) eine aktive Transsexuellenszene gibt, wäre es gut, wenn christliche Leiter/-innen die Auseinandersetzung mit Inter- und Transsexualität weder bewusst noch unbewusst an Kolleg/-innen aus Großstädten delegieren.

Transsexualität	3 definieren richtig
	10 falsch oder sie äußern sich nicht
Transgender	2 definieren richtig
	11 falsch oder sie äußern sich nicht
Transgeschlecht-lichkeit	5 definieren richtig
	8 falsch oder sie äußern sich nicht
Trans*	2 Pastoren definieren richtig
	11 falsch oder sie äußern sich nicht

Geschlechtsumwandlung vs. Geschlechtsangleichung: Der Begriff Geschlechtsumwandlung wird im Rahmen der Transsexualität als irreführende Begrifflichkeit angesehen, da das Geschlecht in der Selbstwahrnehmung nicht umgewandelt, sondern angeglichen wird. Daher sprechen die Betroffenen lieber von Geschlechtsangleichung, da ein Trans*-Mensch die körperlichen und äußerlichen Geschlechtsmerkmale an die eigene innere Geschlechtsidentität angleichen lässt (Batam :18). Ich wollte wissen, ob den Befragten diese Unterscheidung bekannt ist. Alle Befragten haben den Begriff „Geschlechtsumwandlung" im Sinne des medizinisch vorgenommenen Veränderungsprozesses richtig definiert. Der Begriff „Geschlechtsangleichung" wurde von drei Personen richtig definiert, d. h. die Beschreibungen von 9 Personen waren falsch bzw. unterblieben ganz.

Darüber hinaus wurden drei weitere Begriffe ausgewählt, die im Rahmen der Gendersprache häufig verwendet werden.

Geschlechtsiden-tität	10 definierten richtig
	3 falsch
Transvestitismus	7 definierten richtig oder teilweise richtig
	6 (teilweise) falsch oder sie äußerten sich nicht
Queer identity	3 definieren richtig
	2 definieren falsch
	8 äußern sich nicht

Offen bleibt bei dieser Befragung, ob das Wissen der Pastoren und Hochschulabsolvent/-innen dem der Bevölkerung entspricht oder ob es möglicherweise doch einen Wissensvorsprung gibt.[5]

3 Intersexualität und Transsexualität verstehen

Um die Begriffe im Sinne der Inter- und Transsexuellenbewegung verstehen zu können, bedarf es einiger Begriffsdefinition.

3.1 Begriffsdefinitionen

3.1.1 Intersexualität

Menschen, die „geschlechtlich dazwischen" sind, werden als Intersexuelle (ältere Bezeichnungen sind Hermaphroditen oder Zwitter) bezeichnet. Intersexuelle Menschen bevorzugen den Begriff „Intergeschlechtlichkeit", da es nicht um das Thema Sexualität, sondern um das Thema Geschlechtlichkeit geht. Eine eindeutige körperliche Zuordnung zum männlichen oder weiblichen Geschlecht ist dabei nicht möglich (Schieferdecker 2016:7). Daimond (2016:43-54) unterscheidet zwei Typen (offensichtlich so Geborene und verborgene Intersexualität) und 20 Formen von Intersexualität. Andere unterscheiden im Rahmen der DSD-Klassifikation (Differences of sex development) drei (Deutsches Ärzteblatt 2015) oder vier (Raedel 2016, Zentrale Deutscher Kliniken 2016) Klassifikationen. Laut Schätzung der Bundesregierung sind 8000 Deutsche, also 0,01%, als Intersexuelle geboren. Interessengruppen gehen von weit höheren Zahlen aus (Kuby 2012:156). Nach Iff (2013:18) werden in Deutschland pro Jahr 1400-2800 Neugeborene geschlechtsuneindeutig geboren (vgl. auch die Stellungnahme des Deutschen Ethikrates 2012). Nach Strüvel (2008) sind es 160 Personen im Jahr. Eine wirklich stabile Zahlenangabe liegt also nicht vor.

Seit dem 01.11.2013 sind Eltern und medizinisches Personal in Deutschland nicht mehr verpflichtet, einem Baby mit uneindeutigen Geschlechtsmerkmalen ein Geschlecht zuzuweisen. Die Diagnose „Intersexualität" kann, wenn überhaupt, nur durch eine Chromosomenanalyse erfolgen (Zentrale Deutscher Kli-

---

[5] Ein Teilnehmer der internationalen Christian Leadership Conference erklärte bei der Diskussion zum hier ausgeführten Thema, dass er, obwohl er schon viele Jahre Aktivist für die Schwulenbewegung war, auf die Themen Inter- und/oder Transsexualität erst 2015 gestoßen sei.

niken 2016). Das komplizierte Zusammenspiel von Hormonen bleibt dabei jedoch unberücksichtigt, ebenso wie andere körperliche Gegebenheiten wie z. B. die gleichzeitige Anlage von Ovarien und Gonaden.

3.1.2 Transsexualität

Bei der Transsexualität stehen sich geschlechtliche Faktoren gegenüber (Schieferdecker 2016:8). Auch hier geht es nicht um ein Problem bei der Sexualität, sondern um die Geschlechtsidentität, da die betroffenen Personen sich nicht mit dem ihnen bei der Geburt zugewiesenen Geschlecht identifizieren können. Die Bezeichnung „Transsexualität" wird als medizinische Bezeichnung von den Betroffenen zumeist ablehnt. Diese bevorzugen:

Transgeschlechtlichkeit. Dabei weicht das körperliche Erscheinungsbild vom inneren Empfinden ab. Manche verstehen sich als „weder Frau noch Mann" (also als Intersexuelle) und lehnen solche Kategorien gänzlich ab.

Transgender. Mit dieser Bezeichnung werden die sozialen Aspekte des Geschlechts betont.

Häufig wird als Oberbegriff *Trans** gebraucht, weil es für eine Vielzahl von Geschlechtsidentitäten stehen kann – also für mehr als nur Frau und nur Mann.

Die Häufigkeit von Transsexualität liegt zwischen 1:10.000 bis 1:30.000 bei Mann-zu-Frau, also bei 3.000 bis 8.000 Personen in Deutschland, und bei Frau-zu-Mann bei 1:15.000 bis 1:100.000, also bei 800 bis 5.300 Deutschen. Andere Schätzungen sprechen von 1:1000 bis 1:2500 bereits erfolgter Transgender-Transitionen. Dann wäre von 32.000 und 80.000 (also ca. 0,1 %) transsexuellen Menschen in Deutschland auszugehen (Conway 2016).

3.2 Psychische Komponenten durch körperliche Ursachen

Weibliche Gehirne haben typischerweise eine bessere Sprachfähigkeit. Das führt dazu, dass Frauen sozialer und familienorientierter sind (vgl. Swaab, Castellano-Cruz & Boa 2016:26). Männliche Gehirne haben typischerweise ein größeres räumliches Vorstellungsvermögen (Solms 2016:5-22). So bewirkt Testosteron, dass Mädchen schon einen Tag nach der Geburt ihren Blick länger auf Gesichtern halten und Jungen auf beweglichen Teilen (Swaab, Castellanos-Cruz & Boa, 9016:23-42). Bei angeborener Nebennierenhyperplasie ist die Produktion von Testosteron vermehrt. Dies beeinflusst auch das Gehirn von betroffenen Mädchen. Betroffene zeigen im Alter von 4-5 Jahren eher maskulines Verhalten und sind durchschnittlich wilder als andere Mädchen (Daimond 2016:43-54). Wird Testosteron produziert, aber nicht aufgenommen, fühlen sich die Menschen jedoch möglicherweise weiblich. In Gehirnen von Mann-zu-Frau-Transsexuellen sind die Neuronenmengen typisch weiblich, bei Frau-zu-Mann-Menschen typisch männlich (Swaab, Castellanos-Cruz & Boa, 33-34).

Die in der Literatur beschriebene Geschichte von Bruce/Brenda/David Reimer zeigt eins klar auf: Das Gehirn kann man nicht einfach ändern, denn Brenda nahm das ihr im Alter von 22 Monaten zugewiesene Geschlecht nicht an.[6]

3.3 Pränatale Entwicklung

Problematisch ist, dass Inter- und Transsexualität nicht immer klar voneinander abzugrenzen sind. So kann es sein, dass Menschen, die wie Transsexuelle wirken, tatsächlich Intersexuelle sind. Wenngleich der Genotyp im Moment der Empfängnis bestimmt wird (XX oder XY), wird die Frage des Geschlechtes in komplexen Prozessen biologisch entschieden (Solms 2016:5). Bei diesen Prozessen kann es zu Anomalien kommen, die bei der Geburt äußerlich nicht sichtbar sind, da die Ausformung der äußeren Geschlechtsmerkmale im ersten Schwangerschaftstrimenon stattfindet und die Blut-Hirn-Schranke für Testosteron jedoch erst im zweiten Schwangerschaftstrimenon (ab der 14. SSW) überwunden wird. Das bedeutet, dass das Gehirn eines äußerlich männlichen Kindes erst im zweiten Schwangerschaftstrimenon vermännlicht und sich das Corpus Colosum dann kleiner und das Gehirn und die Hypophyse größer ausbilden.[7]

---

[6] Bruce Reimer, geboren 1965, erlitt als sieben Monate alter Junge (ein eineiiger Zwilling) bei einem medizinischen Eingriff eine unwiderrufliche Penisverstümmelung. Die Experten beschlossen mit den Eltern zusammen, aus ihm ein Mädchen, Brenda, zu machen. Die Operation wurde von John Money ab dem 22. Lebensmonat vorgenommen und anschließend die Veränderung pädagogisch und medizinisch konsequent umgesetzt. „Der transformierte Zwilling hatte vor der Pubertät und bevor man ihn mit seiner Sexualgeschichte konfrontiert hatte, massive Schwierigkeiten mit seiner weiblichen Rolle". Mit 18 Jahren ließ er sich einen Penis und ein Skrotum nachbilden, lebte als David und heiratete später eine Frau. Obwohl Brenda wie ein Mädchen aussah und auch so erzogen wurde, reichte das nicht aus, um sich als Frau zu verstehen. Am 4. Mai 2004 beendete David Reimer sein Leben (Pool 1996:212; Wikipedia 2016:David Reimer; Swaab, Castellanos-Cruz & Boa 2016:24-25).

[7] Auch bei eineiigen Zwillingen sind die Gehirne bei der Geburt schon unterschiedlich, weil sich Gehirne selbst organisieren. Das Gehirn ist ein selbstorganisierter Organismus (ähnlich wie bei Schwärmen). Bsp: Siamesische Zwillinge (zwei Köpfe, ein Körper, jede ein Arm, ein Bein): „Wir sind zwei unterschiedliche Menschen!" So ist eben jeder Mensch einzigartig (Solms 2016:6).

Weitere Ursachen für Transsexualität vermutet Swaab in der Geschwisterfolge: jüngere Brüder von Brüdern hätten vermutlich höhere Chancen transsexuell zu werden, weil die Mutter Antikörper gegen Männliches gebildet habe, und auch die soziale Umwelt könne als Ursache gelten. Dazu gebe es aber keine Forschungsresultate. Swaab resümiert: 50% der Faktoren seien genetisch, dazu kämen Hormoneinflüsse, Einflüsse durch Kunststoffe, Rauchen und Geschwisterkonstellation. Außerdem mache die Natur keine Fehler. Alle Anomalien können auch als Variabilität betrachtet werden. Nach Swaab können Menschen nicht entscheiden, homo-, bi- oder heterosexuell zu werden. Das alles werde vom Gehirn gesteuert (Swaab, Castellanos-Cruz, Boa 2016:41).

3.4 Das 5-Facettenmodell – oder: Wie Trans*Menschen verstanden werden können

Um die fünf Dimensionen des Geschlechtsempfindens verstehen zu können, schlage ich ein ausgebautes Modell vor; wohl wissend, dass sowohl Männer, als auch Frauen allesamt keine reine Ausprägung eines Wesens sind, sondern in der Regel individuell mit männlichen und weiblichen Anteilen leben (Iff 2013:36).

Ausgang ist das Modell von Balswick und Balswick (1999), die vier Dimensionen der Sexualität beschreiben:

Natal sex: angeborene physiologische und biologische Eigenschaften, an denen sich entscheidet, ob ein Baby männlich oder weiblich ist.

Sexual identity: Eigenwahrnehmung einer Person, sich als sexuelles Wesen zu verstehen.

Gender role: kulturspezifische Identifikation innerhalb einer bestimmten Kultur inklusive der Fragen zur Gesprächsführung, zu Ausdrucksweisen, Bewegung, Kleidung und Stereotypen.

Sexual orientation: erotische Ausrichtung: Ist ein Mensch heterosexuell, homosexuell oder bisexuell ausgerichtet?

Durch die Veränderungen in den letzten zehn Jahren ist dieses Modell m. E. um die Dimension des rechtsgültigen Geschlechts zu erweitern. Außerdem ist die Dimension der *gender role* inzwischen flexibler lebbar. In Deutschland ist es zum Beispiel für Männer und Frauen heute eher möglich, sich kulturspezifisch frei zu positionieren. Als ich ein Kind war, galt es z. B. für Frauen unschicklich, einen Traktor zu fahren. Frauen, die das machten, galten als „Mannweib". Ebenso war es z. B. für Männer ein Tabu, Geschirr abzutrocknen.

Ein Mann, der das tat, galt als „Waschlappen" und als frauendominiert. Ebenso erinnere ich mich an Kämpfe für einen Kurzhaarschnitt bei Frauen und für „typische Männer-Hosen". Heute sind die Kleidung, die Wahl des Berufs, die Haartracht und vieles andere nicht mehr geschlechtsspezifisch vorgegeben. Allerdings ist gleichzeitig zu beachten, dass Menschen, die ihre äußere Erscheinung komplett verändern, um es ihrem innerlich empfundenen Geschlecht anzugleichen, mit durchaus drastischen Konsequenzen zu rechnen haben.[8] Daher wird die kulturspezifische Ebene, die durch die vorherrschende Kultur eines Landes geprägt ist, als eine von außen gegebene Ebene auch als solche dargestellt. Dabei scheint mir die bekannte Darstellung von männlich und weiblich (♂, ♀) den Ansprüchen nicht mehr zu genügen, weil sich damit die Veränderungen einzelner Dimensionen des Geschlechtsempfindens nicht abbilden lassen.

Der Mensch, der sich auf der kulturspezifischen Ebene (*gender role*) relativ frei positionieren oder bewegen kann, dessen Sexualität häufig durch das biologische Geschlecht bestimmt ist, das rechtsgültige Geschlecht, die sexuelle Identität (*sexual identity*) und die sexuelle Orientierung (*sexual orientation*). Bei einem heterosexuellen Menschen sind biologisches Geschlecht (*natal sex*), rechtsgültiges Geschlecht und sexuelle Identität kongruent. Die sexuelle Orientierung ist auf das andere Geschlecht ausgerichtet.

---

[8] Das Heft „*Trans* in der Arbeit". Fragen und Antworten*" (Batam) ist deshalb als Hilfe für Trans*-Personen geschrieben, die Diskriminierung erleiden.

242

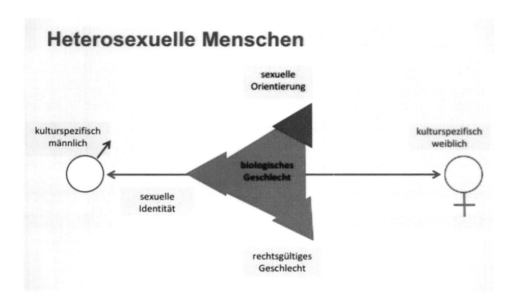

Heterosexuelle Menschen

sexuelle
Orientierung

kulturspezifisch
männlich

kulturspezifisch
weiblich

biologisches
Geschlecht

sexuelle
Identität

rechtsgültiges
Geschlecht

Abbildung 1: Heterosexuelle Person. [9]

Bei homosexuellen Menschen unterscheidet sich alleine die sexuelle Orientierung, welche dem eigenen Geschlecht zugeneigt ist. Der unter dem Künstlernamen Conchita Wurst bekanntgewordene, homosexuelle Thomas Neuwirth gewann 2014 den Eurovision Song Contest.[10] Als Travestiekünstler tritt er mit markant männlichem Bart und zugleich mit langem, feminisiertem Haar, feminin gekleidet und weiblich geschminkt auf. Er spielt in der Öffentlichkeit mit

---

[9] In dem hier favorisierten Modell ist das biologische Geschlecht der Ausgang für das rechtsgültige Geschlecht, welches zumeist bei der Geburt dokumentiert wird. Die sexuelle Identität, die sich ca. im 2. Lebensjahr entwickelt und die sexuelle Orientierung sind dann dem biologischen Geschlecht gleich. In der Darstellung wird Gleiches jeweils mit der gleichen Farbtönung dargestellt. D.h., wenn das biologische Geschlecht, das rechtsgültige Geschlecht und die sexuelle Identität gleich sind, dann werden sie auch in der gleichen Schattierung dargestellt. Bei einem heterosexuellen Menschen ist dann nur die Farbe bei der sexuellen Orientierung anders, weil diese eben zum anderen Geschlecht hin ausgerichtet ist.

[10] Conchita (kleine Muschel) ist ein spanischer Frauenvorname. Wird er in Großbuchstaben geschrieben, ist er ein Verweis auf die Jungfrau Maria und derer unbefleckten Empfängnis. Wird das Wort klein geschrieben, ist es ein Kosewort für die Vulva.

der zur Schau gestellten sexuellen Identität und präsentiert sich – und nur dann – als „Sowohl-als-auch".

Während bei heterosexuellen und homosexuellen Menschen vom biologischen Geschlecht (mit eindeutigen vorhandenen Geschlechtsmerkmalen) gesprochen werden kann, empfiehlt es sich bei Intersexuellen von äußeren Geschlechtsmerkmalen zu reden, die eben uneindeutig sein können. Die sexuelle Identität ist individuell entwickelt und prägt die (unbekannte) sexuelle Orientierung mit.[11] Das rechtsgültige Geschlecht bleibt, wenn die Geburt nach 2013 war, ebenfalls offen.

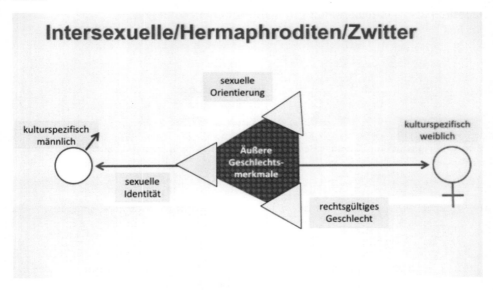

Abbildung 2: Intersexuelle Person/Hermaphrodit/Zwitter.

Andere Menschen bezeichnen sich als transsexuell, könnten aber nach den Erkenntnissen der pränatalen Entwicklung auch intersexuell sein. So wuchs Dorothea Zwölfer als Andreas Zwölfer auf und erklärte ihrer evangelischen Gemeinde 2011 „Ich bin eine transsexuelle Frau" (Potzel 2015). Frau Zwölfer ist verheiratet und ihre Frau ist ebenfalls Pfarrerin. Beide haben einen gemeinsamen Sohn. Frau Zwölfer lebte fast 50 Jahre als heterosexueller Mann. Verändert haben sich die sexuelle Identität und, daraus folgend, das rechtsgültige Geschlecht. Bei einer Konferenz zu „Transsexualität. Eine gesellschaftliche Her-

---

[11] Daher werden diese in der folgenden Graphik ohne Farbgebung dargestellt.

ausforderung im Gespräch zwischen Theologie und Neurowissenschaft" formulierte Frau Zwölfer (2016), dass geschlechtsangleichende Maßnahmen geplant sein. Dann spätestens müsste, statt vom biologischen Geschlecht, von äußeren Geschlechtsmerkmalen die Rede sein.

Noch komplexer ist, was am 09.09.2013 in deutschen Zeitungen zu lesen war: „Das Baby-Wunder des Jahres. Berliner Mann bringt Baby zur Welt" (Bild 2013). Die Süddeutsche Zeitung (2013) titelte „Der schwangere Mann. Väterinnen auf dem Vormarsch: Das ist weniger eine Frage der Medizin als der Psyche". Eine genetische XY-Person, der Selbstempfindung nach ein Mann und rechtlich als Mann anerkannt gilt als weiblicher Mann (Focus 2013).[12]

Bild 1: Beispielhaft hier Thomas Beatie, USA, mit seiner Familie (static.bz-berlin 2013).

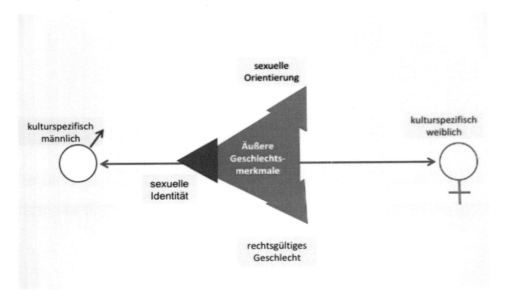

---

[12] In den USA hat bereits 2009 ein Mann, Thomas Beatie, ein zweites Kind zur Welt gebracht (N24 2009).

Abbildung 3: 1. Phase: die sexuelle Identität entspricht nicht den äußeren Geschlechtsmerkmalen.

Dann folgte eine äußere Geschlechtsangleichung und Namensänderung:[13]

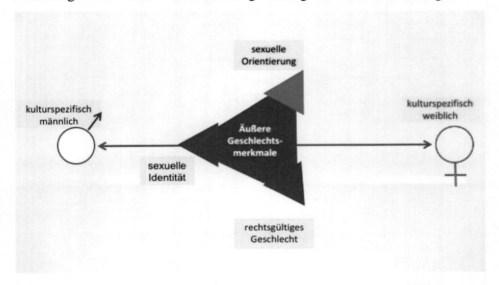

Abbildung 4: 2. Phase: äußere Geschlechtsmerkmale und rechtsgültig Geschlecht werden der sexuellen Identität angepasst.

Mit der Schwangerschaft verändert sich das Bild noch einmal:

---

[13] Die inneren geschlechtstypischen Organe sind davon aber nicht zwingend betroffen. Demzufolge kann eine Person mit den äußerlichen Geschlechtsorganen eines Mannes nach wie vor einen funktionsfähigen Uterus haben und bei entsprechend hormoneller Unterstützung ein Kind austragen.

246

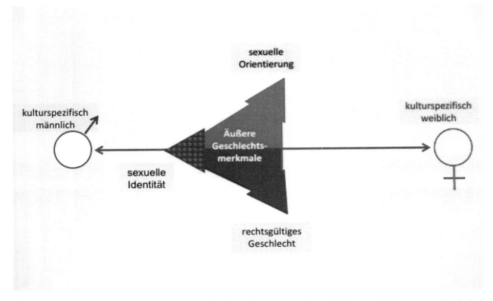

Abbildung 5: 3. Phase: die sexuelle Identität ist wegen der sichtbaren Schwangerschaft bei deutlich männlichem Aussehen uneindeutig geworden.

Rechtsgültig ist es also korrekt, dass ein Mann ein Baby zur Welt bringt kann. Gleichzeitig verwirren solche Meldungen.

Eine noch andere Situation zeigt Norrie aus Australien, die mehrere Jahre vor Gericht dafür gekämpft hat, offiziell als Neutrum zu gelten. Sie sagt von sich: „Untenrum bin ich eine Barbie, oben ein Ken". „Wer über sie spricht, soll `zie´ anstelle des englischen er (he) oder sie (she) und 'hir' statt sein (his) oder ihr (her)" sagen und den Namen Norrie benutzen (Bubrowski 2014). So bleiben sowohl ihre äußeren Geschlechtsmerkmale, als auch ihr rechtsgültiges Geschlecht und ihre sexuelle Identität bewusst verborgen.

3.5 Schlussfolgerungen

Die meisten Menschen werden mit XX-Chromosomen oder XY-Chromosomen und mit den dazugehörigen Hormonen (wenngleich es viele Variationen gibt) geboren und leben in Kongruenz mit ihrem Geschlecht. Manche Menschen werden als offensichtlich Intersexuelle geboren. Andere werden mit einer verborgenen Intersexualität, die nach außen wie eine Transsexualität wirkt, geboren und die erst bei einer Obduktion des Gehirns nachgewiesen werden kann. Diese Menschen werden mit den äußeren Geschlechtsmerkmalen eines Mannes oder einer Frau geboren, fühlen sich aber falsch in ihrem Körper – äußerlich sichtbare Geschlechtsmerkmale und das gefühlte Geschlecht sind inkongruent. Auch wenn man berücksichtigt, dass Transsexualität psychische Gründe haben kann, so bleibt die Tatsache, dass es auch die Folge einer intrauterinen Fehlentwicklung sein kann, die zu Lebzeiten eines Menschen nicht nachgewiesen werden kann.

Kritisch anzumerken ist, dass innerhalb der Transsexuellenbewegung jeder psychische Einfluss der Geschlechtsentwicklung zur Transsexualität hin ausgeschlossen wird. Kunert fordert dazu auf, in erster Linie darüber nachzudenken, was man verhindern dürfe, und nicht in den Vordergrund zu stellen, was gestattet werden dürfe. Alltagstests und Begutachtungen oder Psychotherapiezwang bezeichnet Haupt (2016:75-122) als unmenschlich, entwürdigend und als Diskriminierungsform, weil damit Transsexualität psychopathologisiert werde (Kunert 2016:597-634). Nicolosie (2011) schreibt hingegen, dass es zwar glaubwürdige biologische Einflüsse geben könnte, die *möglicherweise* die vorgeburtliche Entwicklung betreffen, dies aber eine eher seltene biologische Entwicklungsstörung sei. Eher könne davon ausgegangen werden, dass eine Bindungsstörung auch als Geschlechtsidentitätsstörung zu Tage trete, die sich bereits in der frühen Kindheit zeige. So seien Geschlechtsidentitätsstörungen nach wie vor bei der Klassifikation psychischer Erkrankungen, und die unter die Störung der Geschlechtsidentität im Kindesalter (F61.2) fallen, anerkannt.

4 Theologische Diskussion

Wenn Transsexualität neurologisch korreliert, dann dürfe man nicht von einer psychischen Erkrankung sprechen, wie es zurzeit noch geschehe (Ohley 2016:533-556, vgl. Krollner & Krollner 2016). Denn dann handelt es sich um verdeckte Intersexualität. Intersexualität soll als individuelle Variation verstanden werden (und folglich nicht als Krankheit), die eine komplexe Situation hervorbringt und biologische, psychologische und soziale Dimensionen hat (aus einer Stellungnahme des Deutschen Ethikrats 2012). Beides hat auch theologische Dimensionen, denen im Folgenden nachgegangen wird.

Die theologische Diskussion bezüglich (verdeckter) Inter- und Transsexualität ist erst am Anfang, ist aber ebenso komplex, wie es die Sachverhalte sind. Daher bedarf es, gerade im Zusammenhang mit Transsexualität, einer differenzierten Auseinandersetzung (Schreiber 2016:XIII-XXI).

Von liberaltheologischer Seite werden die theologischen Antworten zur Inter- und Transsexualität vermischt und oft aus dem Umgang mit Homosexualität adaptiert. Dem gegenüber steht die ebenso undifferenzierte Ablehnung der gesamten Genderforschung als absurde Ideologie. Zwei, in theologisch konservativen Kreisen populäre Bücher sind Kelle (2015), „GenderGaga: Wie eine absurde Ideologie unseren Alltag erobern will" und Klenk (2015), „Gender Mainstreaming: Das Ende von Mann und Frau?". Mit Bezug auf Genesis 1,27 werden alle Denkansätze der Genderforschung vom Tisch gewischt und neuere medizinische Forschungsergebnisse nicht wahrgenommen, verschwiegen oder abgelehnt.

Hier, wie da, wird nützliche Genderforschung mit der Ideologie sexueller Vielfalt vermischt. Die Konsequenz ist, dass die einen sexuelle Vielfalt durch Genderforschung fördern und die anderen beides absolut ablehnen. In der Tat ist die gesellschaftliche Unterwanderung, die sich vor allem das Ziel der sexuellen Vielfalt auf die Fahnen geschrieben hat, massiv.[14] Gleichzeitig erscheint mir die Vermischung auf beiderlei Seiten höchst problematisch, denn es sollte weder hilfreiche Genderforschung als Vehikel einer Ideologie der sexuellen Vielfalt missbraucht werden, noch sollten neue Forschungsergebnisse abgelehnt werden, weil man die Gefahr einer Ideologisierung fürchtet.

Im Folgenden werden nun verschiedene theologische Positionen dargestellt, um dann in einer alternativen theologischen Positionierung, Hilfestellung für christliche Kirchen/Gemeinden und Werke geben zu können, damit diese mit inter- oder transsexuellen Menschen einen menschlich und geistlich hilfreichen Umgang finden können.

4.1 Intersexualität und Theologie

Speziell zum Umgang mit Intersexualität in der Theologie gibt es im angelsächsischen Raum einige Veröffentlichungen, wie den Sammelband der Theologie Cornwall (2015) oder die Monographie von DeFranza (2015a) die ich zur weiteren Lektüre empfehle. Beispielhaft werden im Folgenden verschiedene Ansätze skizziert.

Die als konservativ geltende Theologin DeFranza (2015b) argumentiert, dass alle Menschen nach dem Bild Gottes – männlich, weiblich und intersexuell – geschaffen sind und dass es deshalb von Intersexuellen zu lernen gelte. Dabei

---

[14] Das ist besonders heikel, weil gerade die Erziehung von Kindern zur sexuellen Vielfalt hin ein Ziel zu sein scheint. Auf dem Bildungsserver Berlin-Brandenburg (2016) findet man dazu reichlich „Unterrichtsmaterial – sexuelle Vielfalt". Die hierzu unbedingt notwendige Diskussion muss allerdings an anderer Stelle geführt werden.

geht sie von den in der Bibel beschriebenen Eunuchen als biblische Ressource aus (siehe auch Marchal 2015:29-54, Hare 2015:79-98). Aus Respekt für die spezifischen und dringenden Fragen intersexueller Menschen sollen Akademiker die Debatte zur sexuellen Ethik übernehmen. Gleichzeitig will sie verhindern, dass die Anstrengungen der konservativ-religiösen Traditionen zur Bildung, Integration und medizinischer Versorgung für intersexuelle Personen untergraben werden, indem man Intersexualität einfach als eine weitere Farbe im Regenbogen der queeren Sexualtäten betrachtet. Die Interpretation der Intersexualität mit der Queer-Theologie versäume es, die Vielfalt der religiösen Perspektiven unter intersexuellen Personen zu erkennen. Da intersexuelle Menschen eine Vielzahl religiöser Hintergründe haben, und einige auch eine konservative Ethik vertreten, stehen sie trotzdem vor den Herausforderungen, die Intersexualität mit sich bringt. Daher sollten zeitgenössische Christen die komplexen und konfliktreichen Herausforderungen von Intersexualität heute überdenken.

Weitere Ansätze gehen z. B. von der Rolle der Religion auf dem Weg zu Gesundheit und Wohlbefinden aus oder erforschen Intersexualität auf der Erde und im Himmel (Kerry 2015:121-146, Jung 2015:173-196). Jung sieht einen Zusammenhang zwischen der Taufverkündigung in Galater 3,28 und der Christologie, in welcher durch Gottes Gnade Andersartiges eingebunden werden kann (:186). In Christus sind alle eingeladen sich selbst zu erkennen und im Anderen den von Gott geliebten Menschen zu sehen, um so von der Trennung zur Gemeinschaft zu kommen. Denn auch zukünftig, in der Herrlichkeit, werde nicht mehr sexuell differenziert (:163).

Der konservative, deutsche, systematische Theologe Raedel geht von der biologischen Seite aus und sucht theologische Lösungen mit der Anerkennung biologischer Gegebenheiten. Er sieht Intersexuelle als von Gott geliebt und zur Gemeinschaft mit Christus Berufene, die „in der christlichen Gemeinde grundsätzlich durch Glaube und Taufe" Mitglied der Gemeinde werden und in dieser auch mitarbeiten können (Raedel 2015a:152). Sie sollten „(a) ihre spezifische Leibsignatur annehmen lernen und (b) der *Lehre* zustimmen können, dass Gottes ursprüngliche Absicht für den Menschen die Identität als Mann oder Frau ist." (Raedel 2015b).

Weiter formuliert Raedel (2016), dass eine Ehe nur als Bund zwischen einem Mann und einer Frau als einzigem Ort für gottgewollte Sexualität gutgeheißen werden könne. Für Intersexuelle, die eine Ehe eingehen wollten, bedeute dies,

„dass sie sich *stimmig* in einem der beiden Geschlechter beheimaten (können) und die Paar-Konstellation im Ergebnis heterosexuell ist. Intersexuelle haben hier, einfach ausgedrückt, etwas mehr 'Spielraum'". Sie müssten allerdings sicherstellen, dass im Fall der Fortpflanzung,[15] der Ehepartner mit weiblicher Identität das Kind bekomme.[16]

4.2 Transsexualität und Theologie

Während es einige theologische Veröffentlichungen zum Umgang mit Intersexualität gibt, war bisher keine theologische Positionierung zu finden, die sich allein auf Transsexualität bezieht. Das war in der Theologie bisher kein Thema (Klatt 2016).[17] Der evangelische Systematiker Schreiber formuliert: „... dass es schlicht nichts gibt seitens Theologie und Kirche: keine Stellungnahmen, keine theologischen Expertisen zum Umgang mit transsexuellen Menschen als Teil der Gesellschaft. Und auch nicht als Teil der kirchlichen Gemeinschaft. Das ist ein bedauerliches Desiderat". Als erste wissenschaftliche Veröffentlichung gilt daher im deutschsprachigen Raum das Buch „Transsexualität in Theologie und Neurowissenschaften" (Schreiber 2016), welches aus dem Kongress „Transsexualität. Eine gesellschaftliche Herausforderung im Gespräch zwischen Theologie und Neurowissenschaft" hervorging und aus welchem hier bereits mehrfach zitiert wurde.[18] Nun ist es in diesem Werk allerdings auch nicht gelungen, Transsexualität singulär in den Focus zu nehmen. In fast allen Artikeln werden Intersexualität und Transsexualität vermischt und dazu ein gemeinsames Resümee gezogen, bei dem dazu immer wieder auf den Umgang mit Homosexualität zurückgegriffen wird.

Darüber hinaus ist unter den Suchbegriffen „Transsexualität" und „Theologie" eine einzige Veröffentlichung einer Pfarrerin zu finden, die ihren persönlichen Weg vom Mann zur Frau unter dem Angesicht Gottes darstellt als „ein spiritueller Weg der Gottesbegegnung und Menschwerdung" (Bergmann 2011).[19]

---

[15] Intersexuelle sind nicht automatisch unfruchtbar.

[16] Das entspricht im Moment auch deutschem Recht, dass nur eine Frau als Mutter eines Kindes anerkannt werden kann.

[17] Dies wurde auch in einem Gespräch am 10. November 2016 von dem Systematiker Iff an der Theologischen Hochschule Ewersbach bestätigt.

[18] Der Kongress fand vom 04.-06.02.2016 an der Goethe Universität Frankfurt statt.

[19] Interessant ist in dem Zusammenhang außerdem, dass der Weg vom *Mann* zur *Frau* beschrieben wird – also doch binär und festgelegt gedacht wird.

4.3 Intersexualität und Transsexualität in der Theologie

Der katholische Moraltheologe Schockenhoff und Systematiker Dabrock
nähern sich der Inter- und Transsexualität über die Homosexualität. Dabei sieht
Schockenhoff in der Zweigeschlechtlichkeit ein Grundmuster der Bibel, das jedoch von den Menschen individuell ausgelebt werden kann, denn jeder Mensch
sei gottebenbildlich geschaffen (Schockenhoff 2016:565-576). Das dürfe nicht
bewertet werden. Wesentliche Faktoren seien u.a. Freundschaft und Treue. Wo
immer Promiskuität und Mehrfachbeziehungen gelebt würden, sei es problematisch – gleich in welchem Körper. Für Dabrock können LGBTIQA-Formen
nicht mit biblischen Argumenten abgelehnt werden, weil diese in der Bibel nicht bekannt waren.[20] Eine Grundperspektive müsse es sein, den liebenden Gott
in einer verkrümmten Welt zu sehen. Deshalb müssten menschliche Erfahrun-
gen ernst genommen werden. Theologische Normen, die auf Schöpfungsord-
nungen und Fortpflanzung pochten, seinen letztlich nicht christlich (Dabrock
2016:505-516).

Der katholische Moraltheologe Goertz (2016:506-517) nähert sich den „Theologien des transsexuellen Leibes" ausschließlich aus der Perspektive des sexuellen Vollzugs und der damit einhergehenden Zeugungsfähigkeit und folgert,
dass daraus ethisch keine Schlüsse gezogen werden können. Das Sollen sei „im
absoluten Wert der Person, also in ihrer Freiheit, nicht in irgendwelchen Tatsa-
chen ihrer Natur begründet" (:530).[21] Als Mann und Frau geschaffen zu sein
(mit Verweis auf Gen. 1,27) ziele auf Liebesfähigkeit, von der vielleicht der
biblische Text nichts wisse, wohl aber die menschliche Erfahrung und diese sei
sowohl heterosexuellen als auch transsexuellen Menschen zugänglich (:531).
Nicht die menschliche Fortpflanzungsfähigkeit zeichne den Menschen als
sexuelles Wesen aus, sondern die Umsetzung auf menschliche, also personale
Weise (:532).

---

[20] „L" - lesbians; „G" - gays; „B" - bisexuals; „T" - transgender people; „I" - intersex
people; „Q" - queer and questioning people; „A" - asexual people and allies.

[21] Hier zeigt sich auch die innerkirchliche Diskussion in der katholischen Kirche. Goertz resümiert, dass seine Kirche „erst dann zu einer neuen Sicht auf das Phänomen der
Transsexualität kommen kann", wenn sie sich von „ihrer bisherigen sittlichen Bewertung
der Sexualität von Transsexuellen" löst (Goertz 2016:532).

5 Eine alternative theologische Positionierung

Die bisher beschriebenen, noch jungen Ansätze verdienen eine kritisch-würdigende Anerkennung. Gleichzeitig gestalten sich diese Ansätze schwierig. Eine theologische Betrachtung von (verdeckter) Inter- und Transsexualität muss differenziert geschehen und es ist notwendig, dass theologische Maßstäbe angeboten werden. Zugleich:

- Die Suche nach dem im Einzelfall richtigen oder falschen Umgang mit der facettenreichen, individuellen (verdeckten) Inter- oder Transsexualität erscheinen ebenso wenig zielführend, wie eine undifferenzierte, verallgemeinernde Gesamtsicht, egal ob diese nun fördernd oder ablehnend ist.

- Bei transsexuellen Menschen ist es nicht ohne weiteres erkennbar, ob es sich nicht tatsächlich um intersexuelle Menschen handelt. Deshalb kann nicht von jedem/jeder Christen/-in erwartet werden, dass er/sie sich in die Einzelheiten der (verdeckten) Inter- und Transsexualität so vertieft, damit er/sie dem einzelnen Menschen gerecht werden kann. Wohl aber, dass sie, um der Mitmenschen willen, bereit sind, differenziert zu denken, überlegt zu handeln und dass sie etwas nicht nur deshalb ablehnen, weil es ihnen fremd ist oder exotisch auf sie wirkt. Es ist fragwürdig, wenn beispielsweise christliche Leiter/-innen meinen, ein Recht auf das Offenlegen sexueller Praktiken oder Möglichkeiten zu haben und darüber hinaus auch noch meinen, diese bewerten zu können.

- Es ist weder (verdeckt) Inter- noch Transsexuellen zuzumuten, sich im Rahmen einer Gemeinde oder gegenüber einer Gemeindeleitung so zu outen, wie man es normalerweise höchstens beim Arzt oder Therapeuten tut.

Dem an und in sich selbst irritierten Menschen hilft es nicht, wenn er auch noch von Christen/-innen, also von außen, hinterfragt und analysiert wird. Ganz im Gegenteil. Dies führt häufig zu (weiteren) Verletzungen – und das ist wahrlich nicht seelsorgerlich. In erster Linie muss es deshalb darum gehen, den an einem nicht unwesentlichen Punkt seiner Persönlichkeit zutiefst fragenden oder irritierten Menschen, mit seiner Inkongruenz anzunehmen.

Von diesen Vorbemerkungen ausgehend wird im Folgenden der Umgang mit trans- und (verdeckt) intersexuellen Menschen aus der Perspektive der „Toleranz aus Glauben" betrachtet (Eckstein 2010:171-202). Auch wenn sich der

Neutestamentler Eckstein nicht direkt zu den Fragen der Inter- oder Transsexualität positioniert, sind seine Ausführungen jedoch so grundlegend, dass sie
auch auf dieses Spektrum des Menschseins angewandt werden können.

Eckstein skizziert im Rahmen der Toleranz ein Spektrum zwischen „Duldung"
als Minimalforderung und „Anerkennung" und „Annahme" im Umgang mit
Fremdem und Andersartigen. Dabei wirbt er für echte, freiwillige und aus Liebe
und Einsicht geborene Toleranz, die weder religiös, noch politisch, noch ideo-
logisch aufgenötigt werden kann. Gleichzeitig braucht eine umfassende Toleranz unbedingt eine Differenzierung, eine inhaltliche Begründung und eine
Grenze, damit sie nicht in eine pauschale Bejahung abgleitet und alles, und sei
es noch so utopisch, egalisiert wird. Damit muss die Förderung von Glaubensfestigkeit und damit auch der Identität einhergehen. Im Wirklichkeitsbereich
des Glaubens werden Menschen durch Christus aus Gnade versöhnt, angenommen und zur Gemeinschaft mit Gott und untereinander befähigt.

Wenngleich der Begriff der Toleranz sowohl in der Tradition des Alten wie
Neuen Testamentes keine zentrale Rolle spielt, so ist dennoch ihr Sachverhalt
durch die Begriffe „Gnade", „Barmherzigkeit", „Güte", „Menschenfreundlich-
keit", „Annahme" (und andere) bekannt und entspricht einer sowohl alttestamentlichen als auch neutestamentlichen Wesensbeschreibung Gottes. Darin
wird zugleich eine Differenzierung deutlich: Auf der einen Seite Gottes unbe-
dingte, voraussetzungslose Liebe und Zuwendung – also Gottes Bejahung der
„Sünder" – und auf der anderen Seite auf keinen Fall die Verharmlosung oder
Anerkennung der Sünde, die allerdings wiederum gnädig vergeben, aber nicht
gutgeheißen oder anerkannt, werden kann. Uneingeschränkte Liebe und eine
Konfrontation mit der Wahrheit sollen den Umgang mit Menschen prägen. Wer
Jesus zum Vorbild hat, der sich Zöllnern und Sündern, Samaritern, Frauen, gri-
echisch sprechenden Heiden, Fremden, Andersartigen und Ausgegrenzten zu-
wandte, der ist auch heute aufgefordert, die Integrations- und Inkulturations-
leistung der frühen Kirche fortzuführen (:178-196).

Jede radikal gelebte Intoleranz schadet sich selbst und ebenso den Grundlagen
der Gemeinschaft. Intoleranz wird so indirekt gestärkt (:180). (Aggressiv)
Abgrenzen wird sich, wer Angst zum Handlungsleitfaden erhoben hat und sich
bedroht fühlt (:190). Dem gegenüber steht eine aus Glaubensfestigkeit, im Wissen um die eigene Stärke gewonnene Kraft zur Toleranz (187, 197-202). In vielen Gleichnissen werden neue Perspektiven des Handelns aus Liebe, Dankbar-

keit und Einsicht aufgezeigt und so das generelle Ablehnen oder pauschale Misstrauen von Andersartigkeit als beschämendes Vorurteil entlarvt (:191). Gott, der die Menschen sucht, betrachtet die Menschen mit göttlichem Blick, gemäß seinem Wesen.

Konsequenzen, um Versöhnung erreichen zu können:

Insgesamt kann es für christliche Kirchen und Gemeinschaften also nur um eine geistliche Haltung den Menschen gegenüber gehen, die anders sind. Daher werde ich in den folgenden Ausführungen auf einer Metaebene eine Hilfestellung anbieten. Das hat zur Folge, dass die Unterscheidung zwischen (verdeckter) Inter- und Transsexualität entfallen kann.

1. Die Barmherzigkeit des Vaters gilt allen Menschen, da sie alle Geschöpfe des einen Gottes sind. Das gibt ihnen Wert und Würde, ungeachtet ihrer persönlichen Haltung Gott gegenüber und ungeachtet ihrer körperlichen, psychischen und sozialen Verfassung. Gerade christliche Leiterschaft hat den Auftrag, ein Abbild der Barmherzigkeit Gottes zu sein und so Wert und Würde eines Menschen zu fördern.

2. Es besteht die neutestamentliche Aufforderung, dass wir unsere Haltung von dem bestimmen lassen sollen, was uns Jesus Christus vorgelebt hat (Philipper 2,5). Dies sollen besonders christliche Leiter/-innen vorbildhaft, im vollen Bewusstsein dessen, dass sie selbst im Wirklichkeitsbereich des Glaubens leben, umsetzen (:197-202).

3. Dabei spielt es auch eine Rolle, wie transsexuelle oder (verdeckt) intersexuelle Christ/-innen mit der Situation umgehen. Offensiv „missionarische" Aktivitäten für Trans- oder Intersexualität sollten nicht hingenommen werden, wenngleich es den Menschen möglich sein muss – ebenso wie anderen – über ihre inneren Konflikte und deren Folgen zu reden.

Das bedeutet konkret:

Zu Beispiel 1: Die Frau wird nicht aus der Kinderarbeit entlassen, schon gar nicht übereilt. Es darf auch nicht zugelassen werden, dass Kinder verwirrt werden. Da sie schon länger in der Gemeinde mitarbeitet und bis dato nicht bekannt war, dass eine Geschlechtsangleichung stattgefunden hatte, ist davon nicht auszugehen, dass sie andere beeinflusst hat. Es entsteht also erst einmal kein Handlungsbedarf.

Zu Beispiel 2: Wenn erwachsene Personen getauft werden, dann verhalten sich hoffentlich alle Beteiligten erwachsen. D. h. erstens, muss eine Lösung für diesen Einzelfall gefunden werden (und damit nicht die ganze Gemeindeethik und -praxis in Frage gestellt werden). Zweitens ist es erwachsenen Menschen zuzumuten, sich ohne gegenseitiges Anstarren gemeinsam umzukleiden. Möglicherweise dienen Sichtschutzhilfen.

Zu Beispiel 3: Kurzfristig sollten Informationslücken gefüllt werden und deshalb keine schnellen Entscheidungen getroffen werden. Langfristig sollten grundsätzlich sowohl der Missionar als auch seine Familie für die Missionstätigkeit erhalten bleiben. Hier ist weises Vorgehen, besonders in Bezug auf den Missionskontext hin, gefordert und evtl. ein Ortswechsel angezeigt. Wenn die Situation Folgen für die Ehe hat, ist nach den ethischen Regeln der jeweiligen Missionsgesellschaft vorzugehen.

6 Zusammenfassung und offene Fragen

Es bleibt also festzuhalten, dass komplexe körperliche Diagnostik von Intersexualität medizinisch relativ klar zu erfassen ist, wenngleich sie theologische und ethische Fragen aufwirft. Die Situation Transsexueller ist noch komplexer und nicht einfach zu erfassen, weil es sich dabei auch um eine verborgene Intersexualität handeln kann.

Die bereits vorhandenen theologischen Antworten sollten weiterhin kritisch hinterfragt werden und weiter nach guten Hilfestellungen gesucht werden.

Auf jeden Fall sollte aber der Umgang mit (verdeckt) Inter- und Transsexuellen von Toleranz geprägt sein und Fremdes nach dem Vorbild Jesu integriert, statt kritisch abgelehnt, werden.

Gleichzeitig müssen weitere Fragen gestellt werden:

- Auf keinen Fall kann dem einzelnen Menschen abgesprochen werden, ein Geschöpf Gottes zu sein. Aber ist es nicht zu kurz gedacht, wenn Gottes Schöpfung als variantenreich bezeichnet wird (Schreiber 2016:XVI) und dabei unberücksichtigt bleibt, welche Folgen der „Sündenfall" auf die Schöpfung und die daraus resultierende Entwicklung von Anomalien hat?[22] Welche Bedeutung hat die daraus möglicherweise resultierende Degeneration der Menschheit in diesem Zusammenhang? Und wie könnte das so kommuniziert werden, dass Inter- und Transsexuelle dadurch nicht verletzt werden?

- Welche Folgen haben Inter- und Transsexuelle für die Theologie, Anthropologie und Ethik? Und welche Folgen hat es, wenn Inter- und (verborgene) Transsexualität nicht klar voneinander abgegrenzt werden können?

Wie können Gemeinden mit Betroffenen umgehen? Welche weitere Anleitung brauchen Leiter/-innen, Kirchen und Gemeinschaften, damit inter- und transsexuelle Menschen integriert leben können oder gar als Bereicherung gesehen werden?

- Mit welchem speziellen Beitrag könnten Intersexuelle und Transsexuelle Theologie und/oder christliche Gemeinden bereichern?

Bibliographie

Balswick, Judith K. & Balswick, Jack O. 1999. *Authentic Human Sexuality: Finding Wholeness in a Sexually Saturated Society*. Downers Grove: InterVarsity Press.

Batam, Damaris u. a. *Trans* in der Arbeit. Fragen und Antworten: Senatsverwaltung für Arbeit, Integration und Frauen*. Berlin: Landesstelle für Gleichbehandlung – gegen Diskriminierung aus Trans* bei der Arbeit.

---

[22] So wird z.B. niemand einem an Typ-1-Diabetes leidendem Kind absprechen, ein Geschöpf Gottes und daher gottgewollt zu sein. Dennoch wird man das Fehlen von Insulindepots in der Leber als (lebensbedrohliche) Anomalie bezeichnen. Auch die Brachydaktrylie ist eine Anomalie. Es handelt sich dabei um einen Gendefekt, der zwischen 3,4 % und 21 % der Bevölkerung betrifft (auch die Autorin dieses Artikels). Die Kurzfingrigkeit hat im Gegensatz zum Typ-1-Diabetes keine weitreichenden Folgen, aber beides sind Zeichen für das Leben in einer „gefallenen Welt".

Bergmann, Christina 2011. *Und meine Seele lächelt: Transsexualität und Spiritualität: Mein Weg zu einem authentischen Selbst.* Schalksmühle: Pomaska-Brand.

Bild 2013. „Das Baby-Wunder des Jahres | Berliner Mann bringt Baby zur Welt." Aufgerufen am 16. Juni 2016: http://www.bild.de/news/inland/geburt/berliner-mann-brachte-zu-hause-einen-gesunden-jungen-zur-welt-32308812.bild.html.

Bildungsserver Berlin-Brandenburg 2016. Aufgerufen am 07.12.2016: http://bildungsserver.berlin-brandenburg.de/themen/bildung-zur-akzeptanz-von-vielfalt-diversity/sexuelle-vielfalt/lehrkaefte/unterrichtsmaterial/. Aus „Schule unterm Regenbogen: HeteroHomoBiTrans-Lebensweisen im Unterricht an den Schulen im Land Brandenburg". Aufgerufen am 07. Dezember: 2016: https://publishup.uni-potsdam.de/opus4-ubp/frontdoor/index/index/docId/2037.

Bräumer, Hansjörg 2000. „Geschaffen als Mann und Frau". In Cornelia Mack & Friedhilde Stricker. *Begabt & beauftragt: Frausein nach biblischen Vorbildern: Orientierung an der Bibel.* Holzgerlingen: SCM Hänssler.

Bubrowski, Helene 2014. „Unten Barbie, oben Ken." Faz 02.04.2014. Aufgerufen am 16. Juni 2016: http://www.faz.net/aktuell/gesellschaft/menschen/norrie-auf-australien-muss-sich-fuer-kein-geschlecht-entscheiden-12876623.html.

Conway, Lynn 2016. „Wie häufig tritt Transsexualität auf?" Aufgerufen am 14. Juni 2016: http://ai.eecs.umich.edu/people/conway/TS/DE/TSprevalence-DE.html.

Cornwall, Susannah (Hg.) 2015. *Intersex, Theology an the Bible. Troubling Bodies in Church, Text, and Society.* New York: Palgrave MacMillan.

Daimond, Milton 2016. „Transsexualism as an Intersex Condition". In Schreiber (Hg.), 43-54.

Dabrock, Peter 2016. „Why Heteronormativity Should Not Have the Final Word on Sexual Identity. Ethical Considerations form a Protestant Perspektive". In Schreiber (Hg.), 505-516.

DeFranza, Megan K. 2015a. *Sex Difference in Christian Theologie. Male, Female, and Inersex in the image of God.* Michigan/Cambridge William B. Eerdmans 2015.

DeFranza, Megan K. 2015b, „Virtuous Eunuchs: Troubling Conservative and Queer Readings of Intersex and the Bible*". In Cornwall (Hg.), 55.

Deutsches Ärzteblatt. 30. Januar 2015. Aufgerufen am 11. April 2016: http://www.bundesaerztekammer.de/fileadmin/user_upload/downloads/Vorabversion_BAeK-Stn_DSD-Disorders_of_Sex_Development2.pdf.

Deutscher Ethikrat 2012. „Intersexualität" vom 23.02.2012. Aufgerufen am 05. Dezember 2016: www.ethikrat.org/publikaionen/stellungnahme.

Eckstein, Hans-Joachim 2010. *Wenn die Liebe zum Leben wird. Zur Beziehungsgewissheit*. Asslar: SCM Hänssler.

Focus 2013. „Mann bringt zweites Kind zur Welt." Aufgerufen am 16. Juni 2016: http://www.focus.de/panorama/welt/usa-mann-bringt-zweites-kind-zur-welt_aid_406993.html.

Goertz, Stephan 2016. „Theologien des transsexuellen Leibes. Eine moraltheologische Sichtung." In Schreiber (Hg.), 506-517.

Hare, John 2015. „Hermaphrodities, Eunuchs, and Intersex People. The Witness of Medical Science in Biblical Times and Today". In Cornwall (Hg.), 79-98.

Haupt, Horst-Jörg 2016. „Abschied von Trans und Gender – evidenzbasierte Zugänge zu Mustern geschlechtlicher Vielfalt". In Schreiber (Hg.), 75-122.

Iff, Markus 2013. Menschsein in Differenz. Systematisch-theologische Perspektiven zum Genderverhältnis und den Gender-Studien. In *Theologische Gespräche. Freikirchliche Beiträge zur Theologie 2013*, Heft 1. Witten: Bundes-Verlag, 18-36.

Jung, Patricia Beattie 2015. „Intersex on Earth as It Is in Heaven". In Cornwall (Hg.), 173-196.

Kelle, Birgit 2015. *GenderGaga: Wie eine absurde Ideologie unseren Alltag erobern will*. Asslar: Adeo.

Klatt, Thomas 2016 „Entmoralisierung der Geschlechterfrage. Transsexualität in Theologie und Kirche". Aufgerufen am 07. Dezember 2016: http://www.deutschlandfunk.de/entmoralisierung-der-geschlechterfrage-transsexualitaet-in.886.de.html?dram:article_id=345180.

Klenk, Dominik 2015. *Gender Mainstreaming: Das Ende von Mann und Frau?* 2. Auflage. Gießen: Brunnen.

Kerry, Stephen Craig 2015. „Intersex and the Role of Religion on the Path to Health and Well-Being. In Cornwall (Hg.), 121-146.

Kessler, Volker 2009. Ein Dialog zwischen Managementlehre und alttestamentlicher Theologie: McGregors Theorien X und Y zur Führung im Lichte alttestamentlicher Anthropologie. DTh Dissertation. University of South Africa. Pretoria. Aufgerufen am 20. Juni 2016: http://uir.unisa.ac.za/xmlui/bitstream/handle/10500/1384/thesis.pdf?sequence=1&isAllowed=y.

Krollner, Björn & Krollner, Dirk 2016. ICD-Code 2016. Aufgerufen am 06. Dezember 2016: http://www.icd-code.de/icd/code/F64.-.html.

Kuby, Gabriele 2012. *Die globale sexuelle Revolution: Zerstörung der Freiheit im Namen der Freiheit.* Kißlegg: fe-medien.

Kunert, Cornelia 2016. „Geschlechtsidentität und Bewusstsein. Naturwissenschaftliche Fragen und philosophische Positionen" reden, und was das für die Behandlung bedeutet". In Schreiber (Hg.), 597-634.

Marchal, Joseph A. 2015. „Who Are You Calling a Eunuch?! Staging Conversations and Connections between Feminist and Queer Biblical Studies and Intersex Advocacy". In Cornwall (Hg.), 29-54

N24 2009. „«Schwangerer Mann» bringt zweites Kind zur Welt." Fassung vom 16. Juni 2016: http://www.n24.de/n24/Nachrichten/Panorama/d/698492/-schwangerer-mann--bringt-zweites-kind-zur-welt.html.

Nicolosie, Joseph 2011. „Transgender – Kinder mit Störungen der Geschlechtsidentität". In *Buttetin* 01/11. Identitätsentwicklung und Erziehung. Reichelsheim: Offensive Junger Christen.

Ohley, Lukas 2016. „Transsexualität und der virtuelle Körper. Theologische-metaethische Anmerkungen. In Schreiber (Hg.), 533-556.

Oorschot, Jürgen van 2000. „Er schuf sie als Mann und Frau – der Mensch als geschlechtliches Wesen". In Wilfried Haubeck u.a. (Hg.), *Geschaffen als Mann und Frau: Ehe und Sexualität im Spannungsfeld von Gesellschaft und Gemeinde.* Theologische Impulse. Band 2. Witten: Bundes-Verlag.

Pool, Robert 1996. *Evas Rippe: Das Ende des Mythos vom starken und vom schwachen Geschlecht*. München: Knaur.

Potzel, Dieter 2015. „Wie transsexuelle Pfarrer der Schöpfungsordnung den Kampf ansagen. Pfarrer werden nach Geschlechtsumwandlung zu Pfarrerinnen - Hat Gott bei ihnen einen Fehler gemacht?" In Potzel, Dieter (Hg.) 2015. *Der Theologe*. Fassung vom 11.10.2015. Ausgabe Nr. 69. Aufgerufen am 16. Juni 2016, http://www.theologe.de/transsexuelle_evangelische_pfarrer.htm.

Raedel, Christoph 2015a. „Geschlechtsidentität und Geschlechterrollen. Perspektiven theologischer Anthropologie". In Christoph Raedel (Hg) 2015. *Das Leben der Geschlechter. Zwischen Gottesgabe und menschlicher Gestaltung*. Münster: Lit, 119-156.

Raedel, Christoph 2015b. E-Mail vom 24. November 2015, Privatarchiv.

Raedel, Christoph 2016. Intersexualität in der Perspektive christlicher Ethik. Unveröffentlichter Artikel. Privatarchiv.

Schieferdecker, Christina 2016. *Biologische Grundlagen. Transsexualität. Zum wissenschaftlichen Forschungsstand*. Ludwigsburg: ATME.

Schockenhoff, Eberhard 2016. „Sexualität und Katholische Kirche – ein Dauerkonflikt?" In Schreiber (Hg.), 565-576.

Schreiber, Gerhard (Hg.) 2016. *Transsexualität in Theologie und Neurowissenschaften. Ergebnisse, Kontroversen, Perspektiven*. Berlin/Bosten: Walter de Gruyter.

Schreiber, Gerhard 2016. „Vorwort". In Schreiber (Hg.), XIII-XXI.

Solms, Mark 2016. „The Biological Foundations of Gender: Delicate Balance." In Schreiber (Hg.), 5-22.

Static.bz-Berlin 2013. Aufgerufen am 16. Juni 2016: Quelle: http://static.bz-berlin.de/data/uploads/multimedia/archive/00080/schwanger_mann_beati_80525a-768x432.jpg.

Stüvel, Heike 2008. „Das dritte Geschlecht" vom 21.06.2008. Aufgerufen am 21.12.2016: https://www.welt.de/welt_print/article2129682/Das-dritte-Geschlecht.html.

Süddeutsche Zeitung 2013. „Der schwangere Mann." vom 10.09.2013. Aufgerufen am 16. Juni 2016: http://www.sz-online.de/nachrichten/der-schwangere-mann-2659792.html.

Swaab, Dick F.; Castellanos-Cruz, Laura & Boa, Ai-Min 2016. „The Human Brain and Gender: Sexual Differentiation of our Brain." In Schreiber (Hg.), 23-42.

Westermann Claus 1994. *Biblischer Kommentar: Altes Testament*. 1. Teilband Genesis 1-11. Neukirchen-Vluyn: Neukirchener.

Westermann, Claus 2000. *Der Mensch im Alten Testament. Altes Testament und Moderne*. Band 6. Münster: LIT.

Wikipedia 2016. David Reimer. Aufgerufen am 14. Juni 2016: https://de.wikipedia.org/wiki/David_Reimer.

Wolf, Hans Walter 1994. *Anthropologie des Alten Testaments*. 6. Auflage. Gütersloh: Chr. Kaiser.

Zentrale Deutscher Kliniken 2016. „Intersexualität". Aufgerufen am 14. Juni 2016: http://zentrale-deutscher-kliniken.de/lexikon-deu/Medizin/Genetik/Intersexualitaet.html.

Zwölfer, Dorothea 2016. Mündlich auf der Konferenz: Transsexualität. Eine gesellschaftliche Herausforderung im Gespräch zwischen Theologie und Neurowissenschaft vom 04.-06.02.2016 an der Goethe Universität Frankfurt.

Authors & Editers

Jonathan Andrews has been researching and writing on Middle East affairs since 2003. He is the UK representative of the International Institute for Religious Freedom (Bonn – Cape Town – Colombo – Brasilia – Brussels/Geneva) and chairs the Muslim World Forum operated by Global Connections. He is the author of Identity Crisis – Religious Registration in the Middle East, Last Resort – Migration and the Middle East, and editor of The Church in Disorienting Times – Leading Prophetically Through Adversity, and The Missiology behind the Story – Voices from the Arab World.

Matthias Ehmann is a pastor in the German Bund Freier evangelischer Gemeinden, lecturer in mission studies and intercultural theology at the Ewersbach University of Applied Arts, Germany, and a doctoral student at the University of South Africa. He is married with Tamara and lives in Würzburg, Germany.

Tobias Faix (DTh, MTh, M.A.) is professor of Practical Theology at the YMCA University Kassel and professor extraordinarius at the Department of Christian Spirituality, Church History and Missiology, College of Human Sciences, UNISA. He is the Dean of the Institute empirica for Youth, Culture & Religion.

Randy Friesen is the president of Multiply, the global mission agency of the Mennonite Brethren churches of North America. Multiply is focused on making disciples and planting churches through partnerships with national leaders and churches in 65 countries around the world. Their Building Leaders for Peace camps and programs have equipped hundreds of leaders to be peacemakers in their local communities. Randy and Marjorie have two children and live on the west coast of Canada.

Morten Hørning Jensen (Ph.D., University of Aarhus) is associate professor of New Testament at the Lutheran School of Theology in Aarhus, Adjunct Professor at MF Norwegian School of Theology in Oslo and Research Fellow at the Department of Biblical and Ancient Studies, University of South Africa, Pretoria. He is married to Jeanette and has four kids and lives in Denmark.

Martina Kessler, co-researcher of the University of South Africa (Department of Philosophy, Practical and Systematic Theology); in the direction of the Akademie für christliche Führungskräfte and dean of studies for Stiftung Therapeutische Seelsorge.

Thomas Kroeck graduated in Agriculture at the Justus-Liebig-University Giessen, Germany, and holds an MA in Intercultural Studies of Columbia International University, USA. For his PhD he worked at the International Rice Research Institute in the Philippines. With his wife and three children he lived and worked for 10 years in Tanzania training church workers and coordinated rural development projects. As Project Officer in the German Youth Federation for Christian Endeavour (EC), he was in charge of supporting child development projects in India, Nepal, Brazil and Eastern Europe and also facilitated international youth exchanges. Since 2012 Thomas has been teaching Development Studies cooperating with the University of South Africa (UNISA). He also lectures at MBS, Marburg, and AWM, Korntal, in Germany.

Catherine Morris, BA, JD, LLM, is an adjunct professor in the Faculty of Law at the University of Victoria, Canada. She is also an adjunct professor at Carey Theological College, Vancouver, Canada. She teaches negotiation, conflict resolution, peacebuilding, and international human rights in academic and other settings. She is the managing director of Peacemakers Trust, a non-profit organization for research and education on conflict transformation. Her international work has included assignments in Thailand (since 1994), Cambodia (since 1995), Honduras, Myanmar, Bolivia, Rwanda and Europe. Her publications include works on dispute resolution, religion and peacebuilding, and reconciliation. This paper was revised and updated in early 2018 during a community sabbatical at the Centre for Studies in Religion and Society, University of Victoria.

Ester Petrenko is academic dean of the Latvian Biblical Centre, Associate Professor at the Norwegian School of Leadership and Theology, Extraordinary Senior Lecturer at Northwest University (South Africa) and Greenwich School of Theology (UK), and research fellow at St. John's College (University of Durham, UK). She is married to Vitali and has a son called Lukass, and they live in Latvia.

Johannes Reimer is professor of mission studies and intercultural theology at the Ewersbach University of Applied Arts, Germany and the University of South Africa. He is Global Director of the Peace and Reconciliation Network of the World Evangelical Alliance (WEA). He is married with Cornelia, is father of three children and lives in Germany.

Christof Sauer is professor for Religious Freedom and Research on Persecution of Christians at Freie Theologische Hochschule Giessen, Germany, part-time Professor of Religious Studies and Missiology at Evangelische Theologische Faculteit Leuven, Belgium, and Professor Extraordinary at Stellenbosch University Theological Faculty, Departmental Group Practical Theology and Missiology. He is also the founding co-director of the International Institute for Religious Freedom. His doctorate in Missiology at Unisa, South Africa, was concerned with mission history in Egypt. His postdoctoral habilitation thesis on martyrdom and mission at Wuppertal Protestant University included an examination of the situation of the Coptic Orthodox Church in Egypt in the 20th century.

Christoph Stenschke teaches New Testament at Biblisch-Theologische Akademie, Bergneustadt, Germany. Stenschke also works as professor extraordinarius in the Department of Biblical and Ancient Studies at the University of South Africa and is a prolific writer. He is an ordained minister in the German Baptist Union and serves on the local city council. He is married with Helene, is father of two children and lives in Germany.

Marcus Weiand is the director of the Institut Compax for conflict transformation in Switzerland. He studied theology und politics in Basel and Tübingen and earned his doctorate in social ethics at King's College London.

Hans-Georg Wünch is academic Dean and lecturer of Old Testament at Theologisches Seminar Rheinland (Rhineland School of Theology) and Prof. extr. at the Department of Biblical and Ancient Studies at the University of South Africa. He further teaches Biblical Hebrew at the Ewersbach University of Applied Arts. He is married with Bettina, is father of two children and lives in Germany.

Cobus van Wyngaard is lecturer in Systematic Theology in the Department of Philosophy, Practical and Systematic Theology at the University of South Africa. He is an ordained minister of the Dutch Reformed Church in the inner city of Pretoria. He is married to Maryke, is father of three children and lives in South Africa.

Interdisziplinäre und theologische Studien

im Auftrag der Gesellschaft für Bildung und Forschung in Europa (GBFE) hrsg. von
Tobias Faix, Volker Kessler und Debora Sommer

Martina Kessler; Werner Schäfer; Michael Utsch (Hg.)
Menschen begleiten: individuell – ganzheitlich – geistlich
Geschichte, Methoden und Beispiele der Therapeutischen Seelsorge
Bd. 2, 2018, 234 S., 34,90 €, br., ISBN 978-3-643-14139-2

Oliver Merz
Vielfalt in der Kirche?
Der schwere Weg der Inklusion von Menschen mit Behinderung im Pfarrberuf
Bd. 1, 2017, 224 S., 29,90 €, br., ISBN 978-3-643-80251-4

LIT Verlag Berlin – Münster – Wien – Zürich – London
Auslieferung Deutschland / Österreich / Schweiz: siehe Impressumsseite

Theology in the Public Square
Theologie in der Öffentlichkeit
edited by/hrsg. von Prof. Dr. Heinrich Bedford-Strohm (Universität Bamberg, Germany),
Prof. Dr. James Haire (Charles Sturt University, Canberra, Australia), Prof. Dr. Helga Kuhlmann
(Universität Paderborn, Germany), Prof. Dr. Rudolf von Sinner (Lutheran School of Theology, Sao
Leopoldo, Brasil) und Prof. Dr. Dirkie Smit (University of Stellenbosch, South Africa)

Traugott Jähnichen; Pascal Bataringaya; Olivier Munyansanga; Clemens Wustmans (Eds.)
Dietrich Bonhoeffer
Life and Legacy
This volume is the documentation of a workshop at the "Dietrich Bonhoeffer Centre for Public Theology" in Kigali, that took place in February 2018 and discussed what can be gained from Bonhoeffer's
theology for contextual theologies in Africa as well as in Europe. The core feature of the workshop in
February 2018 was a competition in which students from Butare/Huye presented the findings of their
examination of Dietrich Bonhoeffer's life and work. The prize-winning contributions are documented
in this volume. Papers from the European perspective were contributed by doctoral candidates and
students of the Ruhr University Bochum, and the chairing and commentary of the event was shared
amongst Dr Clemens Wustmans (Berlin), Dr Christine Schliesser (Bern), the President of the Pres-
byterian Church in Rwanda, Dr Pascal Bataringaya (Kigali), the Dean of the Theological Faculty of
the Protestant Institut of Arts and Social Sciences, Olivier Munyansanga, Ph.D. (Huye/Rwanda), and
Prof. Dr Traugott Jähnichen (Bochum).
Bd. 11, 2019, 190 S., 29,90 €, br., ISBN 978-3-643-91106-3

Heinrich Bedford-Strohm; Tharcisse Gatwa; Traugott Jähnichen;,
Elisée Musemakweli (Eds.)
African Christian Theologies and the Impact of the Reformation
Symposium Plass Ruanda February 18 – 23, 2016
"African Christian Theologies and the Reformation Legacy" may seem to have little to do with each
other. But there are shared perspectives. One of the strongest heritages of the Reformation for Christianity was to return to the central role given to the Bible, translated in local dialects. Christianity
expanded thanks to the translation of the Bible in vernacular languages worldwide. Most importantly,
the people who had been victims of prejudices of race supremacy could now have access to God in
their own language, culture and idioms without intermediaries. It is largely thanks to Bible translations that the majority of those churches in Africa born of European mission activities continued to
develop positively after the end of the colonial age, and that independent African churches emerged.
Bd. 10, 2017, 460 S., 39,90 €, br., ISBN 978-3-643-90820-9

Heinrich Bedford-Strohm; Pasal Bataringaya; Traugott Jähnichen (Eds.)
Reconciliation and Just Peace
Impulses of the Theology of Dietrich Bonhoeffer for the European and African Context
Bd. 9, 2016, 242 S., 29,90 €, br., ISBN 978-3-643-90557-4

Katrin Kusmierz
Theology in Transition
Public Theologies in Post-Apartheid South Africa
Bd. 8, 2016, 360 S., 54,90 €, br., ISBN 978-3-643-80101-2

Heinrich Bedford-Strohm
Liberation Theology for a Democratic Society
Essays in Public Theology. Collected by Michael Mädler and Andrea Wagner-Pinggéra
Bd. 7, 2018, 344 S., 39,90 €, br., ISBN 978-3-643-90458-4

LIT Verlag Berlin – Münster – Wien – Zürich – London
Auslieferung Deutschland / Österreich / Schweiz: siehe Impressumsseite

Frieden – Versöhnung –Zukunft: Afrika und Europa

Schriften der GIUBUNTU Peace-Academy

hrsg. von Prof. Dr. Klaus Baumann (Universität Freiburg), Prof. Dr. Rainer Bendel (Stuttgart/Tübingen), P. Déogratias Maruhukiro, PhD (Universität Freiburg)

Déogratias Maruhukiro
Für eine Friedens- und Versöhnungskultur
Sozial-politische Analyse, ethischer Ansatz und kirchlicher Beitrag zur Förderung einer Friedens- und Versöhnungskultur in Burundi
Bd. 2, 2020, 360 S., 34,90 €, br., ISBN 978-3-643-14444-7

Klaus Baumann; Rainer Bendel; Déogratias Maruhukiro (Hg.)
Gerechtigkeit, Wahrheitsfindung, Vergebung und Versöhnung
Zur Friedensarbeit von Politik und Kirchen in Nachkriegsgebieten
Bd. 1, 2020, ca. 240 S., ca. 29,90 €, br., ISBN 978-3-643-14443-0

LIT Verlag Berlin – Münster – Wien – Zürich – London
Auslieferung Deutschland / Österreich / Schweiz: siehe Impressumsseite

Religion – Geschichte – Gesellschaft
Fundamentaltheologische Studien
hrsg. von Johann Baptist Metz (†) (Münster / Wien), Johann Reikerstorfer (Wien)
und Jürgen Werbick (Münster)

Hans-Gerd Janßen; Julia D. E. Prinz; Michael J. Rainer (Hg..)
Theologie in gefährdeter Zeit
Stichworte von nahen und fernen Weggefährten für Johann Baptist Metz zum
90. Geburtstag

Johann Baptist Metz (* 5. August 1928) hat seine Theologie im intensiven Austausch mit Philosophie, Geschichte, Rechts-, Politik- und Sozialtheorie, Jüdischem Denken und Welt-Literatur & Kunst
gewonnen und entfaltet – und so nicht nur in der theologischen Diskussion prägende Spuren hinter-
lassen. Seine Gottesrede lässt sich nicht aus den Katastrophen in Geschichte und Gesellschaft her-
auslösen, sondern bleibt im Kern herausgefordert angesichts der weltweit steigenden Gefährdungen:
interkulturell, sozial, politisch, ökonomisch, ökologisch ... !
Dieser Band führt 150 kompakte Stellungnahmen zusammen, die Zeit-Zeichen setzen: die Beiträ-
ger_innen loten aus, in wieweit sie der Neuen Politischen Theologie und J.B. Metz als Person prägende Inspirationen und bleibende Impulse für ihre eigene Sicht auf Philosophie, Theologie, Geschichte,
Gesellschaft, Recht, Politik, Bildung und Kunst verdanken: eine ungewöhnliche Festschrift voller
Überraschungen und weiterführender Anstöße.

Bd. 50, 2. Aufl. 2019, 600 S., 39,90 €, br., ISBN 978-3-643-14106-4

LIT Verlag Berlin – Münster – Wien – Zürich – London

Auslieferung Deutschland / Österreich / Schweiz: siehe Impressumsseite